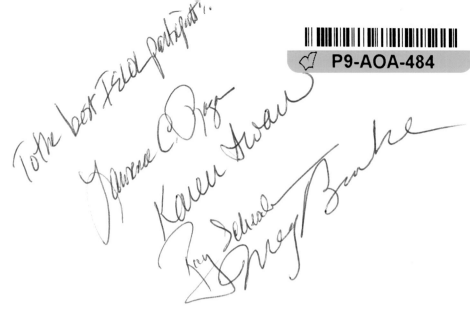

To the best FELD participants...

Lawrence C. Ragan

Karen Swan

Ray Schroeder

Greg Bowie

LEADING THE E-LEARNING TRANSFORMATION OF
HIGHER EDUCATION

Phillip,
You are our
future
Greg

Phillip
Best wishes
Ray

Good luck
Phillip,
Karen Swan

ONLINE LEARNING & DISTANCE EDUCATION
Leadership, Innovation, Policy, & Practice

Additional titles in our
ONLINE LEARNING AND DISTANCE EDUCATION series
edited by Michael Grahame Moore

ASSURING QUALITY IN ONLINE EDUCATION
Practices and Processes at the Teaching, Resource, and Program Levels
Edited by Kay Shattuck
Publication date: Fall 2013

CULTURE AND ONLINE LEARNING
Global Perspectives and Research
Edited by Insung Jung and Charlotte Nirmalani Gunawardena
Publication date: Spring 2014

WEB 2.0 FOR ACTIVE LEARNERS
by Vanessa Dennen
Publication date: Fall 2014

LEADING THE E-LEARNING TRANSFORMATION OF HIGHER EDUCATION

Meeting the Challenges of Technology and Distance Education

Gary Miller, Meg Benke, Bruce Chaloux,

Lawrence C. Ragan, Raymond Schroeder,

Wayne Smutz, and Karen Swan

Series Foreword by Michael Grahame Moore

Published in association with

ONLINE LEARNING™
CONSORTIUM
FORMERLY THE SLOAN CONSORTIUM

STERLING, VIRGINIA

COPYRIGHT © 2014 BY
STYLUS PUBLISHING, LLC

Published by Stylus Publishing, LLC
22883 Quicksilver Drive
Sterling, Virginia 20166-2102

In association with
The Online Learning Consortium, Inc. (formerly the Sloan Consortium)
P.O. Box 1238
Newburyport, MA 01950-8238

PUBLISHER'S NOTE
After publication of this book, the Sloan Consortium (Sloan-C)
formally became known as the Online Learning Consortium.
This information has been updated in the frontmatter and on the
cover. However, all other references to the organization throughout
this text remain as they appeared in the first printing.

Library of Congress Cataloging-in-Publication Data
Leading the e-learning transformation of higher education : meeting
the challenges of technology and distance education / Gary Miller
[and six others].—1st ed.
    p.   cm. —
Includes bibliographical references and index.
ISBN 978-1-57922-795-1 (cloth : alk. paper)
ISBN 978-1-57922-796-8 (pbk. : alk. paper)
ISBN 978-1-57922-797-5 (library networkable e-edition)
ISBN 978-1-57922-798-2 (consumer e-edition)
1. Education, Higher—Computer network
resources.   2. Education, Higher—Effect of technological
innovations on.   3. Internet in higher education.
4. Distance education   I. Miller, Gary.
LB2395.7.L39 2014
378.1'7344678—dc23
                                                            2013013284

13-digit ISBN: 978-1-57922-795-1 (cloth)
13-digit ISBN: 978-1-57922-796-8 (paper)
13-digit ISBN: 978-1-57922-797-5 (library networkable e-edition)
13-digit ISBN: 978-1-57922-798-2 (consumer e-edition)

Printed in the United States of America

All first editions printed on acid-free paper
that meets the American National Standards Institute
Z39-48 Standard.

Bulk Purchases

Quantity discounts are available for use in workshops and for
staff development.
Call 1-800-232-0223

First Edition, 2014

10   9   8   7   6   5   4   3

In Memoriam

The authors wish to dedicate this book to the memory of our friend, colleague, and coauthor, Dr. Bruce Chaloux, who died in September 2013 as this volume was being prepared for publication.

For the past three decades, Bruce has been recognized as a pioneer and leader in the field of media-based distance education, helping to shape policy and innovative practice in our field from the era of satellite to the Internet age.

Bruce led the Sloan Consortium, an international organization dedicated to the growth, expansion, and integration of online learning into the mainstream of higher education. Prior to his leadership of the Sloan Consortium, Bruce served for 14 years as the director of student access programs at the Southern Regional Education Board (SREB), where he founded and oversaw SREB's 16-state Electronic Campus, which now includes 2,000 degree programs from 300 colleges. Bruce also led extended campus programs at Virginia Tech.

Bruce is perhaps best known in our community for his significant achievements in guiding the public to promote online and lifelong learning. For the past three decades, he was a leading advocate for practitioners to help find solutions to state, regional, and national problems and issues and led engagement between government agencies and practitioner communities. From 1982 to 1984, he directed Project ALLTEL (Assessing Long Distance Learning via Telecommunications), a two-year study cosponsored by the Council on Postsecondary Accreditation and the State Higher Education Executive Officers Association. The goal was to develop policies and procedures for accrediting bodies and state authorizing agencies for the evaluation of instruction delivered via telecommunications. Most recently, he worked to enhance reciprocity between states for online learning, having recently been named to a national commission for implementation.

Bruce was widely recognized for his leadership by the professional community. In 2010, he was named to the Inaugural Class of Sloan-C Fellows. Most recently, in 2013, Bruce was honored by the National University

Telecommunications Network with their highest honor, the Distinguished Service Award. He was inducted posthumously into the International Adult and Continuing Education Hall of Fame in November 2013.

Bruce took great pride in his role as codirector of the Institute for Emerging Leaders in Online Learning (IELOL), a partnership between the Sloan Consortium and the Penn State World Campus that he encouraged and in which he taught for the past five years. Through IELOL, Bruce and his colleagues—many of this author team included—helped to empower a new generation of leaders in our field. His family has established a scholarship to support future IELOL participants.

Bruce lived his life enthusiastically and fully. His engaging spirit endeared him to everyone he met. His quick wit, smile, and genuine interest in people won over all who he met. We, the authors of this book, were both friends and colleagues of this wonderful man. We hope that this book will be one way in which Bruce's contributions will continue to shape our community well into the future.

CONTENTS

FOREWORD
Michael Grahame Moore
ix

PREFACE
Leading Change In Distance Education
xi

PART ONE: LEADING CHANGE
Making the Match Between Leadership and Institutional Culture
1

1. E-LEARNING AND THE TRANSFORMATION OF
HIGHER EDUCATION
Bruce Chaloux and Gary Miller
3

2. THE IMPACT OF ORGANIZATIONAL CONTEXT
Bruce Chaloux and Gary Miller
23

3. LEADING CHANGE IN THE MAINSTREAM
A Strategic Approach
Gary Miller
38

4. LEADERSHIP IS PERSONAL
Wayne Smutz
48

PART TWO: ENSURING OPERATIONAL EXCELLENCE
75

5. ENHANCING E-LEARNING EFFECTIVENESS
Karen Swan
77

6. SUPPORTING FACULTY SUCCESS IN ONLINE LEARNING
Requirements for Individual and Institutional Leadership
Lawrence C. Ragan and Raymond Schroeder
108

7. OPTIMIZING STUDENT SUCCESS THROUGH
STUDENT SUPPORT SERVICES
Meg Benke and Gary Miller
132

8. MOVING INTO THE TECHNOLOGY MAINSTREAM   149
   Raymond Schroeder and Gary Miller

9. OPERATIONAL LEADERSHIP IN A STRATEGIC CONTEXT   162
   Raymond Schroeder

PART THREE: SUSTAINING THE INNOVATION   **175**

10. POLICY LEADERSHIP IN E-LEARNING   177
    Bruce Chaloux

11. LEADING BEYOND THE INSTITUTION   200
    Meg Benke and Gary Miller

12. FORESEEING AN ACTIONABLE FUTURE   210
    Gary Miller, Meg Benke, Bruce Chaloux, Lawrence C. Ragan,
    Raymond Schroeder, Wayne Smutz, and Karen Swan

    AUTHORS   235

    INDEX   241

FOREWORD

Michael Grahame Moore, Series Editor

T his book about distance education and leadership is the first in a series of books about online learning and distance education published by Stylus. Plans for forthcoming books include such subjects as quality assurance, culture and online learning, access for disabled students, teaching science, and teaching online in elementary and secondary (K–12) schools. This series aims to fill a gap in the literature, the space between the academic scholarly research literature, such as my own *American Journal of Distance Education* on the one hand, and on the other hand, the vast swamp of information awaiting the student on the Internet, minimally organized, and with no mechanisms for control of quality. Students and especially practicing instructors at the K–12 level, in colleges and universities, and training in the workplace have been asking for a new resource that is authoritative but also accessible. This series seeks to meet that need. Our aim is to provide in each book in the series a thorough description and considerable analysis of one of the major topics in this very large field, each written by authors who are able to draw on research and scholarship and at the same time are able to relate this to the practical challenges facing policy makers and leaders, teachers, students, and administrators in their everyday implementation of online distance learning and teaching.

Online learning is the most evolved form of distance education and offers unprecedented opportunities for innovation in teaching and learning, especially in how our institutions are structured and managed. Thus, from that perspective, it should be obvious why the first book in our series deals with leadership. I have been eager for this topic of leadership to be the focus of the first book, after spending all my professional life in this field of distance education and having experienced and observed how directly innovation in every aspect (including all future book titles in the series) has been accelerated or impeded by the quality of the leadership provided by the administrations in our institutions, as well as that at state and federal levels. I have no doubt, of course, that we must continue to study the dynamics of learning and teaching in all their many dimensions, but I am certain that successful application of what we know and discover will, as in the past, be impossible without better administrative leadership, and perhaps of even greater importance, policy leadership. Successful, full capitalization of the potential of modern technology is simply not possible unless deans, department heads, university presidents, and others in similar roles, including at the state and federal levels, understand, have the vision to see the potential, and have the courage to implement essential and often far-reaching changes in how human and other resources are applied. That is what this book is about: how the challenge of bringing about institutional change has been addressed in some of the country's major institutions, including Empire State University, Pennsylvania State University, University of Illinois, and Virginia Tech. While referencing research and theory, the core of this book is *experience*, the experiences and insights of seven veteran administrators who at varying times over the past two decades stepped up to the plate and attempted to make a difference in their institutions. Never before has such real-world experience been compiled into one volume as here, and consequently I am thrilled to have this opportunity of introducing Gary Miller as first author of *Leading the e-Learning Transformation of Higher Education* and to thank him and his colleagues for their willingness to share their lifetimes of knowledge with us in this first book in this series.

Michael Grahame Moore
Distinguished Professor Emeritus of Education
The Pennsylvania State University

This book is about leadership—the leadership of online distance education in the context of its increasingly mainstreamed role in American higher education. As such, this book focuses specifically on the role of the online distance education leader in effecting change in the broader institution, as higher education adapts to the needs of a new era, the information society.

While online distance education is still a relatively new phenomenon in our institutions, distance education itself has been part of American higher education since 1892 when it was introduced as correspondence study, one of the many ways higher education innovated to meet the needs of the Industrial Revolution. Throughout the twentieth century, distance education embraced new technologies and spawned other innovations, such as the open university movement. However, the introduction of the World Wide Web in the mid-1990s stimulated what has become a transformation not only in distance education but also in higher education generally. With its ability to provide access and innovate with teaching methods online, e-learning has greatly expanded the range of undergraduate and graduate degree programs that can be taught at a distance. It has also been embraced by many new colleges and universities that had no previous involvement in distance education. At the same time, the impact of e-learning is also being felt on traditional campus-based programs, blurring the traditional distinctions between distance education and resident education.

This transformation has required that distance education leaders develop new leadership skills that will allow them to innovate successfully in the mainstream of their institutions. The purpose of this book is to provide insights into the challenges facing the field for a generation of emerging leaders who can expect that much of their career will be devoted to continuing this transformation.

Organization and Structure

Leading the e-Learning Transformation of Higher Education is organized around major themes pioneering leaders developed for the Institute for Emerging Leaders in Online Learning. It also reflects the Five Pillars of Quality Online Education that Frank Mayadas developed for the Alfred P. Sloan

Foundation (for more on this, see Chapter 1). The book is divided into three distinct sections.

Part One: Leading Change: Making the Match Between Leadership and Institutional Culture

The first Sloan pillar of quality addressed is access, which relates to the role of online distance education in an institution's fundamental mission and institutional strategy. This section provides a broad institutional context for leading an online distance education unit.

Chapter 1, "e-Learning and the Transformation of Higher Education," sets the stage for understanding the role of the online distance education leader as a change agent. It explores the historical roots of distance education as a response to the needs of industrialization, the dimensions of the current transformation now under way as higher education adapts to the information society, and the role e-learning is playing in that transformation.

Chapter 2, "The Impact of Organizational Context," uses the personal experiences of the authors and the perspectives of leaders in five very different kinds of higher education institutions to demonstrate how organizational mission and culture affect the role of the leader.

Chapter 3, "Leading Change in the Mainstream: A Strategic Approach," looks at several sources to understand the traditionally decentralized shared governance culture of higher education and its implications for the online distance education program leader. It adopts the ethical realism philosophy of international affairs as a touchstone for leading change in this environment.

Chapter 4, "Leadership Is Personal," offers the perspective of one leader whose professional journey has led him to the conclusion that leadership is not only personal, but that the values and beliefs of the individual leader determine all other aspects of leadership.

Part Two: Ensuring Operational Excellence

The Sloan pillars of quality include three that deal with ensuring effective operations: learning effectiveness, faculty satisfaction, and student satisfaction. This section includes individual chapters on each of these three success criteria, as well as two chapters that explore the mainstreaming of online learning from a technological and strategic planning perspective.

Chapter 5, "Enhancing e-Learning Effectiveness," examines the inherent need to adapt pedagogical approaches to the unique opportunities and constraints of a new medium in adopting online technology for training and learning. This chapter takes the position that any such efforts should be grounded in detailed evidence of the inputs, processes, and outcomes of online courses and programs.

Chapter 6, "Supporting Faculty Success in Online Learning: Requirements for Individual and Institutional Leadership," examines the leader's twofold responsibility for ensuring faculty success in this new environment: preparing individual faculty members to effectively participate in online course instruction, and creating an institution-wide system to support and encourage faculty participation.

Chapter 7, "Optimizing Student Success Through Student Support Services," discusses how online distance education brings new students to our institutions who may not have direct physical access to traditional student support services and who may require support services that are not typically provided to campus-based students.

Chapter 8, "Moving Into the Technology Mainstream," surveys the development of information technology as part of the basic infrastructure of higher education and discusses leadership issues related to making online learning technology part of the institutional mainstream.

Chapter 9, "Operational Leadership in a Strategic Context," explores the interrelationships between operational leadership and strategic leadership at the institutional level.

Part Three: Sustaining the Innovation

The final Sloan pillar of quality addressed in this book relates to the ongoing institutional commitment to online learning. This section looks at the online distance education program leader's role in ensuring sustainability and scale through leadership that goes beyond internal operational excellence.

Chapter 10, "Policy Leadership in e-Learning," considers how online distance education has expanded and has raised fresh questions about a wide range of policy issues at the institutional level, but also at state and federal levels and among a variety of accrediting bodies. This chapter looks at those issues and how the distance education leader can become involved in their resolution.

Chapter 11, "Leading Beyond the Institution," discusses opportunities for leadership. Leading a distance education program also involves participating in broader professional communities beyond the institution. This can bring new insights into how to enhance the leader's program and also help ensure broader acceptance of online learning among key external constituents. This chapter looks at opportunities for leadership in three arenas: professional associations, accrediting organizations, and government and related policy arenas.

In Chapter 12, "Foreseeing an Actionable Future," the authors give their personal views on a wide range of issues that may affect the future of online distance education.

PART ONE

LEADING CHANGE
Making the Match Between Leadership and Institutional Culture

The basic purpose of a distance education program is to provide better access to the institution's academic programs for students who otherwise may not be able to fully participate in a program. This goal addresses the fundamental mission and purpose of the institution itself, a fact that is especially important in the era of online distance education, which has blurred the traditional distinctions between learning on campus and at a distance. The online distance education program leader in this environment must be sensitive to the broader institutional environment in which the distance education program functions and must be prepared to be a change agent.

The chapters in this section explore the broad institutional context for today's distance education operation, leadership challenges, and perspectives on how to lead and effect change, in the context of today's higher education culture.

In Chapter 1 Bruce Chaloux and Gary Miller, whose careers in distance education span changes in technology and policy over four decades, provide an overview of the changing social and institutional context in which distance education operates, starting with a brief history of distance education in the United States. This chapter closely examines the emergence of online learning, the nature of the current societal changes that are disrupting the higher education community, and external and internal policy issues that affect the development of online learning as part of a new higher education mainstream.

In Chapter 2, also by Chaloux and Miller, we visit with distance education leaders at five very different institutions to better understand the impact of organizational mission and culture on how distance education operates and how distance education leaders respond to leadership issues.

1

Chapter 3 looks at higher education as a complex, highly decentralized social organization. Gary Miller applies two approaches to strategic leadership from very different realms: Jim Collins's *Good to Great and the Social Sectors: A Monograph to Accompany Good to Great* (New York, NY: HarperCollins, 2005) and the ethical realism philosophy of international affairs. He then goes on to explore how these strategies can be adapted to help distance education leaders be successful as strategic change agents as online learning enters the mainstream of our institutions.

In Chapter 4, Wayne Smutz argues that leadership begins and ends with the leader—that leadership is personal—and presents his own personal leadership journey at The Pennsylvania State University World Campus to demonstrate the power of the individual in the complex world of a research university.

1

E-LEARNING AND THE TRANSFORMATION OF HIGHER EDUCATION

Bruce Chaloux and Gary Miller

E-learning has been a disruptive change in American distance education and, indeed, for distance education worldwide. It has brought into the field many institutions that had no previous involvement in distance education. It has stimulated the creation of new higher education organizations, including for-profit universities. And, in the process, it has brought into leadership roles academics and other professionals for whom distance education is a new venture and who have little connection with the preexisting distance education community. For that reason, we begin this book on leadership with an overview of the field, starting with a brief history of distance education in the United States, followed by a survey of the many aspects of higher education that are being transformed with the full flowering of the information society. The chapter concludes with a summary of the leadership challenges facing the field.

A Historical Perspective

For many higher education professionals, distance education is viewed as a recent phenomenon, launched by the e-learning innovations of the 1990s. The roots of e-learning run much deeper; distance education in its earliest form in the United States was correspondence education dating from the 1890s and was created because of the need to find new ways to extend access to agricultural education at the height of the Industrial Revolution. The evolution of distance education is the story of how our college and university leaders have sought to use a variety of the strategies and technologies of the day over more than a century and a half to help their institutions adapt to dramatically changing social needs. A long view of the evolution of distance education is essential to understanding the leadership challenges facing the field today, as online distance education emerges as one key to how higher education generally will adapt to a new cultural environment. As we begin our look at the leadership challenges associated with the current transformation of higher education, a quick look backward will help us understand the challenge of leadership in today's e-learning environment.

Distance Education and the Industrial Revolution

The Industrial Revolution began in the 1850s as a transportation revolution —from steamships that created new markets for U.S. goods to railroads that opened the continent for rapid development. Industrialization sparked a twofold transformation. First, growing industry stimulated urbanization as people moved from rural areas to rapidly growing cities to work in the new mills and factories. Second, at the same time, the United States experienced a massive immigration as new citizens came from all over the world, attracted by the promise of a fresh start in the new industrial democracy.

These factors, in turn, stimulated a transformation in American higher education. Policy makers recognized that the industrial economy would require new kinds of professional skills in the workforce, engineers, managers, scientists, city planners, and so forth. Also, a serious concern was that given the burgeoning immigrant population, the country would need to pay more attention to primary and secondary education so the children of immigrant families would acculturate to their roles as citizens of a democratic society. Moreover, new kinds of public higher education institutions were needed and indeed emerged in response to this challenge. Traditionally, higher education had been focused on the liberal arts and the preparation of students for the clergy and other traditional professions and was accessible only by the wealthy and socially elite. The Industrial Revolution demanded new institutions that could serve the growing middle class. The Morrill Land-Grant Act of 1862, now considered a cornerstone of higher education in the U.S., had as its stated purpose:

> without excluding other scientific and classical studies and including military tactic, to teach such branches of learning as are related to agriculture and the mechanic arts, in such manner as the legislatures of the States may respectively prescribe, in order to promote the liberal and practical education of the industrial classes in the several pursuits and professions in life.

Federal lands in each state were sold, and the proceeds were used to establish a land-grant college in each state to focus on the mechanical and practical arts, along with normal schools designed to produce the teachers needed by the growing public schools. In the end, the Morrill Act of 1862 and the Second Morrill Act of 1890, which created many of the historically Black colleges and universities, established the foundation for U.S. higher education for the next century, including the emergence of the distance education movement.

The Roots of Distance Education

When The Pennsylvania State University, the University of Chicago, and the University of Wisconsin launched the first tertiary-level correspondence programs in the United States in 1892, the country was a generation into the Industrial Revolution and in the midst of a social transformation the likes of which had not been seen since the Renaissance. Only the year before, in 1891, the federal government had announced the western frontier was officially closed; the United States was settled coast to coast. However, there was also a concern that the nation would not be able to sustain industrialization and the urbanization and immigration that fed it unless it was accompanied by a revolution in agriculture. The land-grant colleges took the lead on improving agricultural production, but policy makers were worried about how to keep them down on the farm. Rural life was isolated and hard, especially when compared to the growing consumer luxuries of urban life—electricity, telephones, and public transportation. One solution was to create a communication lifeline for rural families by extending home delivery of mail to rural areas, called Rural Free Delivery. It also provided a new delivery system that higher education institutions could use to reach learners. Although it was still experimental when the three institutions (two of them land grants, the third a new research university, all products of the Industrial Revolution) launched their first distance education programs in 1892, it was the genesis of modern university outreach efforts.

For much of the first half of the twentieth century, correspondence study led the development of distance education in the United States. Most public programs were housed at land-grant institutions. Some focused on agriculture and related issues, and were centralized in continuing education units and offered a wide variety of undergraduate courses. Some also offered high school courses via correspondence. While institutions competed with each other, they also collaborated, producing integrated catalogs, for instance, and licensing print-based course materials to each other.

The Coming of the Information Revolution

If the Industrial Revolution began as a transportation revolution, the information revolution began as a communications revolution. By the late 1950s and into the 1960s, institutions around the nation, especially community colleges (themselves a product of the late industrial period), began using local public television stations (some of which were owned by community colleges, school districts, or public universities) to extend access to college course lectures. Early efforts such as *Sunrise Semester* showed the promise of using technology to reach learners remote from traditional campuses and established a base of institutional experience that paved the way for today's e-learning efforts. A new form of distance education emerged—the telecourse—which combined recorded video lectures with traditional textbooks and study guides that contained discussion and assignments, and in some cases, occasional class meetings. Throughout the 1960s, telecourse delivery tended to be limited to the broadcast area of the local public television stations. In the 1970s, however, the coverage range extended as states built public television networks and as colleges gained control of local cable TV access channels.

Several projects emerged that demonstrated the potential of reaching remote students, such as the Appalachian Educational Satellite Program. Funded by the Appalachian Regional Commission, it used the experimental Applications Technology Satellite-6 (ATS-6) of the National Aeronautics and Space Administration to deliver telecourses and other educational programs in areas such as nursing and teacher education and firefighter training to a multistate area along the Appalachian Mountains. It demonstrated the potential of satellite technology to bring higher education and K–12 support units together across state boundaries to serve widely dispersed adult student populations.

The telecourse format also underpinned a major international venture in open and distance education: the formation of the British Open University in 1970. Now called the Open University (OU) of the United Kingdom, it combined video programs produced by the British Broadcasting Corporation (BBC) with highly developed printed materials and original readings to produce interdisciplinary courses delivered to adult learners throughout the United Kingdom through BBC broadcasts, complemented with classroom sessions at regional study centers. The OU became a model for the development of open universities throughout the world. In the United States, the International University Consortium for Telecommunications in Teaching was created by the University of Maryland University College to adapt the OU materials to the North American curriculum and then to license the resulting materials to its member institutions. Other consortia also began to emerge. Community colleges that produced telecourses created the Telecourse People, a consortium of community colleges created to jointly market their programs to other institutions. The To Educate the People Consortium brought together colleges and universities in Michigan with the automobile industry and unions to extend education to working people in that industry.

In 1978 satellite delivery took center stage as the Public Broadcasting Service (PBS) began to distribute its programs to public television stations via satellite and make its excess capacity available to educational institutions to deliver other kinds of educational programs. PBS established the Adult Learning Service to be a national aggregator of telecourse distribution. PBS-ALS acquired the distribution rights to telecourses from many different institutions and then, through its network of local PBS stations, licensed local institutions to offer the courses for credit when they were broadcast locally. In the early 1980s, the Annenberg Foundation granted $150 million to the Corporation for Public Broadcasting to support the development of high-quality telecourses in an effort to ensure that all adults would have access to key elements of the undergraduate curriculum.

While prepackaged telecourses dominated media-based distance education at the undergraduate level, some graduate schools, especially in engineering, began to use telecommunications to extend live classes in engineering and the sciences to workplaces near graduate schools. As satellite technology became more readily available, a variety of national higher education/industry partnerships emerged, such as the National Technological University and the National University Degree Consortium. The National University Teleconference Network was developed to provide a means to coordinate national delivery of noncredit professional training programs, while the Agricultural Satellite (Ag*SAT) Corporation (later renamed the American Distance Education Consortium) was created to use satellites to deliver agriculture-related training among cooperative extension services nationally and internationally.

Online Learning Emerges

By the early 1990s, live, interactive, telecommunications-based delivery was becoming a major trend in distance education. As technology shifted from satellite to telephone lines, lowering the cost of infrastructure and the cost per minute of delivery, many thought this would be the future of distance education. This changed in 1993 when the University of Illinois launched the first Internet web browser. Within three years, the World Wide Web had become an international phenomenon, and the modern e-learning environment was established.

There had been experiments with development of online degree programs before the web browser. Two examples illustrate the kind of innovations that were under way. In the early 1990s, for instance, The Pennsylvania State University incorporated computers and telephones into a synchronous delivery system to offer its master of adult education degree to students in Mexico and Europe. Around the same time, the University of Maryland University

College launched a baccalaureate degree in nuclear science as a contract program with several major energy companies; it used a version of the PLATO (Programmed Logic for Automatic Teaching Operations) computer system. However, the advent of the World Wide Web greatly lowered the cost of entry and stimulated a number of early experiments, many built as for-profit entities. Many of these early attempts failed. Columbia University's Fathom and AllLearn—a collaborative effort among the universities of Oxford, Princeton, Stanford, and Yale—were two examples of very visible experiments that failed in part because they were not rooted in the institutions' culture and mission and instead focused on visions of financial success during the dot-com bubble.

However, in 1996 the Western Interstate Cooperative for Higher Education, a regional collaborative of governors of 14 western states, announced the formation of the Western Governors University in an attempt to use the online environment to better serve the widely scattered populations of these states. This stimulated other states, regions, and institutions to take a serious look at online learning as a way to advance their core mission of providing access to education. Western Governors University ultimately focused its work on competency-based programs. However, the initial energy on a multistate online initiative stimulated institutions in other states to act.

The Sloan Five Pillars of Quality Online Education: Standards for a New e-Learning Community

The first decade of the twenty-first century was marked by the rapid growth in enrollments in online programs, the near ubiquitous adoption of e-learning by colleges and universities (particularly public institutions), and lately, the influx of proprietary institutions into the e-learning market. Online learning moved distance education into the mainstream of higher education and made it a central focus of a growing number of institutions.

Online learning has proven to be a truly disruptive innovation in the distance education community. For instance, it has attracted institutions that had no prior tradition in distance education and, as a result, no familiarity with the history research in the field. Often the starting point for online learning initiatives was with individual academic departments and faculty. As a result, a new leadership community was needed to help define the quality parameters for online distance education. In the United States, the development of this new community was spurred on in large part by the Alfred P. Sloan Foundation, which launched its asynchronous learning networks initiative in the mid-1990s, providing more than $40 million to help institutions launch mission-centered, sustainable online learning programs. The foundation's initiative resulted in the creation of a new professional community (the Sloan Consortium), a refereed journal (*Journal of Asynchronous Learning Networks*), and a strong research base. It supported the first national survey of online learning designed to document enrollments and to capture responses from institutional leadership. Published annually for eight years, the survey provides the most comprehensive information about online enrollments and challenges in the United States. Moreover, the Sloan Foundation's initiative established a framework for institutions to address quality. Defined metaphorically as *pillars* for online learning by the foundation's lead online learning officer, Frank Mayadas, the Five Pillars of Quality Online Education have been embraced by the community: access, cost-effectiveness and institutional commitment, learning effectiveness, faculty satisfaction, and student satisfaction (Moore, 2002). Together, the pillars of quality map the territory of leadership responsibility in this new arena.

Access represents the vision that online distance education will provide the means by which all qualified and motivated students will be able to complete courses, degrees, or other programs in their discipline of choice. This pillar begins with ensuring technical quality. However, quality in access also means ensuring that prospective students are aware of online learning opportunities available to them through marketing, branding, and program information through the web and other media. Access also requires that curricula are available in their entirety, that online programs have adequate options, clear program information, and seamless access from readiness assessment to navigation within courses and access to learning resources. Access also involves three areas of student support: academic support in the form of tutoring, advising, and library resources; administrative support, such as financial aid and disability services; and technical support, including a help desk that is available when students tend to study. The access pillar, then, requires a leadership involvement in delivery technology, marketing and public information, curriculum and program design, learning resources, and academic, administrative, and technical support. These elements are fundamental to an effective online learning service.

Cost-effectiveness and institutional commitment are factors that contribute to the institution's ability to sustain its commitment to an online learning program over time. It deals, in part, with the balance between high quality and cost-effectiveness. The goal is to control fixed and variable costs, not only for the delivery of a course but to recover its original development costs and the cost of updating the course over time. Leaders take responsibility for continuous improvement of processes and policies and for developing cost-effectiveness metrics, comparing costs and benefits of different delivery modes across diverse disciplines and program levels (undergraduate versus graduate for instance), and tracking retention rates, faculty workload and compensation, technology and infrastructure costs, and satisfaction levels. These metrics can be used to develop strategic plans for marketing that focus not only on generating new student enrollments but also ensuring the long-term loyalty of students, employers, and other constituents. Moving from initial innovations to achieve a sustainable level of operations may also require ongoing review of institution-wide policies that inhibit growth or cost-efficiency.

Learning effectiveness refers to the instructional quality of online learning: Is the online student's learning equivalent to that of traditional on-campus students? This requires that instructors and course developers work together to ensure that courses take advantage of the unique characteristics of online technology. Ensuring quality in this area means that leaders must involve their organization in a variety of functions, from instructional design to faculty development, assessment, and retention, and other factors that reflect learning outcomes.

Faculty satisfaction means broad acceptance by faculty for the use of technology and online pedagogical strategies that enhance the teaching and learning environment. More specifically, it addresses the need for faculty to find value in their online learning experiences and be assured that the quality is sound and that the technology helps them to meet learning objectives. A variety of factors help to measure faculty satisfaction, in particular, high-quality and continuous faculty-student and student-student interaction, the pace of student learning, achievement, and the freedom associated with online learning. It also includes rewards and recognition for course development and instruction, workload considerations, online instructional support, and student learning outcomes.

Student satisfaction is student acceptance of learning outcomes, enjoyment for the technology-based learning environment, the levels of interaction with faculty and students, and that expectations are met or exceeded. While distance education historically served students who otherwise did not have easy access to traditional campus-based offerings, dramatic enrollment increases suggest other students are seeking online programming. More and more students are enrolling in online courses for convenience and for balancing work, family, and study responsibilities, in addition to a growing number of students who live on or close to campus.

The pillars serve as a useful tool in framing the transformation of the higher education landscape. They also illustrate the scope of the challenge facing institutional distance education leaders, who, in order to address all five dimensions of quality, must either build services in each area or work with existing support units to ensure quality.

Disruption: The Nature of the Current Transformation

If Rural Free Delivery was the information highway of the nineteenth century, providing a national delivery system for the first generation of distance education, the World Wide Web has marked the road ahead for the Information Society. At the same time, the societal implications of the Information Revolution have proven to be as profound in the twenty-first century as the changes brought about during the Industrial Revolution, but even more rapid in their impact on education. Online learning is both part of the disruption and part of the response.

Globalization. Perhaps the most visible dimension of the current revolution is that global communications have eliminated geography as a natural barrier. Immigration, which helped to fuel industrialization and democratization in the 1800s, has been replaced by globalization in the information era. We now have a global communications system, a globally distributed workforce and, as a result, a global supply chain for a wide range of products and services. This includes higher education, which can be viewed as a commodity and has been developed as such by several countries that export online learning programs and services.

Redefining community. Globalization is also forcing individuals and organizations to redefine *community* at many levels. Traditionally, we tend to think of communities as local. A community is a village or a neighborhood of people who live interdependent lives. You may own the town bank, but my son teaches your daughter in the local school. The kids we went to school with grow the food we eat, run the shops where we buy what we need, attend the same churches, and so on. In a globalized economy that kind of highly localized interdependence is harder to find. The process of reperceiving our understanding of community and how communities are interdependent in today's world is a critical issue. In his book *The World Is Flat*, Friedman (2005) calls this "Globalization 3.0" and suggests that the flattening of the world is a product of the convergence of the personal computer and fiber-optic microcable with the rise of workflow software.

Innovation. The rapid pace of technological and social change is forcing employers to put greater emphasis on top-down and bottom-up innovation to stay competitive. Knowledge is no longer an end in itself but is increasingly a lifelong and a just-in-time experience. Workers are expected to find information, evaluate it in the context of their work, and apply it to solve problems. Innovation has become a core skill in the information society.

Collaboration. A globally distributed workforce and supply chain, combined with the need for continuous innovation, have made collaboration and teamwork critical workplace skills at all levels of an organization. Current technology allows levels of collaboration never seen before that support professionals from different countries to compare results, undertake testing/assessments, and to seek solutions in a very different work environment. This developed earlier in the higher education research community and is now occurring in instructional activities.

Emergence of the skills society. Some have begun to call the information society a knowledge society, which is less about how quickly information reaches people and more about how information brings people and ideas together in new ways. We are beginning to realize that in reality the knowledge society is a skills society, a shift that will have a significant impact on education at all levels. Officials in U.S. government have realized the strategic importance of preparing a workforce for this new environment, and they have set a goal for the number of high school graduates who enter postsecondary education and complete a credential to increase from the current level of 39% to 60% by the year 2020. Reaching this goal will require not only greatly expanded access to higher education but also an increase in the percentage of high school graduates who are prepared to go on to college. This challenge has spawned a new market of students—adults with some college but no degree—many, if not most, of whom cannot be served by traditional campus programs.

The Impact on Education

Just as the Internet has enabled globalization at many levels, it has eliminated geography as a limiting factor in the relationships between educational institutions and their students and faculty. Increasingly, many institutions that do not have a history or tradition in distance education are able to serve students well beyond their traditional service areas. At the same time, they can provide more convenient access to students on and near campus. Moreover, a growing number of traditional students are opting for online versions of courses. While the reasons may not always be academic, acceptance of the legitimacy and quality of online learning is growing.

Expanding impact. While land-grant universities and community colleges, the two ends of the public higher education spectrum, continue to dominate the distance education environment, many new institutions have entered the field. *Changing Course* (Allen & Seaman, 2010), the tenth annual study of the impact of online learning conducted by the Babson Survey Research Group, noted in 2010 that more than 6.7 million U.S. students (32% of all higher education students) reported taking at least one online course during the fall 2011 term, which is a 9.3% rate of growth that far exceeds the less than 0.1% overall decrease in the higher education student population (pp. 4, 17).

As these data suggest, the impact of online learning is being felt not only in distance education but across traditional campuses as faculty begin to blend online elements into otherwise traditional courses. The resulting hybrid courses, in which online activities replace between 20% and 80% of classroom activity, provide greater flexibility for students and faculty while also introducing new pedagogical elements. Similarly, blended programs, which mix a significant percentage of fully online and hybrid courses with some traditional classroom experiences or residencies, increase practical access for students who live near a campus but who must mix study with job and family commitments.

The result is an increasingly complex context for online learning at institutions, many of which do not share a long history of distance education and as a result are not organized to support this new relationship with students. While an institution's initial focus might be on the technology of delivery, once a program is up and running, other questions become critical to sustainability and scalability. These issues, which include student support, faculty support, learning effectiveness, and policy, and their implications for leadership are explored in more detail in subsequent chapters.

New institutions. The information revolution is also stimulating new kinds of institutions to meet the expanding need for professional education in a knowledge society. Most visible are for-profit companies that offer either fully online or blended learning experiences at undergraduate and graduate levels. Most have sought regional accreditation, the gold standard of higher education quality in the United States, which opens doors to federal grant programs. Indeed, the top three recipients of federal financial aid are for-profit companies. This has stimulated increased federal concern about financial aid and student recruiting, which could have an impact on the field in general. The national policy implications are explored in depth in Chapter 10.

New opportunities for collaboration. Just as technology has eliminated geography as a barrier between institutions and students, it is allowing institutions to find new ways to work together to meet student needs. The open educational resources movement is stimulating faculty members to make their online learning content available to faculty at other institutions around the world. Institutions are collaborating to offer online degree programs they would not be able to sustain individually as a way of better serving the needs of students in their traditional service areas and to reach new student populations. During the late 1990s, a number of networks, many funded by the Sloan Foundation, also began working on collaborative online learning. In New York a regional consortium initially led by State University of New York (SUNY) Empire State College became a statewide entity led by the system administration. The SUNY Learning Network was particularly successful in leveraging online learning with community colleges. Collaboration is also emerging beyond state boundaries. One example is the Great Plains Interactive Distance Education Alliance, through which research universities in the Midwest use online learning to offer degree programs in agriculture and the human sciences they would have difficulty offering individually. In this environment, online learning leaders must be able not only to lead their operational functions associated with online delivery, but they must learn to lead beyond the institution, helping to identify partnership opportunities and informing their institution about developments in the field. This challenge is the focus of Chapter 11.

New students. The U.S. Department of Education's goal of increasing the percentage of high school graduates who go on to college to 60% by 2020 means increasing the total student population by almost 50%. That level of growth, and the need for rapid response, will greatly exceed the current campus capacity. Online distance education will become increasingly important as a strategic response to this need.

Another factor is the student population itself. Today, traditional and nontraditional students tend to be part of what Diana Oblinger (Oblinger & Oblinger, 2005) of EDUCAUSE has called the "Net Generation," students born in or after 1982 who have grown up with the Internet as a daily factor in their lives. In *Educating the Net Generation*, Oblinger and Oblinger note that as college students the Net Generation demonstrates distinctive learning preferences, including

- A predisposition to work and learn in peer-to-peer teams.
- A structured environment that sets well-defined parameters and priorities, so that they can achieve a goal.
- Engagement and an experiential learning environment that encourages interactivity and inductive discovery—making observations, formulating hypotheses, figuring out rules.
- A comfort with image-rich environments, rather than with text and with doing things rather than just talking about things.
- Learning within the context of solving real-world problems and focusing on "things that matter." (p. 2.7)

The oldest of members of the Net Generation turned 30 in 2012. Increasingly, the adult part-time learner, who is the target of most online programs, will consist of Net Generation students who have these learning preferences.

New pedagogy. Providing access, convenience, flexibility, and cost-effectiveness will continue to be important issues, but the emerging leadership question for the next decade or so is how can educational institutions help individuals learn how to build and sustain new communities built around collaboration and sharing of knowledge to solve local and, increasingly, global problems? For distance education leaders, the challenge is more focused: How can we use what we've learned about online distance education to help transform our institutions to meet the needs of this emerging society?

Institutional Leadership Issues: Lessons From the Association of Public Land-grant Universities Study

In 2009 the Association of Public Land-grant Universities (APLU) published an intensive study of the leadership factors that contribute to a successful e-learning initiative at public research universities (McCarthy & Samors, 2009). The report notes that the two-part benchmarking study "was designed to illuminate how public institutions develop and implement the key organizational strategies, processes, and procedures that contribute to successful and robust online learning initiatives" (p. 5). The first part of the study included 231 interviews with key people at 45 institutions who represented at least 100,000 online enrollments. Interviewees included presidents and chancellors, chief academic officers, online learning administrators, faculty leaders and professors, and online students (p. 10). The second part was a faculty survey sent to more than 50,000 faculty members across the teaching spectrum—full-time and part-time, tenure track and non–tenure track, those who had taught online and those who had not. APLU received nearly 11,000 completed surveys from faculty at 69 institutions.

The final report (McCarthy & Samors, 2009) included several general observations about effective e-learning programs:

- Online learning programs may work most effectively as a core component of institutional strategic planning and implementation.
- Online learning initiatives benefit from ongoing institutional assessment and review because of their evolving and dynamic nature.
- Online learning activities are strengthened by the centralization of some organizational structures and administrative functions that support and sustain the programs.
- Online learning programs overseen by academic affairs units may be more readily accepted and may be more easily integrated into the fabric of the institution.
- Online learning programs need reliable financing mechanisms for sustainability and growth.

- Online learning programs succeed with consistent and adequate academic, administrative, and technological resources for faculty and students.
- Online learning programs have the capacity to change campus culture and become fully integrated if presidents, chancellors, chief academic officers, and other senior campus leaders are fully engaged in the delivery of messages that tie online education to fundamental institutional missions and priorities.

The report's recommendations emphasized the critical importance of communication, with all faculty and administrators, campus leaders, administrators, and faculty working together to ensure and improve quality, and for administrators to better understand what motivates faculty to teach (McCarthy & Samors, 2009). The report also recommended that administrative and academic governing bodies regularly reexamine institutional policies regarding faculty incentives and develop strategies to acknowledge and recognize faculty investment of time and effort in online courses compared to face-to-face teaching (p. 6).

The interviews with campus leaders and the faculty survey suggested four broad leadership strategies for a successful program: developing the online initiative within the context of institutional strategic planning, developing an organizational structure that recognizes shared authority for different aspects of the program, designing a financial model that ensures sustainability for administrative and academic investments, and communicating within the academy in a way that dispels myths and builds a sense of community.

Strategic planning. The study (McCarthy & Samors, 2009) noted the critical role institution-wide task forces or advisory councils have played in successful online learning initiatives. Several of the campus leaders interviewed noted "the benefit of maintaining standing committees or task forces after online programs have been established and have begun to grow and mature. These oversight groups address new or unforeseen issues that arise or examine and advise campus leaders on proposed changes in financial and administrative structuring, or policies and procedures" (p. 16). Typically, such groups should be charged by the president, the provost, or the faculty senate.

The report emphasized, "While many issues appear to be resolved prior to launch, the Commission believes that campus leaders must remain sensitized to the many issues that may resurface or emerge in previously unanticipated ways once a program is underway or as it has matured" (McCarthy & Samors, 2009, p. 18). Among the issues advisory councils or task forces should monitor are enterprise and unit-level technology needs, academic oversight, program scope, financing for all aspects of the program (including faculty and student resources), nonfinancial faculty and student support, and quality control and assessment (p. 18).

Designing the organizational structure. Traditionally, higher education operates in an environment of decentralized academic authority and centralized administration and support services. The report (McCarthy & Samors, 2009) identified three essential elements that should be considered in developing the organizational structure:

- administrative oversight and faculty support housed within academic affairs, which could be organized as a new central administrative unit or a new charge to an existing unit;
- curricular control as a fundamental responsibility of academic departments, always, the report notes, residing in academic affairs; and
- technological elements as the responsibility of Information Technology units.

The report notes there is no single organizational home for the instructional design function, which supports faculty in developing courses but also works closely with the technology itself (p. 23).

Developing sustainable funding and allocating institutional resources. The report noted that at the broadest level,

> institutional participant observations and faculty respondent data together indicate that campus leaders must consider multiple approaches to institutional resource allocation, including strategies that take into account the difference between resources needed to start a program and resources needed to sustain and/or grow a program. (McCarthy & Samors, 2009, p. 24)

The APLU commission defines *institutional resources* as "the combination of financial, administrative, and technical allocations made to support online learning initiatives" (McCarthy & Samors, 2009, p. 24). The commission emphasizes that

> upfront funding for online programs is essential for the development of robust strategic online initiatives. Further, institutions must provide the necessary resources to sustain and to grow established online initiatives. This ongoing need for funding holds true for institutions that are in "start up mode" or "re-start mode" with their online learning efforts, as well as for those running more mature programs. (p. 25)

The commission discovered that institutions have diverse ways to recover costs. Some have created new fees attached to registration costs for online learning. Others have developed various kinds of revenue-sharing models to distributed tuition revenue in order to cover costs. Still others have established separate tuition levels (for online courses (McCarthy & Samors, 2009, p. 26).

Equally important to the success of a program are the nonfinancial resources provided to faculty. Three areas were seen as especially important for leaders to address: (a) professional support for course design and delivery, including faculty training programs as well as the availability of instructional designers and media specialists to work with faculty members in course development and delivery; (b) faculty incentives for development and delivery of online content, including stipends, but also including promotion and tenure policies that reward younger faculty members for participating in online course development at the expense of other more traditional activities; and (c) institutional policies concerning intellectual property.

Another important institutional resource is support for the online student. For instance, some institutions assign the online student a special academic adviser who continues to work with the student through his or her entire academic program. The report noted that some campuses use routine student survey instruments to identify the need for these kinds of services (McCarthy & Samors, 2009).

Effective leadership communication. The APLU study found that launching an online program can be a significant cultural and operational change for the institution. As a result, the report states that "a critical and ongoing task for campus leaders is to provide effective leadership and communication of institutional plans and decisions" (McCarthy & Samors, 2009, p. 41). Among the critical leadership skills are the "keen ability to recognize and articulate the value of online learning, relate it to campus mission, and seize organizational changes and planning as opportunities to solidify institutional commitment to online learning" (p. 42).

Part of the communication challenge is to deal with the culture change that often underpins the online initiative. The APLU study found a sometimes marked difference of perception between campus administrative leaders and faculty. With that in mind, it encourages campus leaders directly communicate to dispel myths and to build a stronger communication environment. The following are specific recommendations:

- Campus leaders need to better understand the characteristics of the online teaching populations on their campus and use communication strategies that target and engage all faculty members.
- Campus leaders should maintain consistent communication with all faculty and administrators regarding the role and purpose of online

learning programs as they relate to academic mission and academic quality. Further, campus leaders, administrators, and faculty must all work together to improve the quality—or perceived quality—of online learning outcomes.

- Campus leaders have the potential to expand faculty engagement by better understanding what motivates faculty to teach online.
- Campus leaders and faculty governing bodies need to regularly re-examine institutional policies regarding faculty incentives, especially in this era of declining financial resources. Perhaps most importantly, campus leaders need to identify strategies to acknowledge and recognize the additional time and effort faculty invest in online, as compared to face-to-face, teaching and learning. (McCarthy & Samors, 2009, pp. 47–49)

A Changing State and National Policy Context

Throughout the twentieth century, U.S. distance education courses were subject to very little regulation. States could regulate educational institutions only if they established a physical presence in the state. Distance education—by correspondence study or by telecommunications systems like satellite—was protected by federal interstate commerce regulations. Where distance education was part of a traditional college or university, it was regulated as part of the institution's regional accreditation, itself a product of the Industrial Age. Other institutions, including for-profit providers, were regulated through the Distance Education and Training Council or other professional bodies.

However, the policy context in which online distance education operates promises to be quite different for several reasons. The global nature of the policy challenge was suggested in a European Commission report, *The Future of Learning: Preparing for Change* (Redecker et al., 2011), which noted several factors affecting public policy in education.

The overall vision is that personalization, collaboration, and informalization (informal learning) are at the core of learning in the future. These terms are not new in education and training but will have to become the central guiding principle for organizing learning and teaching in the future. The central learning paradigm is characterized by lifelong and lifewide learning, shaped by the ubiquity of information and communication technologies. At the same time, because of fast advances in technology and structural changes to European labor markets that are related to demographic change, globalization and immigration, generic and transversal skills will become more important. These skills will help citizens to become lifelong learners who flexibly respond to change, are able to proactively develop their competences and thrive in collaborative learning and working environments.

In the United States, several interrelated factors have combined to create a dramatic change in the policy context in which online distance education operates. First, the federal government recognizes that the nation's ability to compete in a global knowledge-based economy requires that a greater percentage of high school graduates earns a college degree. The U.S. Department of Education has set a goal of increasing the rate from the current level of 39% to 60% by the year 2020. This goal has made the government increasingly sensitive to the effective use of federal support for education, including federal financial aid to students, especially in light of the rise of for-profit degree-granting organizations. According to a *Chronicle of Higher Education* article, "for-profit colleges that rely heavily on online education receive nearly 90 percent of their revenue from federal student aid" (Kelderman, 2011, p. B5). The top three recipients of federal financial aid are for-profit companies.

A 2011 EDUCAUSE policy review reported that, while the Department of Education has "reiterated the historical interpretation of state authorization—that is, to participate in federal financial aid programs, an institution had to be authorized to offer postsecondary education *by the state in which it was physically located*," regulations proposed in October 2010 inserted a new requirement for distance education programs (Cummings, 2011, p. 110; emphasis in original). "In essence," the review notes, "the new regulation clearly tied, for the first time, the financial aid eligibility of students in distance learning programs to whether their institutions are authorized by the state *in which the student, not the institution, is located*" (p. 110; emphasis in original).

The rise of for-profit degree-granting organizations has also had an effect on regional accrediting agencies. The six regional accrediting agencies had all developed a common set of standards for online distance education as early as 2001 (Kelderman, 2011). However, some regional accreditors have come under scrutiny as the number of regionally accredited for-profit degree granters has increased. The Government Accountability Office "alleged widespread abuses in the recruiting and enrollment of students at for-profit colleges" (Kelderman, 2011, p. B5), challenging the standards and accreditation review processes of the regional agencies.

The regulation and policy issues are highly interrelated at the state, regional, and national levels. This environment requires distance education leaders at higher education institutions of all types to be ambassadors. They must not only focus on building effective policy and practice at the institutional level, which itself requires a great deal of tact and diplomacy, but they must be prepared to represent their institution's needs with external agencies and simultaneously translate regulatory concerns within the institution and help construct institution-wide responses. A more detailed discussion of policy issues can be found in Chapter 10.

Coupled with these myriad factors, a larger financial cloud hovers over the world economy. In the United States this portends radical changes in federal support for education. Public institutions in most states are witnessing reduced state support, are increasing tuition and fees, and are being asked to be more efficient and effective, particularly in regard to degree attainment.

The Leadership Challenge for Distance Education

All these factors will change the landscape of higher education institutions, which will be asked to do more with less. Few believe the current capacity of institutions can respond to the challenge, which opens a window of opportunity for online learning.

A new mainstream. We can envision a broader strategic horizon in which distance education is a key part of a more complex picture, one that includes fully online courses offered to students on campus and at a distance, hybrid courses offered on campus and through continuing education, blended programs that mix distance education and site-based experiences, and more generally, an academic environment in which e-learning is seen as a utility available to all faculty and students. Access will continue to be a critical strategic issue, along with efficiency on campus and, perhaps most important, continuing to develop a new pedagogy that responds to the new needs of Net Generation individuals and their communities.

Strategic focus. Increasingly, online education in all its variations is seen as central to the strategic future of institutions. Allen and Seaman (2010) noted that "sixty-three percent of all reporting chief academic officers said that online learning was a critical part of their institution's long term strategy" (p. 2). The perception was greatest among public universities; almost 75% reported positively on this topic. However, a much higher percentage of for-profit companies actually included online learning in their written strategic plans.

New relationships. Online learning is also blurring distinctions between higher education institutions and other sectors. Online learning facilitates dual enrollment courses in which students simultaneously earn high school and college credit. It also opens new opportunities for partnerships between institutions and employers. The Energy Providers Consortium for Education is an example of industry and education collaborating to build critical workforce skills. It brings together four higher education institutions, a virtual high school, and more than 20 energy companies, unions, and industry associations to offer undergraduate degrees and certificates in areas such as renewable energy, electric power, nuclear power, and electrical engineering.

A chance to lead. The transformation suggested by these trends is an opportunity for those involved with online learning to accept the challenge and lead institutions into a new era, one built to respond to student needs, one built on flexibility that technologies now and those in the future support, one that expands access to quality education, and one that can be more cost-effective and efficient than current models. It is a time for action and bold leadership in higher education.

References

Allen, I. E., & Seaman, J. (2013). Changing course: Ten years of tracking online education in the United States. Needham, MA: Babson Survey Research Group.

Cummings, J. (2011). Online learning challenges: State authorization, federal regulation. *EDUCAUSE Review, 46*(6), pp. 110–111. Retrieved from http://net .educause.edu/ir/library/pdf/ERM11610.pdf

Friedman, T. L. (2005). *The world is flat: A brief history of the twenty-first century.* New York, NY: Farrar, Straus & Giroux.

Kelderman, E. (2011, November 11). Online programs face new demands from accreditors. The Chronicle of Higher Education, pp. B4–B5.

McCarthy, S., & Samors, R. (2009). *Online learning as a strategic asset.* Retrieved from http://www.aplu.org/document.doc?id=1877

Moore, J. C. (2002). *Elements of quality: The Sloan-C framework.* Needham, MA: Sloan Consortium.

Morrill Act, 7 U.S.C. § 301 et seq. (1862).

Morrill Act, 26 Stat. 417, 7 U.S.C. 321 et seq. (1890).

Oblinger, D., & Oblinger, J. (2005). *Educating the net generation.* Retrieved from http://www.educause.edu/educatingthenetgen

Redecker, C., Leis, M., Leendertse, M., Punie, Y., Gijsbers, G., Kirschner, P., . . . Hoogveld, B. (2011). *The future of learning: Preparing for change.* Retrieved from http://ipts.jrc.ec.europa.eu/publications/pub.cfm?id=4719

2

THE IMPACT OF ORGANIZATIONAL CONTEXT

Bruce Chaloux and Gary Miller

In 2006 Miller and Schiffman noted, "Most institutions began their online learning programs with one of two goals in mind: (1) to extend access to degree programs to new off-campus students or (2) to improve the quality of teaching for existing students on campus. Initial emphasis on access or quality typically drove early decisions about organization and funding" (p. 15). Similarly, decisions about organization and business models affect how the online learning program leader operates in different types of institutions. This chapter explores the implications of organizational and business models for distance education leadership in several different institutional environments.

Understanding the Unique Position of the Online Learning Leader

Online distance education leaders often hold positions in their institutions that are rare if not unique. While some distance education programs reside fully in an individual academic department, many distance education programs are centrally administered, institution-wide delivery systems that work with multiple academic units to design, deliver, and support faculty and students in diverse programs that reflect many different disciplines. There are few positions like this in most traditional higher education institutions. We asked how the online distance education function is organized in several different institutions to see what the leadership implications might be. The most obvious conclusions are that there is no single way to organize the function and that leaders must understand and work within the context of their organizational structure and culture to achieve change in that culture. However, reviewing different models to compare and contrast their structures and the leadership challenges faced in different institutional settings can be instructive.

23

As part of a Pennsylvania State University and Sloan Consortium leadership development program (the Institute for Emerging Leadership in Online Learning), we developed a set of questions to help participants prepare for the program. Every online program leader should be able to answer these questions about the role of the online distance education program at his or her home institution and the opportunities and restrictions on leadership in that environment. It can be a helpful guide for leaders.

1. What is your institution's vision for online learning? How does it fit with the institution's overall mission and goals?
2. Where does the online learning unit sit within your institution? What is the reporting line from you to the President/Chancellor/Chief Administrative Officer?
3. What is the unit's relationship with academic units and faculty who teach in other learning environments?
4. What is your governance structure? Who sits on the unit's internal leadership team? If you have an institution-wide governing/steering/advisory committee, who sits on this?
5. What are your institution's financial goals for online learning? How have these been articulated and approved?
6. How are costs—the unit's and related operational and academic costs— recovered? What happens to after-cost revenue?
7. How are the various support functions—technology, student support, faculty support, registration, and so on—organized? What functions are organized centrally at the institutional level? What are organized within a central online learning unit? What are distributed to individual academic units?
8. Where is policy about online learning made and approved? How are policy issues resolved?
9. What is the organizational culture in which the online learning initiative functions at your institution? Is it similar to or different from the organizational culture in other parts of the institution? Do the differences or similarities matter? How?
10. What are the most significant leadership arenas for online learning at your institution: administrative (organization, finance, etc.), academic (program approval, faculty relations, etc.), technology, or other?

Five Institutional Models

Using this general framework, we asked executive-level leaders at five very different institutions to answer these questions to illustrate how organizational structure shapes leadership opportunities and restrictions. While different in size, scope, and structure, they share a common feature: All have highly successful online learning programs and have demonstrated leadership crucial to that success. Our institutions included the following:

- a major research (R1) land-grant institution;
- a small regional state university;
- a large state college with an adult-focused mission;
- a large two-year community college online-only institution; and
- a large for-profit online-only institution.

The responses were as diverse as the institutions, but common elements emerged and provided a helpful framework for leadership for any institution engaged in online learning. These elements are presented in the final section of this chapter.

The Pennsylvania State University World Campus

Established in 1855, The Pennsylvania State University (Penn State) is one of America's leading state universities, a land-grant university that enrolls more than 95,000 students—some 45,000 on its main campus in University Park; over 34,000 more on several commonwealth campuses around the state; and nearly 10,000 in the World Campus, Penn State's online campus. The World Campus operates as an administrative delivery unit, delivering degree and certificate programs from Penn State's core academic units. It was developed in the context of a mature university-wide outreach function that dates from the early years of extended education. Penn State was a pioneer in distance education, offering some of the nation's first correspondence courses in the 1890s and leading in the production and delivery of educational television, satellite, and interactive video services before the Internet era. In addition to distance education, the Outreach function includes a variety of continuing education delivery services, ranging from academic conferencing to evening programs and specialized training programs for industry. Outreach is an administrative unit, with no academic authority, so the World Campus works with all academic units to offer degree programs online. In addition, the World Campus is not the only way the university uses online technology and methods; some colleges have their own instructional development functions, and a central information technology services unit maintains the university-wide technology infrastructure and support services that serve the traditional campuses and the World Campus.

The World Campus executive director reports to the vice president for outreach, who reports to the president.

University of Illinois at Springfield

The University of Illinois at Springfield (UIS) is the smallest of three campuses that constitute the University of Illinois system, the other two being the flagship University of Illinois at Urbana-Champaign, and the University of Illinois at Chicago. The three institutions enroll over 70,000 students. Founded as Sangamon State University in 1969, then renamed UIS in 1995, it is a regional university that enrolls over 5,000 students, a number reached in large measure because of an expanding online program that enrolls some 1,400 students, more than one quarter of the entire student body. The online program was established as a *mirror* campus, meaning all programs available on campus are also available online. This has propelled enrollments and made UIS's online efforts a central part of the institution's mission and focus. All online activities are centralized in the office of the associate vice chancellor and director of the Center for Online Learning, Research and Service, who reports to the vice chancellor for academic affairs. As with Penn State, the online initiative reflects the shared governance model of traditional higher education institutions: while the administrative functions are centralized, the unit works across academic units to develop and deliver programs; academic authority rests with the academic units.

Empire State College

A component institution of the State University of New York (SUNY), Empire State College was founded in 1971 with a distinctive nontraditional flavor. Initiated by Ernest Boyer, it was founded on the same principles of the British Open University, which was emerging at the same time. The philosophy included having full-time faculty responsible for developing distance-learning curricula but arranging courses so that delivery of the studies could also be done with part-time faculty. It developed within SUNY as a special-purpose institution focused on adult learners. The college enrolls some 20,000 students, with the online program serving nearly half the college's enrollments, including international students. It has been using distance education (starting with print) since the late 1980s. The Center for Distance Learning is led by a dean and is a centralized online learning unit and an undergraduate academic programming unit, with full-time faculty members serving as area coordinators, managing a cluster of related courses. Graduate programs report through the Center for Graduate Studies. Both centers report through the provost's office.

Rio Salado College

Established in 1978 as one of 10 institutions in the Maricopa Community College System in Phoenix, Arizona, Rio Salado College has focused on reaching underserved students initially using distance and now online learning to become the largest unit in the system. The college enrolls about 70,000 students annually, 43,000 of which take courses online with a full-time faculty of 33, supplemented by a part-time or adjunct faculty of 1,500 and nearly 650 administrative/support staff. Another defining feature of Rio's model is that classes begin most Mondays, 48 times a year. It is a model that has proven to be effective, as its enrollment numbers suggest. At Rio Salado College, online learning is not a separate unit, but an integrated function supported by all divisions of the college. The vice president of academic affairs serves as the college's chief academic officer and reports directly to the college president. The vice president of academic affairs oversees instructional design and support leaders and is the liaison between residential and adjunct faculty to ensure the academic integrity of the institution.

American Public University System

The American Public University System (APUS) represents one of the new emerging for-profit higher education organizations that have arisen as one part of the transformation of higher education in the information society. All its courses are offered online, and all faculty teach only online. It was established in 1991, initially as the American Military University. It added American Public University and became a system in 2002. The system enrolls more than 100,000 students, the majority of whom are in the military, which is in keeping with its initial student market. It is led by a president and chief executive officer to whom all the supporting academic and administrative functions report. Institutional governance is provided by a board of trustees, and shareholder governance is provided by a board of directors. Both boards approve the annual budget and strategic plan.

The Impact of Business Models

The business model for the online distance education function has a significant impact on the leader's scope of control and ability to influence broader institutional change. Just as there is no single organizational structure for distance education, business models vary widely based on institutional type, organization, and funding. Following are some examples of different models and their impact on the leader's role.

Penn State World Campus is charged to generate new students and, in the process, generate new revenue for the university. It is set up as a cost center within the broader university. It is required to recover all costs, including costs of academic units that offer courses and to return a portion of gross revenue to participating academic units. All costs are recovered through tuition revenue from enrollments. Revenue goals are tied to enrollment goals, which are set to more than double between 2012 and 2021. A revenue sharing plan returns a percentage of gross tuition revenue to the academic unit that generated the enrollment; if funds remain after all costs are recovered, they are invested into improvements or in growth opportunities.

At Rio Salado College, where online learning is integrated into the mainstream business structure, the college has no direct control over tuition rates and so must depend on increased enrollments to generate new revenue. Online learning is seen as one means to expand the student population served. After-cost revenue accrues to the central administration, and the executive council of the college determines how funds are allocated according to the college's strategic plan.

UIS, which represents a third variation on the public college/university, uses a financial model that lies somewhat between that of Penn State and Rio Salado College. Like Penn State's World Campus, its goal is to be self-sustaining without the use of state-appropriated dollars. Like Rio Salado, tuition revenue is retained and distributed by the chancellor's and provost's offices. However, it also uses an online learning course fee in addition to the standard tuition. This fee is distributed across several stakeholder groups, including the academic unit that generated the fee, the online operating unit, information technology, marketing, and the library.

Empire State College represents another business model. Like some of the other institutional cases, it is self-sustaining, with net revenues distributed to support other college activities through an annual budgeting process.

APUS, a for-profit provider, also has a highly centralized business model. The budget for online learning is guided by a high variable-cost ratio and a low fixed-cost ratio. This encourages growth to maintain profitability. Net revenues (which in this environment are defined as revenues less operating costs and income taxes) are reinvested in technology and facilities.

In the end, each of these five institutions is driven by enrollments and the success of their online programs is measured, in financial terms and in other ways, by serving more students. However, the business model—how operational functions are staffed and managed, how costs are managed, and how revenue is distributed—affects the scope of influence for the online leader and determines formal and informal relationships and communication paths the leader must maintain in order to be effective.

A Vision for Online Learning

The success of the five institutions can be attributed to many factors. Some bring a long history of outreach through distance learning; others have developed programs to serve niche (albeit very large) markets. Still others have devised creative strategies and delivery models that make learning opportunities more accessible. But without exception, responses from the five participating leaders clearly indicated there is a vision for online learning for the institutions or units charged with online learning programs that drive their activities.

Vision comes from leadership and is defined by institutional mission statements that make it clear that online programming is important and in some instances critical to long-term success. These five institutions have secured this ground, but they are in the minority, as shown by a study conducted for the Sloan Consortium by I. Elaine Allen and Jeff Seaman (2011). In a series of annual surveys, the researchers asked questions of chief academic officers about the importance of online learning for their future efforts. Historically, this percentage has approached 80%, that is, institutional academic leaders believe online is critical to their future programming efforts. But there is a gap, as Allen and Seaman describe it, between what the academic leaders believe and their institutions' planning processes. Moreover, the gap seems greatest in the public sector and less so in the for-profit sector. The figures from the latest report are telling: Figure 2.1 depicts the criticalness of online education to long-term strategy by type of institutional control; Figure 2.2 depicts the inclusion of online learning in strategic plans, also by type of institutional control.

In a series of earlier surveys conducted for the Association of Public and Land-grant Universities–Sloan National Commission on Online Learning

Figure 2.1 Online Education Is Critical to the Long-Term Strategy of My Institution by Institutional Control, Percent Agreeing—Fall 2009 to Fall 2011.

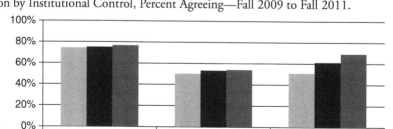

Note: From *Going the Distance: Online Education in the United States* (p. 8), by I. E. Allen & J. Seaman, 2011, Wellesley, MA: Babson Survey Research Group.

Figure 2.2 Online Education Is Critical to the Long-Term Strategy of My Institution by Institutional Control—Fall 2010 to Fall 2011.

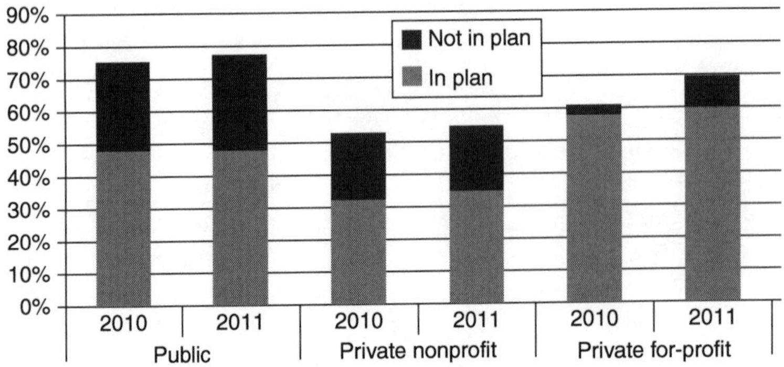

Note: From *Going the Distance: Online Education in the United States* (p. 9), by I. E. Allen & J. Seaman, 2011, Wellesley, MA: Babson Survey Research Group.

(which also included a survey of some 10,000 faculty, the largest such study ever conducted), the researchers described the gap in the following way:

> All three surveys of campus leaders revealed a striking gap: Close to, or more than two-thirds of the responding CEOs recognized that online programs are strategically important to the institution, yet close to, or less than one-half of the respondents actually included online programs in the campus strategic plan. This gap exists even at a time when the number of students taking at least one online course continues to expand at a rate far in excess of the growth of overall higher education enrollments. (McCarthy & Samors, 2009, p. 9)

This suggests an area of need and a challenge for leaders of online programs to educate those who set the strategic direction of institutions. Online leaders must work to have a voice in the strategic planning process, either directly or through others who have a vested interest in the success of the online program and who understand the issues. In this area, as in most, leaders cannot limit their scope to the immediate operational tasks, but, as we shall see, they need to reach out and participate in the broader leadership community in their institutions.

Program Development and Leadership

Organizational structure and business models also have an impact on how program development decisions are made and how programs are developed and managed. In turn, this affects how leaders relate to others in the broader organization.

At single-purpose organizations, like Empire State College and APUS, decisions about curricula tend to be made centrally. APUS president Wally Boston reported,

> There are no faculty members who teach in other learning environments at our institution. New programs are surfaced by the faculty and deans, brought to a Curriculum Committee for preliminary approval, the Executive Committee for review and approval, and then the Board of Trustees for final approval. (personal communication, November, 25, 2012)

Similarly, at Empire State College, faculty are organized around common areas of study, even though they are distributed in a number of different centers and units across the state of New York. The Center for Distance Learning, according to dean Thomas Mackey, "serves as both a centralized online learning unit and as an academic programming unit," with full-time faculty members serving as area coordinators (personal communication, January 16, 2012).

Some other institutions develop programs in a more complex environment that reflects on-campus program development patterns and the tradition of shared governance. At Rio Salado College, president Chris Bustamante said that faculty chairs are responsible for the development, implementation, and evaluation of the college's curricular offerings, whether online or in person (personal communication, November 20, 2012). At Penn State World Campus, program development decisions are a shared responsibility, with the academic unit and the World Campus proposing programs to the Faculty Senate and Graduate Council as appropriate. This reflects the fact that the World Campus invests funds directly in program development and is ultimately responsible for marketing the finished product.

It is noteworthy that three of the institutions—APUS, Empire State, and Rio Salado—have more nontraditional faculty structures (meaning a heavier reliance on part-time and adjunct faculty) and do not have the governance challenges of more traditional institutions with predominantly full-time faculty, as is the case at Penn State and UIS. Still, the challenges of faculty development and quality control are common across the five institutions. In some cases, the online leader may be able to organize professional development programs and mandate them for faculty who develop or teach courses online. In more decentralized environments, the leader may need to work with a centralized faculty development unit or offer incentives to faculty to participate in programs. It is important that the online leadership create an understanding that professional development is critical to long-term success and encourage support from administration and faculty governance, especially in more decentralized environments.

Student Support Services

One of the ongoing challenges for any institution engaged in online learning is the provision of support services for learners at a distance. Traditional campus-based models typically include an array of services that are offered only during normal weekday business hours for students who seek help. This simply does not work for the online learner who may not have physical access to a campus and who often must take courses and use support services in the evening and on weekends and may not live in the same time zone as the instructor or other students. Online students learn at different times, and their service needs don't conform to traditional working hours. They don't have the opportunity to walk to the bursar's office to pay a fee or drop by the writing center for assistance with a project report. The question of how to structure support services for online students has become a new challenge for many institutions, and it is one our five institutions have met.

In actuality, changes in support services driven by the need to serve students away from campus have created effective new service approaches for campus-based students as well. Institutions have moved more and more services into an online environment, allowing students to pay a bill, drop or add a course, access library materials, or pay a parking fine at their convenience and on their schedule. Virtual offices now handle many of these services, providing support 24 hours a day and 7 days a week that frees the student and the service units from in-person processing of many mundane, although important, activities.

Our five institutions have either restructured (Penn State, UIS) or designed from the start (APUS, Empire State, Rio Salado) services that can be accessed by their learners when convenient for them. APUS and Rio Salado have completely transformed traditional academic terms into shorter, more online-student-friendly, formats. They have found ways to overcome barriers and solve problems even when staff at traditional financial aid and registrar's offices said it couldn't be done.

For the online learning program leader, the challenge is to become the voice of the student with existing institutional support services and an advocate for either adapting existing services to meet student needs or for creating separate services for online students. While the organizational structure will define to some extent how the response takes shape, it remains the leader's responsibility to articulate the vision of support for online students and to build a community to implement the vision.

Institutional Culture

The responses to the question about institutional culture, particularly as it relates to online programming, evoked some of the more interesting comments from our leader responses. The challenge was greatest at the institutions that have a traditional campus culture (Penn State and UIS) and the least at those where online learning was the norm and there was no culture clash with the traditional campus (APUS, Rio Salado). Empire State seemed to be in the middle of this continuum as an institution that has many characteristics of APUS and Rio Salado but also has a longer history and is a part of a larger state system, which moved it toward Penn State and UIS.

Respondents noted that establishing a culture around an online program within an institution where one already exists is difficult and ongoing. Penn State World Campus executive director Wayne Smutz made the following observation:

> This is a complex question. The World Campus is integrated within Penn State. So, it in many ways reflects the culture of the University. However, because the World Campus serves students at a distance and has a separate administrative structure that is linked to the central academic culture but is still separate, it has freedom and flexibility. In reality, the World Campus operates both within the University and outside of it. The ability to operate at least to some extent outside of the University is critical. The World Campus operates within a highly competitive environment. It must be extremely responsive to its students who can easily leave to attend other online institutions. (personal communication, January 13, 2012)

Thomas Mackey from Empire State said:

> The Center for Distance Learning is similarly structured to other learning centers in some ways but the scale of the operation has required a rethinking of the traditional learning center model. As with other learning centers the organizational model is relatively flat, with considerable input from faculty, professionals, and support staff. The overall mode is collaborative in which the dean consults with standing committees, faculty teams, a director's group, an associate dean group, and task forces that address current issues relevant to the center, such as educational planning, open education, global strategies, and social learning. (personal communication, January 16, 2012)

And Ray Schroeder from UIS made this observation:

> The organizational culture in the online learning initiative is more collegial, collaborative, entrepreneurial and less bureaucratic and territorial than some other areas of the university. The Center for Online Learning, Research and Service as well as the Community of Practice in e-Learning promotes this open climate and culture. In part, this culture has enabled the online learning initiative to grow rapidly and thrive, even in difficult fiscal times. (personal communication, January 12, 2012)

Leaders at institutions where there was no rooted institutional culture had the advantage of creating one built around online students. Christopher Bustamante of Rio Salado College noted: "The organizational culture at Rio Salado College embraces all aspects of learning. Online learning is a primary focus of the institution; consequently, there is not a variance related to how online learning initiatives are viewed" (personal communication, November 20, 2012). Similarly, Wallace Boston of APUS simply stated: "There is no other culture" (personal communication, November 25, 2012).

With the preponderance of online programming from traditional campuses that expand their programming activities to students at a distance, the culture challenge epitomized by Wayne Smutz likely describes the norm. Finding a way to integrate the preexisting academic culture and the new attitudes required for a successful online program under one larger institutional banner is not easy, but it will likely be the most significant institutional leadership challenge administrators will face as online learning matures in their institution.

These different aspects of organization combine to have a significant impact on the distance education leader's scope and ability to effect change. In cases where the online learning unit is a separate administrative function and not integrated into the traditional academic units, the leader must become a diplomat, working across traditional power structures. Raymond Schroeder, founder of the online program at UIS, came to the task from a long career on the faculty that included a term on the Faculty Senate and president of the faculty union. "I approached the initiative in 1997 as I think any senior professor would," he recalls. "I saw that it belonged in the mainstream academic structure of the university. I approached it as simply a modestly different delivery path for the curriculum" (personal communication, January 12, 2012).

By contrast, Penn State World Campus was set up as a delivery unit in the university's administrative outreach unit; all courses and programs are offered by the mainstream academic colleges. As a result, the World Campus executive director had to develop new relationships with academic deans and department heads across the institution. Executive director Smutz notes, "I must spend considerable amounts of time interacting with and working with academic units. I sit on the Faculty Senate. I sit on the Academic Council for Undergraduate Education. Our director of Graduate Programs sits on the Graduate Council" (personal communication, January 13, 2012). In addition, a World Campus Steering Committee includes representatives from academic units as well as central support units.

Several conclusions could be drawn from the responses of the leaders of the five institutions who participated in these mini case studies. They provided a richness of responses that can help online leaders in their own organizational settings. We have drawn the following six leadership considerations from comparing and contrasting the five institutions.

First, mission is mission critical. No institution that has online learning as a significant part of its current or emerging strategy will be successful if the mission of the institution does not clearly recognize it. Too often the online program strategy is not driven by mission. The strategy developed by the online learning program leader should follow a clear mission statement. Put this on the agenda of your executive leadership team, and if you are leading that team, make it your top priority.

Second, educate up and down. To achieve the first goal, leaders must educate those above, around, and below on the values of online learning. You must educate those who serve as board members who craft or at least sign off on the mission. You must educate those who provide support services that help make online operations run smoothly. Finally you must educate faculty, or in many environments, help faculty educate each other, and provide them with the training and support they need to ensure you have a top-notch online program.

Third, culture can be changed. This is not easy, especially if you have an existing traditional campus culture to change. Moreover, it won't be quick. That said, in a growing number of institutional examples, represented by our group and a number of other institutions, the culture has been changed, or amended, to accommodate online programming efforts. Unless you are an online-only institution, find the cultural compromise, as Penn State and UIS have done, that builds on the current culture but recognizes the online world and its importance. Integrating an innovation into the mainstream culture of a highly centralized social institution like higher education is not a one-time task or a short-term tactic. It requires a constant, ongoing commitment to the success not only of the online program but of the broader institution as it adapts to changing conditions. This, ultimately, may be what defines a new generation of leaders in the field.

Fourth, online leadership is imperative. Despite the phenomenal growth of online learning in the past decade, it is still a young field, and even though it is moving to the mainstream of higher education, it has not yet matured at most institutions. To keep it moving in that direction, online leadership is an imperative. We note that none of the leaders from our five institutions grew up in the online environment. Indeed, most had more traditional academic career paths that led to online administration. This will change in the coming years; institutions should focus greater attention on developing the next cadre of online leaders from those currently engaged in online learning.

Fifth, leaders must shape policy (and not vice versa). From their responses to our questions, the leaders at these institutions clearly took an active role in shaping policy to support their programmatic needs instead of allowing current policy (based upon a traditional campus-based model) to shape their programming. Certainly, many options are possible, depending on the institution's overall policy structure. For instance, Rio Salado College has demonstrated that institutions can administer financial aid even when courses start each week; institutions can also effectively manage the enrollment of thousands of online learners with different start times. The online leader can, and in some situations must, change policy. More on this can be found in Chapter 10.

Sixth, the online leadership imperative cannot be deferred. There is an online leadership imperative now, a time to build on the growth and development, quantitatively and qualitatively, of online learning. With enrollment increases in online learning far outstripping traditional enrollments, with greater access to more powerful and cheaper learning tools, and with the next wave of students ready to reach our campuses having already engaged in online learning in one form or another, now is the time for leadership to emerge.

The Challenge of Leading Change

The five model institutions reflect one additional leadership aspect that is critical to the continuing development and acceptance of online learning—leading change in one's institutions. Beyond being change agents, these leaders exhibited change leadership. As Spiro (2009) noted,

> Change can be a dynamic and positive force for creating new strategies and putting them into action, stimulating creativity, diversity, learning and growth. But change . . . is a deliberate disruption of the status quo. While the need for change will often be apparent to many or most of those affected, opposition, resistance, and unanticipated consequences are likely to emerge. . . . Even positive change can be stressful. An effective change leader can maximize the opportunities of change while minimizing the risks. (p. 1)

In the ever-changing higher education world with the demands of an expanding student clientele, increasing competition in the online space, tightened budgets, increasing costs, and a global set of institutions ready to serve the market, bold leadership has never been more important. The challenges to lead change in online learning will continue to increase. Leadership must meet that challenge.

References

Allen, I. E., & Seaman, J. (2011). *Going the distance: Online education in the United States, 2011*. Wellesley, MA. Babson Survey Research Group.

McCarthy, S., & Samors, R. (2009). *Online learning as a strategic asset. Volume I: A resource for campus leaders*; a report on the Online Education Benchmarking Study conducted by the APLU-Sloan National Commission on Online Learning, August, 2009. Washington, DC: Association of Public and Land-grant Universities.

Miller, G., & Schiffman, S. (2006). ALN business models and the transformation of higher education. *Journal of Asynchronous Learning Networks, 10*(2), pp. 15–21.

Spiro, J. (2009). *Leading change handbook: Concepts and tools*. New York, NY: Wallace Foundation.

3

LEADING CHANGE IN THE MAINSTREAM

A Strategic Approach

Gary Miller

The new generation of online distance education professionals must learn to be a part of the broader institution. As noted in the first two chapters, higher education itself is in a period of dramatic change, with different types of institutions responding differently based on their own traditions, missions, and cultures. This chapter suggests ways distance education leaders can gain insight into their institutions to better serve as change leaders.

Many leaders in the first generation of online distance education have spent much of their careers on the periphery of their institutions. Many of these early pioneers, for instance, came from continuing education units or information technology units or from faculty roles in academic departments. Their experience often did not prepare them for the complexity of leading from within the mainstream. Increasingly, however, online learning leaders are at the institutional leadership table with their counterparts in research, graduate education, international programs, and undergraduate education. Increasingly, their work has an impact on promotion and tenure and other faculty policies and on policies affecting admissions, financial aid, intellectual property, and the university's technical infrastructure. Never before has the need been greater for distance education professionals to understand the broader academic environment in which they work and for other academics to become familiar with what online distance education can offer as academic units struggle to meet the challenge of change.

The challenge of leading within the mainstream requires a new way of thinking about leadership. Unfortunately, most of the management and leadership literature that has been used in the field is derived from the commercial sector, perhaps because distance education often is seen by mainstream academics as a self-standing business arm of the university or as a separate initiative altogether. Ultimately, higher education is more of a social organization than a traditional business organization. If online distance education is to take its proper place within the academic mainstream, online learning leaders will need to see themselves in a new light—as academic innovators rather than as cash cows.

This chapter looks at a somewhat different set of literature to provide a new context for online learning professionals to understand their relationship to the broader institution where they work and practice leadership as the unique institution of higher education goes through a period of radical change. We begin with a look at management theorist Jim Collins's (2005) view of leading in what he calls the *social sectors* and then look at leadership in a very different environment—the ethical realism philosophy that dominated a generation of leadership in U.S. international affairs. Underpinning the discussion is the notion that higher education by its nature is best seen not as a business but as a unique social organization in our culture.

Focus on Mission

Jim Collins (2005) is one business thinker who realized the differences between the needs of commercial organizations and social organizations. He begins *Good to Great and the Social Sectors* with the observation, "We must reject the idea— well-intentioned but dead wrong—that the primary path to greatness in the social sectors is to become 'more like a business'" (p. 1). A key difference is that in business, money is the end goal, while in the social sectors, money is a means to an end. As Collins puts it, money is an input rather than an output. Clearly, most online learning units are expected to sustain themselves and generate revenue that can be reinvested in new academic programs, but the activities that generate this revenue can be sustainable only to the extent that they first contribute to a larger mission of the institution. Many institutional experiments in online learning foundered on that basic issue: the online experiment was not sufficiently tied to the institutional mission to carry it beyond the financial startup risks. "The whole purpose of the social sectors," Collins notes, "is to meet social objectives, human needs, and national priorities that *cannot* be priced at a profit" (p. 19). Having a meaningful mission that is clear and well understood across the institution, and is congruent with the overall institutional mission, is critical. Collins defines *greatness* in this context using three criteria:

1. *Superior performance.* This can be measured in many ways. In a distance education operation in a traditional institution, the measures might relate to student satisfaction and achievement, faculty satisfaction (perhaps measured by the number of faculty who work in

multiple delivery environments), or client response. It might also be measured by the revenue the online program returns to academic units that sponsor programs. Regardless, it is safe to say that distance education units can no longer expect to provide "superior performance" in isolation from other parts of the university that increasingly depend on their performance for revenue, students, external partnerships, and opportunities for academic innovation.

2. *Distinctive impact.* Are the online distance education programs seen as models for other academic units, for innovation in on-campus instruction, or for peer institutions? Are their policies and procedures widely accepted and cited? Do graduate students study the programs? Do employers seek out opportunities to work with the unit? In effect, what is the "brand reputation" of online distance education at the institution and how does that brand reflect on the overall institutional reputation?

3. *Lasting endurance.* This might be measured by the long-term impact of innovation through sustainable programs, full-time faculty who have continuing commitments to online courses as part of their regular workload, and so forth.

Collins (2005) developed, as a "pivot point" for planning around these goals, what he dubbed the "hedgehog concept" (p. 17), a means by which a unit can define itself to focus on long-term results. He describes the hedgehog concept for social organizations as a Venn diagram (p. 19) in which the three elements are

1. *What you are deeply passionate about.* This speaks to the core purpose of online distance education in the university. As such, it should be inclusive (defining what is within your purview) and exclusive (enabling unit administrators to say no when necessary). It is how you want the online distance education mission to be regarded in the university and the community. It defines the area in which the online unit will be the champion across the institution. The response will vary by institution. In some cases, it might be the connector role itself; in others it might be the adult learner (which would then exclude a distance education role in youth education). It is important that the definition of the unit's passionate focus be carefully articulated and, where the unit is embedded in a broader organization, tied to the general institutional mission.

2. *What you can be best in the world at doing.* This represents the areas in which the unit should be expected to excel, with the understanding that activities not within this circle might be done outside the unit,

by an academic unit or by another administrative unit. In this sense, defining what you are also entails defining what you are not, so it is important to take care not to be overly restrictive on the one hand or, on the other hand, to be too inclusive that you lose definition. This also helps to identify other university units whose involvement and support are essential for success in distance education. At the same time, this part of the hedgehog concept suggests that the distance education program must also reflect what the institution itself is best in the world at doing. For instance, the institution should lead with the programs that are most likely to succeed with distant students and that have the best opportunity to be recognized as high quality by employers, professional associations, and other stakeholders.

3. *What drives your resource engine.* This defines how the unit plans to recover its costs, return revenue to the university or individual academic units, and provide investment funds for future projects.

In a changing institutional environment, a hedgehog statement can help communicate to staff and to others in the institution the unique role and scope of authority for the online learning unit and can be the basis for establishing enduring, trusting relationships with other units. The hedgehog should be fully discussed in the unit so there is strong loyalty to these three core defining dimensions of distance education in the institution. At the same time, it is essential that the hedgehog is not focused entirely on internal issues, but that it reflects the connector function and includes the role of distance education in bringing university resources to meet external needs.

Leading in the Mainstream: Ethical Realism and the University

Defining the hedgehog helps set the stage for the online learning function, but real work begins as units implement their vision and mission. Here, operating in the mainstream during times of great change presents very complex challenges. Given all the changes occurring in the communities we serve, in our institutions, and in the means of developing and delivering their programs, distance education leaders find themselves facing a world that is often chaotic, where the old rules no longer fit and where comfortable assumptions are no longer valid.

In short, we are in an era when higher education is transforming itself to meet the challenges of a new social construct, with online learning increasingly recognized as a factor in this transformation. In this context, online learning leaders should view the institution more as a social organization in which there are multiple points of formal authority and informal influences that often lead to competing views about how to accomplish the institution's mission. In their book, *Ethical Realism*, Anatol Lieven and John Hulsman (2007) looked at similar issues in terms of international affairs, attempting to return international thinking "to the everyday world where Americans and others do their best to lead ethical lives while facing all the hard choices and ambiguous problems that are the common stuff of our daily existence" (p. 53). Their findings, which are rooted in the realism movement developed in the mid-twentieth century by Reinhold Niebuhr, Hans Morgenthau, and George Kennan, are instructive to online distance education leaders who find themselves thrust into a complex and shifting leadership community. I wrote about the value of ethical realism as a way to understand the leadership challenge facing professionals in continuing education (Miller, 2008). The example is especially relevant to leading change in online learning today.

Lieven and Hulsman (2007) argue that leadership should be based in a set of principles or values that guide action: prudence, patriotism (better stated for our purposes as *institutional loyalty*), responsibility, study, humility, and a decent respect of the views and interests of others (p. 53). These are the values that allow a leader in a complex social organization to set a vision-based strategy for the future:

Prudence. Lieven and Hulsman (2007) note that prudence is especially important when launching radical and dangerous new ventures (p. 67). *Prudence*, as they use the term, is about the underlying moral duty of leadership, the virtue of shaping goals and making decisions that don't require perfection but instead result in sustainable decency. It involves challenges for leaders to consider the consequences of their actions on the broader community, in this case, the university itself and other stakeholders, and that they have a Plan B in case things don't turn out according to Plan A (p. 67). In other words, prudence requires that we not be wedded to one particular mechanism but to the goal and to a workable and institutionally reasonable path toward the goal.

This is especially important in today's distance education arena. With the old organizational boundaries fading, distance education leaders increasingly are asked to innovate in areas that have a potentially dramatic impact on other parts of the university community. Prudent leadership demands that these leaders not act in isolation but instead bring together representatives of the university units who might be affected by an innovation to build a change community that looks at the total impact of a program. That community should develop a hedgehog description of the innovation and focusing on the mission and goals as the constant, explore multiple scenarios and alternative courses of action and then decide on a path forward.

Loyalty. Lieven and Hulsman (2007) note that patriotism (loyalty in our context) "is attached to the interests, the values, and the honor" of the organization (p. 80). Loyalty to the organization means appreciating the many elements that make higher education a social institution "as they actually exist, warts and all" (p. 81). It "fuses with the other virtues of ethical realism to produce the flexibility, calm, and perspective necessary" for long-term success (p. 82).

Humility. Reinhold Niebuhr, one of the founders of ethical realism, is the author of the "Serenity Prayer," which was later adopted by Alcoholics Anonymous. It goes like this: "Grant us the serenity to accept the things we cannot change, the courage to change the things we can, and the wisdom to know the difference" (Lieven & Hulsman, 2007, p. 70). This epitomizes how ethical realists think about the need for humility in our leaders.

This principle presents an interesting dilemma for distance education leaders. Online learning leaders are expected to innovate and find new ways for the institution to connect with the community by opening access to new students. In doing so, however, they must involve aspects of the university community that lie beyond their direct control and that may be affected by their innovation (Miller, 2008, p. 147). As Lieven and Hulsman (2007) define it, the principle of humility requires the leader to understand the need to engage others who are affected by their work, bringing them into the planning process so that they become active participants in the innovation. This helps us avoid a narrow view of online learning and of the university itself, allowing a clearer view of the strengths and weaknesses of the institution and the online innovation so that we can improve those things that must be changed. In *The Art of the Long View*, Peter Schwartz (1996) argues that to operate in an uncertain world people needed to be able to *re-perceive*—to question their assumptions about the way the world works, so that they could see the changing world more clearly (p. 9). This requires a shared commitment and, ultimately, a shared strategic vision.

Study. One side effect of prudence is that it forces us to recognize that we may not fully understand the environment in which we are trying to lead. Lieven and Hulsman (2007), paraphrasing Hans Morgenthau, note that "reason is like a lamp that cannot move anywhere by its own power, but is carried around on the back of our prejudices" (p. 74). Innovation must be based not just on an idealistic goal but on information and analysis. Online learning leaders often stand at the gate of the institution. They can bring to the institution important information about external societal and learner needs. At the same time, they must study the institution, listening to and learning from the perspectives of others who are affected by their work and building a strategy based on the facts rather than culture or prejudice.

Responsibility. This principle flows directly from the previous principle of study. Lieven and Hulsman (2007) describe the "ethic of responsibility" as being opposed to an "ethic of convictions" (p. 77). They assert it is the difference between "a morality of results and a morality of intentions" (p. 77). To achieve lasting change, the leader must act not simply on an ideal vision or on the conviction that actions are philosophically correct but on an understanding of what is actually needed to accomplish the goal given the on-the-ground realities of the institution.

Change leaders must anticipate the dangers of unintended consequences, understanding that innovation requires them to work in areas where neither they nor their institutional colleagues may have direct experience. While we are prone to action, we must also be willing to reflect, so that we act with clear knowledge rather than with prejudice, habit, or hubris.

Respect for others. Taken together, the principles of ethical realism add up to a willingness to acknowledge and respect the views and interests of others in the institution. Increasingly, online learning innovations will have implications for other parts of the institution; for those parts to succeed they will need to be seen as successful within the context of the other institutional cultures and interests that are affected by the innovation. Success does not necessarily mean the same thing to everyone. While the administrative delivery unit may define success as financial sustainability, an academic unit may be more concerned about faculty access to research opportunities or the reputation of the department. A financial success that does not address these other perspectives will be short lived.

Lessons From the Profession

Many of these values were reinforced by 30 international open and distance education pioneers who shared their experiences with Canadian researcher Elizabeth Burge (2007) in *Flexible Higher Education: Reflections From Expert Experience.* Among the "hard-won lessons" (p. 61) they report are the need to respect learners, one's colleagues, and one's self as a professional, and, equally important, to respond to those things that deserve respect. These leaders noted, among other virtues

- The importance of self-awareness and self-respect. As one respondent said, "It's about being professional in a profession. . . . It's something about self-accountability as well as enforced accountability" (p. 84).
- Having humility and grace. Burge defines *humility* as "an attitude of mind and knowledge about how innovations are best adopted, as well as respectful listening and thinking strategies that acknowledge the limits

of one's skills" (p. 84). Interviewee Raj Danarajan cautioned leaders not to be tempted "with that arrogance of being far ahead of your time. . . . You owe it to yourself, especially, to slow down and address the concerns of the people of whom you find your self being ahead" (p. 85).

- Being knowledgeable. The interviewees suggested three strategies: (a) "avoid thinking that nothing older than five years is worth reading," (b) "read the literature jumping into action," and (c) "avoid dismissing the work of earlier generations as irrelevant" (p. 85). They also agreed that within one's institution, it is important to understand the complex dynamics—political, financial, and educational—understanding, as interviewee Dan Granger noted, that "being right doesn't win the day" (p. 86).

- Being a creative and critical thinker. The pioneers interviewed advised leaders to be compulsive about the details that underpin operational success, be skeptical at all times, and not look for panaceas. While being critical and skeptical, interviewee Chere Gibson from Wisconsin noted, "We just need to keep learners and learning to the fore; they really are central to the enterprise" (p. 87).

Ethical Realism in Practice

How do these principles come to life in the real life of an online distance education unit? Each institution has its own history and culture, so there are no simple answers to these questions. However, the principles do provide starting points that apply to most situations:

Define mission and vision. This is a leadership responsibility. It may be developed initially by the distance education leadership team or by a small university-wide leadership group. However, once it is developed, it should be tested with distance education staff to be sure they all understand it and can buy into it. A final version should be shared and discussed with the broader university leadership.

Create a diverse, university-wide change community to plan a strategy around the hedgehog. Don't use these colleagues as an advisory committee, but as a planning and implementation committee. An early task would be to develop the hedgehog for online learning using Jim Collins's (2005) work as a guide. This begins with the vision statement (the passion that will drive the unit). The team focuses on the other two dimensions: in what areas the unit should excel and how it will sustain itself.

Study the environment in which the hedgehog concept will be applied. What are the societal factors that should drive decisions on programs and services, that is, what problem are we trying to solve? What are the institutional needs that may drive tactical responses to external needs (e.g., budget, faculty workload, accreditation issues, the fit with the broader institutional mission and strategic plan)? What academic programs are prepared to collaborate? Meet with each dean and key academic leaders to identify areas where there is strong interest, then test those interests against external need, funding opportunities, and market interest.

Develop Plan A and Plan B, and other alternatives if needed. A scenario planning process may be helpful here. In *The Art of the Long View*, Peter Schwartz (1996) notes that scenarios use individual needs as filters to identify driving forces and optional responses in complex, even chaotic times. "By imagining where we are going," he writes, "we reduce this complexity, this unpredictability which . . . encroaches upon our lives" (p. 15). The key is to develop scenarios that are informed by real-world dynamics and not simply by our internal action biases or institutional cultures. Engaging the change community (as well as key staff) in scenario development will help ensure that new ideas and perspectives are part of the process. At the end, it is important to communicate the results widely and listen to reactions.

Schwartz (1996) notes that scenario building is an art, not a science. "We started by isolating the decision we wanted to make. . . . As thinking and exploration continued, the questions were constantly refined. . . . We thought about the key factors that would affect decisions . . . trying to decide which factors were critical. The true work took place in the last step, rehearsing the implications" (pp. 26–27).

Be alert for unintended consequences, and unanticipated opportunities, for the larger institution. Early in the innovation, ask all affected parties to articulate how they will define the success of the innovation and what they would see as failure. Try to imagine consequences in the planning scenarios that will contribute to success or to failure. Once the project is under way, be alert for unplanned negatives and act on them.

Evaluate what is really happening and respond accordingly. Take time to set metrics that will give the university a realistic assessment of impact. Be the champion of actual accomplishment, not of an ideal or aspiration. Maintain a persistent long-term vision, but be willing to move to Plan B if that will get the university to the vision more effectively.

Conclusion

Higher education is one of the oldest continuing institutions in Western culture. Over the centuries it has evolved as a highly decentralized social organization whose central administrative structure provides an organizational umbrella over multiple, and often strikingly different, academic cultures that thrive at their tripartite missions of teaching, research, and service. Online distance education has emerged in a relatively short time as a force that is *disruptive* of the traditional higher education culture and *necessary* as higher education adapts to meet the needs of a society being radically changed by the globalized information revolution. Regardless of one's starting point, the distance education program leader must be prepared not only to lead the online distance education function but to play a role as a change leader during a period of dramatic transition. This requires that the leader, first, understand and appreciate the multiple cultures at work in a traditional college or university and, second, understand and be able to communicate within the institution information about the external forces that are driving distance education. With these two perspectives in mind, the distance education leader can serve an important role as an ambassador of change, on one hand, helping the institution understand the external societal forces at work and how other institutions and stakeholders are responding and, on the other hand, helping external stakeholders understand the institution's needs as it works to better serve the community.

References

Burge, E. (2007). *Flexible higher education: Reflections from expert experience.* Berkshire, UK: Open University Press.

Collins, J. (2005). *Good to great and the social sectors: A monograph to accompany "Good to Great".* New York, NY: HarperCollins.

Lieven, A., & Hulsman, J. (2007). *Ethical realism: A vision for America's role in the world.* New York, NY: Random House.

Miller, G. (2008). Leading in the mainstream: Ethical realism and continuing education. *Continuing Higher Education Review, 72,* 144–150.

Schwartz, P. (1996). *The art of the long view: Planning for the future in an uncertain world.* New York, NY: Doubleday.

4

LEADERSHIP IS PERSONAL

Wayne Smutz

The paradox of effective leadership is that it is simultaneously *"all* about *me"* and *"not* about *me!"* How can this be? Aren't these different ways of being a leader contradictory? Let's explore.

Being an effective leader means (at least from my experience) that effective leadership is *all* about *me!* It's about *my* character, values, and accountability. It hinges on *my* self-confidence, perseverance, and ability to gain respect and to earn others' trust. It's all about the willingness to embrace the collective and lead by example.

At the same time, being an effective leader also means that I embrace the idea that it is *not* about *my* ego, power, or recognition. Nor is it about *my* ideas, decisions, or ability to motivate others.

Upon reflection, however, the apparent contradiction between "It's all about me!" and "It's not about me" is really something else. It represents a series of complementary qualities. For example,

- If I let my ego rule my leadership role, I'm not likely to establish trust with my colleagues.
- If I don't demonstrate accountability, people are less likely to choose to be accountable.
- If I don't have self-confidence, why would anyone choose to follow me?
- If I insist on my ideas instead of the best ideas, how can I expect others to work for the betterment of the whole rather than for themselves?

For me, understanding this perplexing paradoxical nature of leadership is fundamental to becoming an effective leader.

Leadership Is Personal

The personal is the foundation of every other component of leadership. It is reflected in the values and beliefs that an individual brings to the leadership role. The critical nature of this personal dimension is the reason no leadership formula exists. Different types of leaders can be successful. But leadership can only occur if a person is genuine, understands himself or herself, and is true to his or her values and beliefs. This is because leadership fundamentally rests upon integrity and trust.

I have long thought of myself as a leader, but I did not always understand the importance of the *personal* in leadership. I've spent considerable time reading the literature on leadership, which is voluminous and growing by the day. Typically, the professional elements of leadership are addressed rather than the personal dimensions.

When I was in my mid-40s, a little book titled *Let Your Life Speak* by Parker J. Palmer (2000) helped me come to grips with the importance of the personal in leadership. Palmer speaks on the issue of vocation when he writes: "Let your life speak." For me, vocation and leadership are so intertwined that I interpreted these four words in the context of my leadership. Until I chose to let my life speak through my leadership, I was not truly a leader.

A few of Palmer's insights into the personal element of vocation and leadership leapt out for me:

> I must listen for the truths and values at the heart of my own identity. . . . [They are] the standards by which I cannot help but live if I am living my own life. (p. 12)
>
> Our deepest calling is to grow into our own authentic self-hood, whether or not it conforms to some image of who we ought to be. As we do so, we will not only find the joy that every human being seeks—we will also find our path of authentic service in the world. (p. 16).
>
> We are here not only to transform the world but also to be transformed. (p. 97)

This chapter explores leadership in the context of the emergence of online learning in American higher education. It's based on my experience at Penn State. I practice leadership daily, and I've learned some things from that practice. For that reason, I make no apologies for not basing this chapter on research. The phrase, "Leadership is personal," provides a framework for my understanding of leadership as well as its expression.

Elements of that framework include qualities such as opportunity, vision, reaching beyond your grasp, and education as a game changer. Social justice, collaboration, and the worth of every individual also fall within the framework.

Although from my perspective the personal is the most essential aspect of leadership, professional leadership issues also need to be addressed, among which the most critical are

- Context matters—macro and micro
- The core of leadership
  - vision
  - strategy and goals
  - relationships and partnerships
  - organizational culture
- The illusion of control
- Change happens

Woven and intertwined throughout the discussion of these issues are examples of the values and experiences that have shaped who I am. They illustrate the personal nature of my leadership, and demonstrate how who I am inevitably shapes my approaches to leadership. At the conclusion of this chapter, I show how the personal and professional aspects of leadership work together.

Context Matters: Higher Education in the United States

These are transformative, perhaps even revolutionary, times for higher education in the United States. An almost perfect storm of factors are aligning to create an urgency for change. Consider the following:

- Over the past 30 years, higher education tuition has risen faster than the costs of health care, a trend that is expected to continue.
- The federal government's massive investment in student financial aid has led to demands for clear demonstration of learning outcomes. Accrediting bodies are pressing for the systematic articulation and revelation of learning outcomes.
- States increasingly are hard pressed to provide public financial support at past rates, which is unlikely to change as the economy improves because of commitments to K–12 education, entitlements, prisons, and more.
- Access to higher education is being restricted at a time when Americans need postsecondary education more than ever for individual well-being and for prosperity in an increasingly knowledge-based, innovation-focused national economy.
- Colleges and universities are criticized for being highly inefficient and slow to take advantage of available technologies for improving student performance and institutional productivity.

- The United States, which once boasted the highest percentage of populations with postsecondary education, now ranks 12th in the world. Graduation rates from higher education hover around 50%.
- Colleges and universities increasingly have become part of a market-based higher education industry over the past 30 years, unleashing new competition among institutions.
- The for-profit sector in higher education continues to grow and develop alternatives to the traditional modes of operation.
- The emergence and widespread availability of digital technologies provide access to incredible amounts of content and enable almost unlimited interaction among individuals who are not in the same location.

Online learning and an increased role for technology in the educational process have the potential to meet some of these challenges and drive key changes in higher education.

One potential key change is the role of faculty, which has historically been the core of the university. Faculty shape and construct curriculum; they develop criteria to determine who succeeds and who fails. Their needs are what shape the way universities function—what's important and what's not. Will such a paradigm survive the current challenges higher education faces?

A paradigm shift that places students, rather than faculty, at the center of the university has the potential to transform higher education, which has existed in its present form for nearly a thousand years.

LEADERSHIP IS PERSONAL
Opportunity

My brother and I are products of opportunity.

My father and mother completed their formal education with the end of high school. Dad earned a living as an auto body repairman, and mom was a home-maker. I always sensed they felt the sting of not being highly educated. They saw great value in education, and consistently communicated to my brother and me that a college degree was key to our having a better life. They were unwavering in this message and made it clear that they would be there to help us. We were dedicated students, and my brother and I eventually both earned PhDs.

My brother and I are not smarter than my parents. I know that well. They gave us access to opportunities they did not have so we could develop our intellectual abilities and talents. I've seen the difference that such opportunity can make. As a consequence, one of my core leadership values is to provide others with access to opportunities.

Online learning and digital technologies could completely alter the way education is delivered: changing where learning occurs, who has access to content, how learners and faculty interact, and how learners interact with each other. It could have an impact on determining when learning interventions should occur, on measuring learning outcomes, and more. Such a shift represents a major threat to traditionalists, although it is far from clear how well this threat is perceived. For leaders, these times represent opportunities, threats, and unending challenges.

Context Matters: Penn State's World Campus

The Pennsylvania State University entered the distance learning arena in 1892 with the delivery of correspondence courses via Rural Free Delivery. One hundred years later it operated an extensive Independent Learning System serving several thousand students across the United States.

The World Campus was created in 1996 as the university's online provider of Penn State distance education. The World Campus was no sudden creation, however. It came into being after Jim Ryan, vice president of Outreach, provided leadership for a deliberate strategy to have Penn State embrace online learning beginning around 1992. As Jim has noted, "The principles of planned change are essential for those who want to facilitate significant organizational change" (J. Ryan, personal communication, April 29, 2012). The Penn State leaders driving for action on the online learning brought both the "philosophy and experience" of planned change, Ryan said. It started with a university task force that was charged with considering possible futures for distance learning at Penn State. A carefully selected and supportive group of faculty who had taught in distance education was core to the task force. The vision created by the task force was subsequently discussed in depth with deans to get their acceptance or at least their willingness not to stand in the way. New and energized leadership for distance education within Outreach was brought on board with the appointment of Gary Miller as associate vice president for distance education and executive director of the World Campus. An AT&T grant provided resources enabling faculty members who supported a new approach to distance education to develop a set of policies related to teaching from a distance. Faculty Senate support and acceptance followed. With this foundation in place, the final step necessary for the launch of the World Campus was support from the new president, Graham Spanier. With a reputation for being forward looking, President Spanier provided his endorsement and offered two important guidelines that framed the birth of the World Campus:

1. If Penn State were to enter online learning, it would be with a full commitment to being a major player.
2. Online education would have to be tied to the core mission of the institution and completely integrated, building on the long tradition established by the Independent Learning System. A credit would be a credit regardless of how it was delivered. Academic colleges would be responsible for programs, courses, and faculty.

Other caveats were that the World Campus would bring new students to Penn State, those who were unable to attend one the university's 24 physical locations, and it could not use state funds or be a drain on university resources. Penn State entered the online education arena in the spring semester of 1997 with 43 enrollments. We hit 3,000 enrollments 3 years later. In 2011–12 we had 47,000 enrollments and are working toward a goal of 120,000 by 2020–21.

Under the leadership of vice president of Outreach Jim Ryan and founding executive director Gary Miller, the World Campus confronted a number of challenges in its first 8 years. The first, and most daunting, was internal to the university. This despite the ground work of support for the World Campus that was provided in the preceding years.

By design, universities are conservative institutions. Movement into the online arena brought out numerous skeptics who voiced considerable doubt about whether quality education could be delivered through the Internet. Consequently, many faculty members who might have been willing to explore teaching in this medium shied away. In addition, faculty who taught online were not receiving credit toward tenure. As part of outreach, teaching for the World Campus was seen as an overload. During its early years, the World Campus existed at the margins of the university.

Another challenge was financial. Given the prescribed limitations on state and university financial resources, two funding sources were critical to early survival. The Sloan Foundation was a key start-up benefactor, and Outreach was able to provide support from revenue generated through its Independent Learning and Continuing Education activities.

Meeting production goals—putting high-quality courses online and meeting deadlines—also was difficult. It highlights a significant change that online learning brings to the university: the need for faculty to adhere to demanding course development deadlines. In the face-to-face environment, faculty can make course changes in real time. But online courses must to be ready weeks prior to the start of a semester, and changes are more difficult. Instructional designers are responsible for working with faculty to facilitate the learning process for online students, and the team approach to course development is a significant shift that represents a challenge to customary university operations.

LEADERSHIP IS PERSONAL
Confidence

"Knowing their abilities with accuracy allows leaders to play to their strengths. Self-confident leaders can welcome a difficult assignment. Such leaders often have a sense of presence, a self-assurance" (Goleman, Boyatzis, & McKee, 2002, p. 254).

I don't remember ever lacking confidence, but someone whom I think of as my mentor gave me a big boost. As a high school teacher and coach, Larry Leslie helped me understand that I was a leader and that leadership can be a difference maker. The teams he coached performed way beyond their natural athletic abilities.

After earning a doctorate and joining the Penn State faculty, Larry invited me to attend Penn State for graduate school. His hand-written invitation to me was a statement of his faith in me and his conviction that I was capable of the highest levels of academic work. It demonstrated his continued belief in me as a leader.

In her book, *Mindset*, Stanford professor and research psychologist Carol Dweck (2008) illustrates the impact of one's mind-set on performance or outcomes. She notes that those who approach a situation with a *growth* mind-set are much more likely to be able to perform, improve, and succeed. Those with a *fixed* mind-set at times don't even try, because they're convinced they can't succeed (Dweck, 2008). Having expectations and creating expectations of success can play an important role in determining how well individuals perform.

Through my leadership, I facilitate understanding of potential and possibilities in all individuals, helping others develop a growth mind-set and encouraging them to develop the confidence they need to succeed.

These were just a few of the leadership challenges Gary and Jim confronted as they introduced significant change into a conservative, tradition-based organization. However, by the end of the 2004–05 academic year, the World Campus could claim some real successes. It had reached the symbolically important enrollment target of 10,000. It had built on the key strategic decision to focus on degree and credit certificate programs at the undergraduate and graduate levels, which helped create college, department, and faculty ownership. More faculty members were starting to become interested in teaching World Campus courses. And, it was fast closing in on being financially in the black for the very first time.

The Professional Core of Leadership: Vision

After Gary Miller retired in 2007, I assumed responsibility for the World Campus. This was not my first involvement with the World Campus, however. I had been director of the market research unit, and I led the development of 10 criteria used to guide the research on offerings. We recommended the five programs that launched World Campus. (Two of those five programs remain strong performers 15 years later in enrollments and revenue, and both have also been recipients of Sloan-C Outstanding Program Awards.)

As the World Campus moved from program selection to program development and delivery in 1996–97, I assumed the role of director of marketing from 1997 until 1999. Finally, I served on the World Campus's Strategic Management Group through the first 5 years of the World Campus. These roles gave me a deep understanding of the World Campus when I took over in 2007.

World Campus had developed a strong foundation by this time. It had a strong pipeline of undergraduate and graduate degree and credit certificate programs, and after a long march to fiscal viability, it was consistently in the

---

LEADERSHIP IS PERSONAL
Reach Beyond Your Grasp

"By framing the collective task in terms of a grander vision, this approach defines a standard for performance feedback that revolves around that vision. Visionary leaders help people to see how their work fits into the big picture, lending people a clear sense not just that what they do matters, but also why" (Goleman, Boyatzis, & McKee, 2002, p. 57).

Sports have had a major influence on my life. I've always enjoyed being physical, and it still is the way I relieve stress—running, swimming, weight lifting.

Exercise has helped keep my weight down, distracted me when I'm dead tired, exercised my heart, and kept my blood pressure at acceptable levels. Those who aspire to be leaders should never underestimate the importance of good health. If you're not present, there's no way you can lead.

I've learned other things from sports as well, including the value in working toward excellence. Sports make excellence seem achievable.

Early in my life I got hooked on winning championships—Little League baseball, Babe Ruth baseball, high school football, basketball, and baseball. In all, I was on six teams that won league championships, and one that emerged as Northern California champion.

Becoming a champion starts with the belief that it is possible. It involves practice, mental preparation, focus, conditioning, relationship building with teammates, and more. Success in sports is built around the idea of being the best at what you do. The belief that you can achieve excellence provides a foundation for everything else.

Myriad ways exist to develop the kind of commitment needed for success, but for me, sports worked. Having learned what it feels like to be the best, it's hard not to want to be that in everything you do.

black. Enrollment numbers showed signs of serious growth. Enrollments had jumped to more than 16,000 by the end of the 2006–07 academic year.

The World Campus leadership challenges were different for me in July 2007, when I assumed overall leadership for World Campus than they were for those who led in the beginning. While issues of credibility, quality, and the marginality were far from settled, questions about the future of World Campus no longer arose. The nature of its role in Penn State's future, however, was not resolved.

In this context, I sensed a need for a clear vision of what the World Campus potentially could be. I believe helping to create a compelling vision is a critical role for every leader. And, it's essential that every organization have one. As the saying goes, if you don't know where you're going, any road will get you there. I spend considerable time on this issue, not only formulating a vision but seeking acceptance and support for it in World Campus and the broader university.

Since 2007, I have worked with the organization to fashion and refine a vision that maps out what the World Campus can be. Our intent is to make a difference. Hence our motto: Impact Pennsylvania, Serve the Nation, Reach the World.

We not only want to make a difference, we want to make a particular difference. Our vision is for the World Campus to provide a uniquely Penn State extraordinary learner-centric education online, to offer excellent academic programs, to attract motivated students, to deliver rich and compelling learning experiences that use the potential of technology, to provide exceptional student support services, and to facilitate transformative learning events. Coupled with this educational vision is a business vision: to create an efficiently run organization that excels at performance by minimizing costs to students and maximizing return to the university. We now refer to this as World Class for World Campus. In adopting this vision, we aim to be the premier online provider of postsecondary education.

Where does vision come from? For me, it's based upon a way of seeing and thinking. The way I approach vision making is rooted in what I learned when studying history and political philosophy. The canvasses these two fields work on tend to be large. For me, thinking as a historian or as a philosopher is about thinking about big issues in order to understand smaller ones. I refer to it as thinking outside in. Any small event or issue is shaped by many, many others. So I learned it is always important to scan the environment widely. What are the forces at play? What factors are in motion? An array of events, issues, happenings all work to create themes and patterns that lead to something. It's important to think and reflect deeply, seeking connections and linkages. It's the interpretation of all of this material that is critical to creating a vision—tying diverse elements into a potential unifying theme. This takes time and leads down many pathways with multiple twists and turns. Ultimately, vision has to be tested with those who are willing to be open and yet constructively critical.

The Professional Core of Leadership: Strategy and Goals

Five overarching goals, or orientations, have been established that embody the strategy we are using to achieve our vision at the World Campus.

Open doorways of opportunity. This is our commitment to access. Our target market is the part-time adult learner who has earned college credits but not a degree. The World Campus offers such individuals a second or perhaps even a third chance, regardless of where they physically reside.

Ensure success, not just access. The World Campus is committed to ensuring that students succeed. Higher educational institutions in the United States have not always made this a priority, as indicated by the low retention and graduation rates. The World Campus aims to be different.

Drive innovative, value-added learning. The World Campus operates in a highly competitive market. Our focus is on providing students with extraordinary learning experiences by continuously enhancing course offerings and the overall learning experience as well as delivering exceptional student support.

Act as one Penn State. Penn State is a large, complex university with processes and systems that can overwhelm students and cost them time and money. The World Campus strives to ensure that its students experience Penn State as a single entity by providing common approaches and efficient service for adult learners. It's not about us. It's about them.

Create lifetime learners. This means urging faculty and instructional designers to produce top-notch, effective courses that also inspire. If learning experiences open new worlds, people are likely to be motivated to continuously learn as well as to build a strong affinity with their extended Penn State family. Certainly this serves the interest of Penn State. As lifetime learners, former students may return for another degree or for professional development or even to contribute financially. But the more noble aspiration here is that learning can transform lives. We aim for nothing less. To that end, we produced a DVD about our students titled *Adult Learners: Stories of Transformation* (http://worldcampus.psu.edu/about-us/video-stories).

Strategy is different from vision but just as necessary. Whereas vision is about collecting elements to create themes and patterns for a constructive interpretation of a desired state, strategy is about shedding whatever gets in the way of a clear focus and precise path to one's objectives. It's about making choices about what you're going to do and what you're *not* going to do to achieve your vision. It is a highly logical exercise of putting pieces together that will get you to your desired end point. My own experience is that colleges and universities struggle with the issue of strategy because they are reluctant to say no and even more reluctant to let go of what may no longer be relevant or necessary. Development of strategy is difficult. Implementation is even harder because of the tug and pull of distractions. While a leader's job is to help develop strategy, I'm convinced the most important role for the leader in the work of strategy is to maintain focus and remind everyone that effective strategy is about choices that fit together logically.

Strategy and goals are also about risk taking. Leaders must take risks. There is never perfect information or perfect understanding of situations to make decision making risk free. And certainly, if leaders are not willing to take risks, they will never take an organization to new heights. Risk taking is not about being careless, however. The kind of risk taking I engage in is what I refer to as *calculated risk taking*. This means: Be clear about the risks

---

LEADERSHIP IS PERSONAL
Education as a Game Changer

I grew up in the mountainous country of rural Northern California, where logging was the primary industry. We lived 300 miles north of San Francisco and 900 miles from Los Angeles, so exposure to the wider world was limited. We didn't get a television until I was eight, and for 10 years, we only received one channel.

My schools were good, and I did well in a high school class of 65. After graduating from high school, I decided to attend college at the University of California, Berkeley, which has high-quality faculty and high-quality students. I wasn't sure about what to expect in terms of academics, but I was certain I would have to work hard to succeed, and I had a growth mind-set that gave me the fortitude to do what was necessary.

I did not foresee that Berkeley would open up new worlds to me. I had never seen a foreign film. I had never seen an original work of art. I had never engaged in extended intellectual debates. I never knew certain fields of study existed (linguistics) or what some were about (cultural anthropology). Through words, oral and written, I discovered things I was unaware of before. And in the process, my life transformed.

I decided I wanted a career in academe so that I could be continuously connected to the life of the mind. It was a decision that would give me the opportunity to engage and interpret the world rather than passively experience it.

The experience of higher education changed my game forever.

you're taking. Evaluate the pros and cons. What are the upsides? What are the downsides? What are the weaknesses in your approach? Ask others for their perspectives on these matters. Then, ultimately, you have to go with what you feel in your gut makes sense. Rarely does this kind of decision making depend upon the number of pros versus the number of cons. It's much more nuanced than that. Experience helps. Failures teach important lessons. That's why it's important to tolerate them.

Context Matters: The Microcontext of Colleges and Universities

Like all organizations, colleges and universities are unique, but they also have commonalities. One fundamental commonality is that a higher education institution's administration shares governance of the college with faculty. The faculty oversees academic matters, such as the curricula and students' academic life, and administrators oversee budgets, physical plants, fund-raising, and so on. It may look like a clear boundary, but in practice, it's not always the case.

Colleges and universities are thought by some to be hotbeds of radicalism, and while those elements exist (as they should), in general these institutions are extremely conservative.

That is a result of at least a couple of contextual factors. One is the issue of shared authority. With a distributed governance structure, it can take a long time to make decisions, or perhaps it's better to say to reach agreement. Neither administrators nor faculty can make the other group do anything.

For example, almost 20 years ago, Penn State formed a partnership with a private company to build and manage a new conference center, the Penn Stater. During a period in which conference enrollments weren't meeting expectations, I was asked to explain "academic culture" to people from the private company. They were dumbfounded to discover that the university president had no authority to order the faculty to start holding conferences at the Penn Stater. Such is the challenge of creating change in colleges and universities.

A second contextual factor that contributes to the conservatism of universities is the nature of scholarship. What seems to be the most frequently used phrase in academic journal articles? How about this: "More research is needed." The kind of work the faculty does—research and teaching—and the education and training they have undergone to get where they are contributes to the slow pace of institutional change. Academics constantly evaluate and criticize others' scholarly work as well as their own. Former Penn State president Graham Spanier, said that "they tend to value tearing ideas apart . . . not necessarily building on them constructively" (Spanier, 2000).

LEADERSHIP IS PERSONAL
Social Justice

I attended Berkeley from 1968 to 1972, and those years were about as eventful as they could be. Berkeley borders Oakland, the seat of considerable Black Panther power at the time, and race issues were extremely sensitive. The Vietnam War was a lightning rod for protest. For one semester in the spring of 1970, the campus was essentially an armed camp—at least it felt that way to students—and sometimes a literal battlefield.

Challenges to the establishment were constant, whether it was the authority of the campus administration, the city administration, corporations, or the state and federal governments.

This environment and my experiences changed me. One of the biggest effects was an understanding of the importance of seeking social justice. Everyone is not born into the same circumstances. Institutions don't treat everyone the same. Not everyone can fight his or her own battles. Who speaks for people under such circumstances? Who steps outside of themselves? I learned at Berkeley that some people do.

I also learned about the importance of passion. Commitment fueled by passion can energize people like nothing else. When something matters, people give their all. That is incredibly important even when facing small challenges, but when the challenges are big, it's an essential ingredient for success. It's the only way people can persevere.

Berkeley taught me that change is always possible. We inherit a world that is constantly evolving. In reality, we make the world we live in. We can be part of actively making it better, or we can choose to simply experience it. It's our choice.

Deborah Tannen (2002) has referred to this as *agonism* or "ritualized opposition" (p. 1653). She notes: "In academic discourse, this means conventionalized oppositional formats that result from an underlying ideology by which intellectual interchange is conceptualized as metaphorical battle" (p. 1652).

Tannen (2000) is convinced that agonism is endemic in universities and is a problem because "academic rewards . . . typically go to students and scholars who learn to tear down others' work, not to those who learn to build on the work of their colleagues" (p. B7).

The most damaging aspect of agonism is that it "produces an atmosphere of animosity that poisons our relationships with each other at the same time that it corrupts the integrity of our research. Not only is the agonistic culture of academe not the best path to truth and knowledge, but it also is corrosive to the human spirit" (Tannen, 2000, p. B8).

Agonism was on full display when online learning was introduced in the mid-1990s and produced substantial challenges. At Penn State, the online learning context was also shaped by two key issues having to do with academics and governance.

The academic decision meant World Campus, with a mission of serving students from a distance and bringing new students to Penn State, would only offer degrees offered by academic colleges and not be set up as a separate entity. This decision was consistent with President Spanier's vision of integration and also with Penn State's independent learning history of treating a credit as a credit regardless of delivery. World Campus had to effectively work with existing academic structures and culture.

The governance decision developed over time. Initially the World Campus focus was on distance students. But as online learning caught on, people became enthusiastic about offering these courses for resident-based students as well. With the emergence of online courses for on-campus students, a new approach to online-learning governance was needed. Eventually two coordinating bodies were established: the Penn State Online Steering Committee and the Penn State Online Coordinating Council (see the organizational chart in Figure 4.1).

The first was a body of deans and senior administrative officers responsible for providing overall coordination, and recommended policy direction to the provost. The second was a body of associate deans and administrative managers responsible for coordinating operational issues. This decision significantly shaped the ways leaders in the online arena have to operate. Context matters.

Figure 4.1 Penn State Online Initiative.

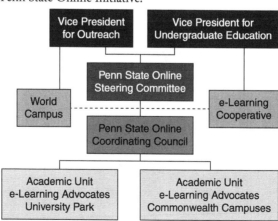

Note: Adapted from Pennsylvania State University (2009).

The Professional Core of Leadership: Relationships and Partnerships

I am amazed by those in colleges and universities who think that power makes things happen. Higher education represents an extreme case of "control as illusion," because all the dynamics are set up to resist, undermine, and sacrifice control for shared governance. And agonism reigns. This often comes up in discussions of people's titles and sounds something like this: "If I were just a (name important title) . . . or if I was positioned this way . . . then I would be able to make something happen."

This illusion of control exists in all organizations, as written about in Max DePree's (1997) *Leading Without Power*, which explores his experience in the corporate world. The idea that leaders can exert control in colleges and universities represents an extreme case of illusion in my experience. This is particularly the case with regard to the relationship between academics and non-senior-level administrative structures, particularly administrative

---

LEADERSHIP IS PERSONAL
The Worth of Every Individual

I am not religious, but I am a spiritual person. I grew up in family that went to church every week. That felt like an obligation to me, and when I left for college, my church-going days ended.

Fourteen years later, I found myself back in a church "meeting." My wife—needing quiet time away from our new twin boys, our three other children, and me—ended up at a silent Quaker meeting. Sometime later, I followed, along with our children.

Quakerism immediately resonated with me because it is based on a belief that every individual has worth. It's known as "the light within." True Quakers make no exception to the worth proposition. That's in part why they are pacifists and against capital punishment.

Quakers are guided by the following tenets: simplicity, peace, integrity, community, and equality. Quakers govern themselves through true consensus—they do not vote. Without consensus, they don't proceed. Without listening deeply to every voice, nothing happens. I can tell you from experience that building true consensus is an extremely difficult challenge.

Having emerged from the formal graduate study of issues such as authority, collaboration, anarchist education, and participation, Quakerism offered a spiritual framework that felt right. While I no longer attend meetings, I think of myself as a Quaker, and I try to act as one. The values remain foundational to me, especially the belief in the worth of every individual.

structures that are often not even seen as core to the University (e.g., Outreach, World Campus).

If control is an illusion, other ways must be found to work and lead in the university environment, especially for those not considered core to the research university. In my experience, developing relationships and partnerhips across all elements of the university has been effective. Rarely do individuals achieve greatness on their own, there are always legions providing support and help.

Winning arguments in the world of academe is incredibly difficult. I talk to my staff about not being drawn into agonism and endless debate, because academics are simply too skilled at it. Typically arguments are centered on winning, not on what is right or what is the truth. Why enter into arenas where the balance of the scale is tipped against you? The ability to develop partnerships in which people bring their diverse skills and talents and are committed and working for the same ends is incredibly rewarding and satisfying. The most essential key to building relationships and partnerships is development of trust. As Goleman, Boyatzis, and McKee (2002) note: "We've seen that result in study after study: Positive groups help people make positive changes, particularly if the relationships are filled with candor, trust, and psychological safety" (p. 163).

Partnerships and relationships require trust to be successful. Underlying trust are the issues of intention and goodwill. Intention is being clear with others about what you want to create, and goodwill is a choice about how you engage with others, even those you don't feel friendly toward. This includes developing an ability to truly see another's perspective, as the Showkeirs (Showkeir & Showkeir, 2008) and others have taught me. These choices and skills are foundational elements for good relationships. They are especially important in an environment characterized by ritualized opposition and no locus of authority.

Also critical to successful partnerships is what I call the *value-add* dimension. When working with faculty, what do we as online educators and staff bring to the table? This is vitally important, because colleges and universities are built around the notion of specialized expertise. When working with faculty, we have to make compelling offers. Too often staff members have not thought about this in any depth and have a hard time with it. But it is absolutely essential.

Related to expertise is the issue of having data to support the case you are making. In research institutions, data rules and opinions may not get you through the door. Data can take many forms: market research, needs assessments, student evaluations, pedagogical studies, research summarized from the literature, and so on. Data won't necessarily win the day alone—expect methodological challenges of all sorts—but you won't get anywhere without the data.

Another approach is to frame an argument in the context of education. One approach that has worked for me at Penn State is focusing on students. World Campus has worked hard to become a learner-centric organization. This is rooted in the question we ask before we make any decision: "What is best for students?" It is a powerful, disarming question. It is extremely difficult to publicly disagree with putting the interest of the student at the center of decision making.

These approaches to building relationships and partnerships are not panaceas, and at times things can get very, very tough. I can't count the times when the World Campus staff or their supervisors talked to me about how they had been "beaten up" or "brought to tears" in the course of discussions with faculty members. Part of our responsibility as leaders in this context is to help our staff develop the capacity to deal with this.

The staff selection process and professional development play a critical role. Developing self-confidence in their talents and capabilities is essential, as is an ability to not take personally the barbs thrown their way. In addition, it is critical that staff is committed to what they are doing. If this work is not their passion, they won't make it. The environment can be brutal.

Leaders help with these issues by selecting staff carefully but also by helping people see that working in the world of online learning in higher education is a choice. While people often don't see themselves as having choices, every day they are deciding what to make of their circumstances (Showkeir & Showkeir, 2008). Helping people develop an understanding of why their choices matter has the added benefit of getting staff to think about commitment and what's important to them. When people see that their commitment is a choice they make, the truth of one's commitment may surface. That's why leaders need honest answers from staff—are they committed or not?

The Professional Core of Leadership: Organizational Culture

People decide according to the value system they espouse, in other words values and attitudes are important because they may shape behavior, and behavior will influence people.
(Bruno, 2008, p. 679)

As human beings, we spend more of our lives in the context of work than in any other activity. And yet, how much time do we spend reflecting upon, thinking about, or actively creating the organizational cultures that play such a large part in our lives? For most of us the organizational culture is probably like water for fish—it's just there. Yet, it affects everything that goes on in an organization.

Culture reflects the values of the organization and sets the tone for interactions. It creates the context for individual growth and development. Culture influences how performance is rewarded and whether taking risks is encouraged. In spite of its critical impact on how work gets done, surprisingly there seems to be very little intentionality with organizational cultures.

When I assumed my current leadership role at Penn State in 2007, there was a 6-month transition period before the previous associate vice president retired. This allowed me the luxury of time to get to know people better and deepen my understanding of the organization. I met with every person, sometimes in small groups, sometimes in larger ones. It was a time for listening, and I did a lot of that.

I don't recall what I thought would come from these conversations, but the discoveries surprised me. Interestingly, it wasn't necessarily new information but rather things that had not pierced my consciousness. What I heard from the staff included the following comments:

- We don't know the goals of the organization.
- We are afraid to voice concerns or disagree with supervisors.
- Organizational hierarchy bogs us down.
- We get information through rumors.
- A lot of back stabbing goes on.
- The units know little about each other and don't interact well.
- We are not allowed to venture far outside our defined roles.

I found these comments sobering. And I felt shaken, considering I had been part of this organization for such a long time and now I was about to be at the helm. How had these concerns become invisible? Had I ignored situations I should have attended to? We had good people and good leaders. Were we so oblivious to the culture that we ran on automatic pilot?

I had no idea what to do to create a different environment. And my initial workload was such that I wasn't focused on fixing the organizational culture. Instead, I plunged into better understanding the work, the people who did it, and the business of online postsecondary education. It became clear we are in a highly competitive arena. Technology has eliminated many of the barriers to entering this business, and many people have seen the opportunities in the marketplace. The for-profits in particular have taken a highly customer service approach to serve the adult learner market that traditional institutions have either ignored or not served well. Smaller colleges looking for new audiences to serve found the adult market attractive as well.

In addition, students, and particularly adult students, have multiple options in the postsecondary education marketplace. They are unwilling to tolerate things they do not like or that cost them money and time. I quickly realized that the World Campus was competing with smart institutions that were positioning themselves to respond quickly to the concerns of these savvy, sophisticated students. That represented a major challenge in the context of a traditional, brick-and-mortar-based institution that was primarily committed to serving young people and reluctant to change.

This competitive landscape was scary and jogged my reflective thinking muscles. It became clear to me that our organizational culture would doom us in the online environment. We had to change.

A significant barrier to change was a hierarchical management structure. This century-old way of organizing business commonly creates an environment where people are afraid to voice concerns and ideas. Formal and informal policies get created that put rigid boundaries on what people can or cannot do. These types of cultures send the message, do what you're told, keep your head down and your mouth shut. Staff initiative is neither prompted nor prized. Many issues, including relatively minor ones, are tossed upward for resolution, which considerably slows decision making. If I took seriously the concerns the staff had raised with me, that is what our organization had become.

These concerns and thoughts were in my head in early 2009 when I found a book at the bookstore titled *Authentic Conversations* by Jamie and Maren Showkeir (2008). It was the first book I have read cover to cover without stopping other than to eat. It spoke directly about the conditions of our culture that I had been worrying about. Although many themes of the book resonated with me, some were particularly riveting:

- The need for everyone in the organization to work for the success of the whole organization.
- Leaders alone cannot save organizations.
- Authenticity is important in organizational cultures because work gets done through conversations.
- To work most effectively, everyone in the organization must be literate about the whole business.
- Everyone is making choices every day. How are these choices serving the organization?
- No one can hold another person accountable. Organizations have to encourage people to choose accountability because they are committed to their work and understand why what they do matters.

I invited the Showkeirs to talk to our entire staff in July 2009. We have been working with them since to dramatically change our culture, not just to be a better place to work but because the competitive nature of our educational business demands a culture that fosters our ability to quickly and successfully respond to the marketplace we are trying to serve—adult learners. I discuss this in detail later in the chapter.

Change Happens: The Role of Core Beliefs, Principles, and Values

One of the most challenging parts of being a leader is that change is constant. A great plan can be developed, but its execution leads to more changes. Or a situation may change dramatically, rendering the plan irrelevant. This has always been the case, but technology has dramatically increased the speed of change. This requires organizations and staff to be extremely nimble.

A major change we had to confront at the World Campus had to do with revenue sharing. Most online institutions, including Penn State, share revenue with academic colleges, institutional administration, or both. Our first model was based on sharing revenue after all costs were covered for academic colleges and the World Campus. While this model worked for budget purposes, it did not work operationally because too much time was eaten up in finger pointing and debating about one another's costs.

The executive director at the time, Gary Miller, led the effort to switch to a gross revenue sharing model around 2005, which aimed to eliminate debates about costs by ensuring that the academic colleges and the World Campus received a certain percentage of the revenue. It was based on the notion that the more each partner controlled its costs, the more revenue would be available to share. It also included a provision based on the amount of work done. For example, if an academic college undertook the instructional design for a program, it received a greater share of the revenue.

This brought most of the acrimony about costs to an end but a different problem surfaced. When gross revenue sharing began, most academic colleges did not do their own instructional design. They discovered that by hiring their own instructional designers the colleges could get more revenue. As colleges began to do this, revenue to World Campus decreased. It became apparent that the World Campus would not be sustainable financially if colleges continued to create their own design shops.

A third model was developed in 2011: revenue distribution categories. This adjusted the percentages of gross revenue so the World Campus would remain viable regardless of who did the instructional design. It also built in an annual review process to determine if the World Campus could survive on less money. This review process could lead to adjustments in percentage distributions without undermining the basic model.

This is an example of how things constantly change. It's reality. But are leaders at the mercy of whatever wind happens to be blowing? They don't have to be. To survive and thrive in these turbulent times, it is critical to stay grounded in principles that can guide decision making regardless of a changing environment. These principles have to be touchstones a leader can return to so that constant change is not what drives the organization. For me, guidance comes from vision, goals, and our commitment to do what's best for the learner and for Penn State. This grounding provides direction and purpose for the staff.

Tying Things Together: Personal Leadership for Student Success

It's important to remember that the more personal the commitment to goals . . . the more likely you are to achieve them. This is where passion and hope—the motivating brain activity inherent in tapping into your dreams—are again so vital to sustainabil(ity). . . . And the more difficult a goal, the more essential one's commitment. (Goleman et al., 2002, p. 147)

I am committed to helping individuals transform their lives through education, and that comes from the things that have shaped me as a person. It is based on my belief in the worth of every individual. It is rooted in my life experiences, of taking the opportunities others offered me so I could create the life I have. A lifetime in education has shown me that given the right support structure, almost everyone has the ability to succeed in higher education. My commitment has been ingrained from what I learned as a student and a lifelong learner—education can be transformative.

As a leader of the World Campus, I work every day to help ensure that we do everything we can to help those who want to help themselves. It starts with access. In many cases our target audience of adult learners has tried and failed at higher education. Given this country's fundamental belief in opportunity and a need for a highly educated workforce to compete economically in this globalized world, we can ill afford to ignore these adult learners.

For those willing to put in the effort to succeed, Penn State's doorway of opportunity has to be open. Access is not enough, however. Student success is essential, and this is why one of our five key goals is ensure success, not just access. To make these words meaningful, we have to put organizational actions behind them. And we do. We remind ourselves constantly: It's not about *us*. It is about the students we serve.

One thing we know about education is that engagement is critical inside and outside the classroom. Faculty members have responsibility for engagement in the classroom, and our director of faculty development works with them to try to ensure that engagement occurs. We're also looking to enhance classroom engagement through learning analytics. But a college education is more than delivering content and courses. We know that what happens outside the classroom is also important. What does that mean for online learning? How do you create a full college experience without a physical campus? As best we can tell, little effort has gone into that facet of online education, and we are trying to change that.

It starts with advising. Developing a personal relationship with online students online is a key engagement point for advisers. Over the last three years, our investment in the Advising and Learner Success unit has tripled. We have also developed a relationship with the tutoring centers on campus to help serve our students who are having difficulty, and we have been pilot testing commercial products as well.

We are also trying things beyond the classroom. One example is the Psychology Club for psych majors. (Penn State has the largest collection of psychology-oriented videos in the world, such as Stanley Milgram's famous work on obedience.) We streamed an outdoor live performance of *Romeo and Juliet* performed by Penn State students to World Campus students. We have a student blog called the Corner of College and Allen, a key street intersection just off the University Park campus. We have streamed a program on football Saturdays, called *Huddle With the Faculty*, which highlights top Penn State professors. Some of the programs will work and some may not, but we'll continue to search for ways to engage our students.

At the World Campus, we do not want a degree to be the end of the line for our students, and we are looking for the keys that will inspire them to be lifelong learners. Certainly faculty can be inspiring, as can other students. In 2010 we began working with our public broadcasting colleagues to embed much more multimedia into our courses. We're trying to engage more of students' senses in the learning process in ways that illustrate concepts or ideas imaginatively and creatively. Our hope is that this type of multidimensional learning experience in time will be so extraordinary that it will be a facilitator of lifelong learning.

If we can help make World Campus students successful, we believe we can build a lifetime connection with them to us and to each other. Indications are that this approach is working. World Campus students join the alumni association at a rate twice as high as any other Penn State campus or college.

Tying Things Together: Personal Leadership for Organizational Success

In getting extraordinary things done in organizations, everyone is important, not just the leader.
(Kouzes & Posner, 1999, p. 133)

LEADERSHIP IS PERSONAL
Collaboration, Partnership, Participation, and Community

Individuals often self-select into fields of study that seem to be right for them, and I was no different. My undergraduate major was American history.

I was fascinated by who we are as a people and why. As an individual with German heritage, I also was interested in understanding the Holocaust and wrote a senior thesis on the Nuremburg laws of 1935. My graduate work moved in a slightly different direction, largely based on my experience at Berkeley.

For my master's, I studied political philosophy—from the Greeks to contemporary thinkers. Given my interest in alternative ways of education, I wrote a thesis on anarchist education. What does education look like without authority structures?

In my doctoral program, I focused on nontraditional forms of education (e.g., community schools, community colleges, unique colleges such as the short-lived Black Mountain College). My dissertation was on boundary spanning in the context of institutional collaboration between universities and professional associations.

Throughout these formal degree programs, themes began to emerge, most clearly at the graduate level. Four of the most important were collaboration, partnership, participation, and community. All are about bringing people together around common causes. These themes continue to be touchstones for me.

The World Campus can't help students be successful unless we succeed as an organization. Colleges and universities traditionally have not been thought of as businesses. Faculty had no need to understand the business side—that's what administrators were for. Times are changing.

The highly competitive environment puts increasing pressure on organizations offering postsecondary education online to be innovative, adaptive, and looking forward. Perhaps in the twentieth-century manufacturing context, command-and-control management models made sense. In the new world we must thrive in, World Campus needs to be a nimble, innovative organization. This reflects who I am and has influenced my leadership. One example is my effort toward a less hierarchical organization.

As executive director, I cannot make the organization successful by myself. People in the organization must understand the vision and goals, strategy, and the core values. They must understand the challenges and contribute to finding solutions. They have to comprehend financial statements. They need to see the connection between their contributions and those of their colleagues to the overall organization outcomes. Otherwise, how can they maximize their contribution?

People need the ability to make decisions on the spot and base them on what is best for the business as a whole. They are capable of doing that if we develop their business literacy and create trust. It's the only way we can build a culture in which everyone in the organization owns the whole World Campus.

We are working to create a transparent culture where everything but personnel matters is open for inspection and discussion. Pledging transparency is a demonstration to your staff and others that you trust them. I've instituted staff chats where staff can ask me anything but personnel matters. My pledge is to give them answers or, if I don't know the answers, to find them. This can be scary for me and for staff members who are unaccustomed to having a canvas to paint any question they want. In fact, we have found that employees have a hard time overcoming their cautiousness.

Once you begin sharing information, many people will start to ask questions, creating additional opportunities to create business literacy. We have instituted monthly business literacy sessions that focus on helping staff understand various parts of the business. One session, for example, was devoted to demonstrating how students are, in fact, the ones who pay our salaries. At another meeting, I asked staff what the size of our budget was. Most had no clue, and why would they if they had never been given the opportunity to learn about it? As they begin to understand the financial picture, we expect that they will also become much more sensitive to the income and expense sides of our budget.

We have developed a six-session workshop on adult learners that all our staff will be taking. An added benefit is that all our staff members will have the experience of being adult learners. They go through the registration process, do reading, use our learning management system, interact with other students, take tests, and so on.

A flatter organization is a new way of working. It asks each person to be personally accountable to everyone else. It asks the individual to proactively make a difference through outstanding service, identifying problems, and collaborating on solutions. This can be discomfiting. Yet I believe that in the past we haven't nearly taken full advantage of the wide range of talents and experience our staff offers.

The personal in my leadership in this context is about helping all staff achieve their full potential for the benefit of the World Campus and for themselves, because I believe there is much in people that they've never been allowed to give.

How do you make it happen, especially when most people have spent their educational and work lives in environments that did not encourage the flowering of potential? One of the ways we are doing this is using the philosophy of Showkeir and Showkeir's (2008) *Authentic Conversations* to change the culture. *Authentic Conversations* is an intentional way of being and acting that affects everything you do. It starts with conversations and how you engage in them.

We've asked all staff to read the book, and have offered everyone the opportunity to take a 2-day workshop based on the book and the work of the authors. Staff members were not required to take it, but 95% of them have.

As a longtime educator, I know that behavior rarely changes as a result of just reading a book or taking a workshop. Instead, we need to encourage staff to use the skills they learned in the workshop to create a new environment for conversation. It's hard for everyone. We acknowledge that and encourage risk taking by trying out the skills. I've asked the directors who report to me to find ways they can model the behaviors and communicate commitment to what we are doing. It is not easy for any of us.

We're about 3 years into the process right now, and I have stated that it will take at least 3 to 4 years to evolve. It's been incredibly frustrating at times, exhilarating at others. But I see progress, which keeps me and others going.

Conclusion

We spend way too much of our very short lives working and not doing something that matters to us. I have told people: "If you don't have a passion for what we do, please go find work that you are passionate about. You do have a choice! Exercise it."

Passion and commitment are just the beginning. We drive hard in the World Campus. Much is expected of us, and we expect much of ourselves. We have big goals—we truly want to be the premier university provider of extraordinary online education. We are approaching the enrollment target of 50,000 set for the World Campus 7 years ago and have set a new goal of 120,000 enrollments by 2020–21. We want to continue to become more efficient so we don't keep pushing the price of education up for our students.

So in the context of the organization, my leadership is personal.

It's about extending opportunity for students and for staff.

It's about reaching beyond one's grasp to achieve what may seem impossible.

It's about creating a compelling vision that reflects the values of the university and expresses the fundamental beliefs that I and my colleagues truly believe in.

It's about setting challenging goals that help us get better as individuals and as an organization.

It's about building confidence as people realize their potential through education and work.

It's about a belief in the transformative power of education inside and outside the classroom and through professional development.

It's about recognizing the worth of all individuals and finding a way to make a difference in their lives.

It's about creating, collaborating, and forming partnerships.

It's about authenticity in our personal, educational, and work lives.

I cannot lead in any other way than through the self-awareness of who I am. I urge all aspiring leaders to consider knowing themselves as they take on the challenge and the responsibility that comes with followers.

References

Bruno, L. F. C. (2008). Personal values and leadership effectiveness. *Journal of Business Research, 61*(6), 678–687. Retrieved from http://www.sciencedirect.com.ezaccess.libraries.psu.edu/science/article/pii/S0148296307002433

DePree, M. (1997). *Leading without power: Finding hope in serving community.* San Francisco, CA: Jossey-Bass.

Dweck, C. (2008). *Mindset: The new psychology of success.* New York, NY: Ballantine.

Goleman, D., Boyatzis, R., & McKee, A. (2002). *Primal leadership: Realizing the power of emotional intelligence.* Boston, MA: Harvard Business School Press.

Kouzes, J. M., & Posner, B. Z. (1990). *The leadership challenge: How to get extraordinary things done in organizations.* San Francisco, CA: Jossey-Bass.

Palmer, P. J. (2000). *Let your life speak: Listening for the voice of vocation.* San Francisco, CA: Jossey-Bass.

Pennsylvania State University. (2009). Penn State online governance: Penn State online initiative. Retrieved from http://weblearning.psu.edu/governance

Showkeir, J., & Showkeir, M. (2008). *Authentic conversations: Moving from manipulation to truth and commitment.* San Francisco, CA: Berrett-Koehler.

Spanier, G. (2000). *State of the university address.* University Park: Pennsylvania State University.

Tannen, D. (2002). Agonism in academic discourse. *Journal of Pragmatics, 34*(10/11), 1651–1669. Retrieved from http://www9.georgetown.edu/faculty/tannend/TANNEN%20ARTICLES/PDFs%20of%20Tannen%20Articles/agonism%20in%20academic%20discourse.pdf

PART TWO

ENSURING OPERATIONAL EXCELLENCE

Online distance education is a complex, multifaceted enterprise. Leading that enterprise requires that the leader achieve operational excellence and strategic development. The Five Pillars of Quality Online Education highlight several areas of operational excellence: learning effectiveness, faculty satisfaction, and student satisfaction. This part examines the leadership issues in these three critical operational areas as well as challenges moving from a strictly operational perspective to a more mainstream, strategic context.

In Chapter 5, "Enhancing e-Learning Effectiveness," Karen Swan examines the intersection between online technology and new learning theories, in particular the link between the opportunities offered by the combination of digital technologies and constructivist theory. In this context she introduces the Community of Inquiry framework, probably the most widely accepted model of learning processes in online environments. Swan argues for the critical importance of the distance education leader's understanding the differences and similarities between online and classroom learning, and for collecting data on their local contexts to improve learning effectiveness through data-based decision making. She maintains that data should be collected on the inputs and processes of online learning, not just its outcomes. Thus the chapter explores sources and instruments that might be used in such endeavors.

Online technology presents new challenges for faculty members who teach online. In Chapter 6, "Supporting Faculty Success in Online Learning," Lawrence C. Ragan and Raymond Schroeder provide a detailed analysis of individual professional development and institutional support services that can help faculty members succeed in this new environment and be recognized for their work.

Student satisfaction in online distance education goes well beyond what happens inside a course. According to the Sloan Five Pillars of Quality Online Education, student satisfaction is measured by the extent to which students are happy with their overall experience in an online program. With Gary Miller, in Chapter 7, "Optimizing Student Success Through Student Support Services," Meg Benke, from Empire State College, calls on her long experience in student support services to discuss what it takes to ensure that students are satisfied with their total experience in an online distance education program. She focuses on the organizational and leadership challenges involved in creating a student-centered environment that promotes retention and success. The chapter includes two case studies to illustrate effective leadership in this arena.

In Chapter 8, "Moving Into the Technology Mainstream," Raymond Schroeder and Gary Miller focus on one of the most fundamental leadership issues: how to integrate the operating platform for online distance education into the institutional mainstream as online learning becomes a pervasive practice in higher education. Schroeder, whose professional roots are in public broadcasting, discusses the evolution of learning technology over the past two decades, current trends in the use of learning management systems on campus, and the issues associated with mainstreaming the distance education platform. He then looks at leadership strategies for navigating in the institutional mainstream.

Part Two concludes with a discussion of the challenges faced by operational leaders as they move to a more strategic role. In Chapter 9, "Operational Leadership in a Strategic Context," Raymond Schroeder surveys the many facets of operational leadership and key aspects that allow the operational leader to become a strategic leader. This chapter sets the stage for Part Three: Sustaining the Innovation.

5

ENHANCING E-LEARNING EFFECTIVENESS

Karen Swan

The calls for more accountability in higher education, the shrinking budgets that often force larger class sizes, and the pressures to increase degree-completion rates are all raising the stakes for colleges and universities today, especially with respect to the instructional enterprise. As resources shrink, teaching and learning is becoming the key point of accountability. (Brown & Diaz, 2011, p. 41)

While there is considerable evidence that effective leadership makes a significant difference in student achievement in the K–12 environment (Waters, Marzano, & McNulty, 2003), similar research linking leadership in e-learning to student success does not exist. Indeed, similar research has not been undertaken at postsecondary levels at all, most likely because student learning at institutions of higher education has not been subject to the same scrutiny as it has in K–12 schools. This state of affairs is changing rapidly, however, driven to no small extent by the rise of online education, and student achievement at postsecondary institutions is increasingly being questioned. The effectiveness of e-learning, therefore, is an issue that e-learning leaders must take very seriously.

This chapter explores what e-learning leaders should know about learning effectiveness. Because there are still many who doubt the efficacy of e-learning, I first review current evidence that students learn at least as much if not more in online classes as they do in traditional face-to-face classes. I then briefly examine the notion that the online medium is better suited for new pedagogical approaches and suggests constructivism as an epistemological foundation for much online teaching. However, learning is an extremely complex activity, and all learning contexts are unique. In this chapter I thus advocate for e-learning leaders making themselves particularly knowledgeable about their own unique e-learning contexts through the collection and analysis of empirical data. I describe the role of learning analytics and data-based decision making and advocate for exploring the inputs and processes of learning as well as learning outcomes. Two different approaches to ensuring quality in the design of online courses are described, along with several approaches to measuring learning processes including the Community of Inquiry (CoI) survey. Finally, I identify a variety of outcome measures that are useful in this environment.

e-Learning Versus Traditional Classroom Instruction

At its most basic, the goal, the product, the raison d'être of education is learning. Ensuring and enhancing learning effectiveness must thus be of prime importance to all higher education leaders, especially in light of the growing national concern about the value of a college education. Ensuring and enhancing learning effectiveness must be particularly important to e-learning leaders because in spite of the fact that we have over a decade of evidence that students learn as much or more from online classes than they do from traditional teaching and learning (Arbaugh, 2000; Bernard, Abrami et al., 2004; Blackley & Curran-Smith, 1998; Cavanaugh, 2013; Fallah & Ubell, 2000; Johnson, Aragon, Shaik, & Palma-Rivas, 2000; Maki, Maki, Patterson, & Whittaker, 2000), a majority of higher education faculty continue to believe that e-learning is inferior to face-to-face learning. Indeed, an Association of Public and Land-grant Universities survey of over 10,700 faculty members at 69 colleges and universities found that 70% of all respondents believed e-learning was less effective than traditional instruction (Seaman, 2009). In fact, even 48% of responding faculty members who had developed or taught at least one online course thought e-learning was inferior, while just 15% of this group thought it was superior to learning in traditional classrooms. Only 6% of the total population surveyed believed e-learning was superior.

The first learning effectiveness task for an e-learning leader, then, often involves justifying the efficacy of learning online. If nothing else, e-learning leaders should familiarize themselves with two large-scale studies that provide strong evidence that online students learn as much or more and are more engaged than students learning in traditional face-to-face environments.

U.S. Department of Education Meta-Analysis

The first of these is a meta-analytic study comparing the learning outcomes of online and blended learning with traditional instruction. The study was commissioned by the U.S. Department of Education and conducted by a group of researchers from the Center for Technology in Learning at SRI International led by Barbara Means (Means, Toyama, Murphy, Bakia, &

Jones, 2009). The researchers reviewed over a thousand studies on online learning that compared learning outcomes between online and face-to-face instruction published between 1996 and 2008. From these they selected 46 studies, all of which involved higher education from which effect sizes could be generated. Effect sizes were computed or estimated for a final set of 51 contrasts. Among the 51 individual study effects, 11 were significantly positive, favoring the online or blended learning condition, and two were significantly negative.

The findings of the meta-analysis revealed a positive effect of +0.21 ($p < .01$), or about one fifth of a standard deviation, for the online and blended learning conditions together relative to traditional learning, and a larger effect of +0.35 ($p < .001$), or slightly over one third of a standard deviation, for the blended condition alone. This effect size is a good bit larger than that for studies comparing purely online and purely face-to-face conditions, which had an average effect size of just over +0.14 ($p < .05$). The findings provide robust evidence that students generally learn at least as well and perhaps slightly better in online environments than they do in traditional face-to-face ones. They quite clearly show that greater learning results from education which combines e-learning and face-to-face elements than they do from traditional, face-to-face education alone.

National Survey of Student Engagement

Similar sorts of conclusions can be drawn from recent analyses undertaken by researchers from the National Survey of Student Engagement (NSSE, 2009). Questions about three types of technologies commonly used to support teaching and learning—learning management systems (LMSs), interactive technologies (social and collaborative applications such as wikis, blogs, and virtual worlds), and high-tech communications (including discussion boards, text messaging, and networking sites as well as e-mail)—were included in the versions of the NSSE survey administered to 31,000 students attending 58 institutions. Controlling for age, gender, major, Carnegie classification, and number of fully online courses taken, the researchers used regression analyses to assess the relationship between the use of Internet technologies and student engagement in college classes.

They found that Internet technology use was positively related ($p = .001$) to all three categories of engagement measured by the NSSE survey, that is, NSSE benchmarks (academic challenge, active and collaborative learning, supportive campus environment, student-faculty interaction), deep approaches to learning (higher order thinking, integrative learning, reflective learning), and self-reported learning outcomes (personal and social development, practical competence, general education). The use of course management technology was most strongly related to student-faculty interaction and self-reported gains in personal and social development. The use of interactive technologies corresponded most strongly with students' self-reported learning gains and the supportive campus environment benchmark. The use of high-tech communications was strongly correlated with every NSSE measure (NSSE, 2009). The researchers concluded that their results demonstrated a significant and meaningful relationship between course technology use and learning and other gains; technology use may in fact represent another important concept under the umbrella of student engagement (Chen, Guidry, & Lambert, 2009).

Paradigm Change

Indeed, we have good and ample evidence that students learn at least as much, and often more, from online classes than they learn in traditional classroom environments. At present, it is important for e-learning leaders to be conversant with that literature to answer the charges of critics. However, comparisons of e-learning and learning from traditional instruction gloss over real differences in the online medium that might be uniquely supportive of particular ways of knowing and learning. For example, Parker and Gemino (2001) compared student learning between traditional and online versions of a course in systems analysis and design for business majors. Although there were no significant differences in final exam scores between classes, on closer examination they found that students in the traditional classes scored significantly higher on the technical parts of the exam, while students in the online sections scored significantly higher on the conceptual parts of it.

More research of this type is certainly called for, but more important, research that explores the learning potential of different approaches in e-learning environments is critical. The unrelenting concern with comparisons of traditional and online delivery draws our attention away from needed explorations to concentrate on issues that have really already been settled. Indeed, perhaps the biggest obstacle to innovation in online learning is thinking things can or should be done in traditional ways (Twigg, 2001).

Henry Jenkins (2006) writes that media are characterized not only by the technologies they employ but also by the cultural practices that surround their use. Similarly, what distinguishes e-learning from the distance education of a previous era is not just the digital technologies it is named after, but more important, the pedagogical approaches such technologies uniquely offer. Where distance education was materials and teacher centered, online learning is student centered; where distance education focused on independent study, online learning focuses on collaboration; where distance education was grounded in behaviorist psychology, online learning is grounded in constructivist theories of learning.

E-learning leaders should familiarize themselves with such approaches for two important reasons. First, if they are to manage learning effectiveness across courses and programs, leaders need to be familiar with foundational theories and with national and international models for designing instruction and for evaluating learning effectiveness. Second, leaders must be able to represent these issues to the institution at large, especially when reporting to academic governance groups, and when working on institutional policies that relate to learning effectiveness in such areas as faculty development and support, technology requirements, student support, instructional design, and evaluation. Leaders cannot be experts in everything, but they must be familiar with the unique attributes of the online learning environment to help it reach its full potential in a broader institutional culture.

Constructivism

Constructivism is the name given to a set of epistemological alternatives to objectivist theories of knowledge that share the notion that we impose meanings on the world rather than discover the meanings extant in it (Duffy & Jonassen, 1992). Constructivists hold that meaning is constructed in our minds as we interact with the physical, social, and mental worlds we inhabit, and that we make sense of our experiences by building and adjusting the internal knowledge structures in which we collect and organize our perceptions of and reflections on reality. Social constructivists further contend that such knowledge construction is facilitated through social interaction (Vygotsky, 1978), with some social constructivists viewing cognition as distributed among the thinking individual, interacting others, and cognitive tools (Brown, Collins, & Duguid, 1989).

While constructivism, then, is first and foremost a learning theory and not a theory of instruction, particular conceptualizations of learning suggest corresponding pedagogical approaches. According to constructivists, no matter how we are taught, all learning occurs in our minds as we create and adjust our internal mental structures to accommodate our ever-growing and ever-changing stores of knowledge (Piaget, 1957). Constructivists thus believe that all learning is an active process, that it is unique to the individual, and that it is, accordingly, intimately tied to individual experience and the contexts of that experience, no matter how or where it takes place. Such beliefs have obvious pedagogical implications. Most important, they shift the pedagogical focus from knowledge transmission to knowledge construction; that is, from teaching to learning.

This shift in focus is particularly well captured in *How People Learn* (Bransford, Brown, & Cocking, 2000), a publication of the National Research Council that summarizes research on learning and its educational implications from a constructivist perspective. The central pedagogical tenet of *How People Learn* is that educators should not be focused on instructional design but rather on the design of learning environments. Although this distinction may appear merely semantic, it is not. Bransford, Brown, and Cocking urge replacing a traditional concern with the design and delivery of instruction and instructional materials with design approaches that focus on the creation of environments that foster and support active learning in collaborative communities. Constructivist learning environments, they argue, should be learner centered, knowledge centered, assessment centered, and community centered. E-learning leaders would do well to consider advocating for constructivist approaches and ensuring their courses meet these criteria.

CoI Framework

The CoI framework (Garrison, Anderson, & Archer, 1999), which is one of the most widely used models of online learning, is grounded in a collaborative constructivist view of higher education. The CoI framework is a process model that assumes that effective online learning requires the development of a community (Rovai, 2002; Shea, 2006) that supports meaningful inquiry and deep learning. The CoI framework has been quite widely used to inform research and practice in the online learning community, and an increasing body of research supports its efficacy for describing and informing online learning (Arbaugh et al., 2008; Swan, Garrison, & Richardson, 2009).

Building from the notion of social presence in online discussion, the CoI framework represents the online learning experience as a function of

Figure 5.1 CoI Framework.

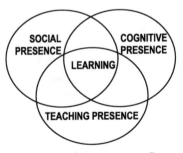

Note: From Critical Inquiry in a Text-Based Environment: Computer Conferencing in Higher Education, by D. R. Garrison, T. Anderson, & W. Archer, 1999, *The Internet and Higher Education, (2/3).* Adapted with permission.

the relationship between three presences: social, teaching, and cognitive (see Figure 5.1). The CoI framework suggests that online learning is located at the intersection of these three presences; that is, all three presences are necessary for learning in an educational context to take place.

Social presence refers to the degree to which participants in online communities feel socially and emotionally connected with each other. A number of research studies have found that the perception of interpersonal connections with virtual others is an important factor in the success of online learning (Picciano, 2002; Richardson & Swan, 2003; Swan, 2002; Swan & Shih, 2005; Tu, 2000). Research also suggests that these elements are strongly affected by teaching presence—instructor behaviors (Shea & Bidjerano, 2008; Shea, Li, Swan, & Pickett, 2005) and course design (Swan & Shih, 2005; Tu & McIsaac, 2002).

Teaching presence is defined as the design, facilitation, and direction of cognitive and social processes for the realization of personally meaningful and educationally worthwhile learning outcomes (Anderson, Rourke, Garrison & Archer, 2001). Researchers have documented strong correlations between learners' perceived and actual interactions with instructors and their perceived learning (Jiang & Ting, 2000; Richardson & Swan, 2003; Swan, Shea, Fredericksen, Pickett, Pelz, & Maher, 2000), and between teaching presence and student satisfaction, perceived learning, and development of a sense of community in online courses (Shea et al., 2005). In fact, the body of evidence attesting to the critical importance of teaching presence for successful online learning continues to grow (Garrison & Cleveland-Innes, 2005; Murphy, 2004; Swan & Shih, 2005; Vaughn & Garrison, 2006; Wu & Hiltz, 2004) with the most recent research suggesting it is the key to developing online communities of inquiry (Shea & Bidjerano, 2008).

Cognitive presence describes the extent to which learners are able to construct and confirm meaning through course activities, sustained reflection, and discourse (Garrison et al., 1999). Although some researchers have found that cognitive presence rarely moves beyond exploration (Garrison & Arbaugh, 2007; Kanuka & Anderson, 1998; Luebeck & Bice, 2005; Murphy, 2004), students did progress to resolution in studies in which students were challenged to do so and in which explicit facilitation and direction were provided (Meyer, 2003; Murphy, 2004; Shea & Bidjerano, 2008; Wang & Chang, 2008).

Learning Analytics and Data-Based Decision Making

It is plainly important for e-learning leaders to stay conversant with the literature on online learning research and with best practices in the field. This isn't easy because staying conversant is an ongoing activity, made especially so by a constantly changing technology culture. It is also clear, however, that learning is an extremely complex activity, and all learning contexts are unique. All e-learning leaders, therefore, should become particularly knowledgeable about e-learning in their own unique context. An understanding of the e-learning field in general provides ideas for innovation; an understanding of one's own context is the foundation for intelligent decision making. An understanding of one's own context, moreover, can no longer be grounded solely in networking and intuition; it must also be grounded in data.

We have passed from an industrial to an information age. One consequence of this move is the information overload envisioned by Vannevar Bush (1945) over a half century ago. The growth of data often seems to threaten the ability of organizations to make sense of it. However, the gargantuan amount of available data also has enabled the development of new techniques that have changed the very ways businesses are managed (Brynjolfsson, Hitt, & Kim, 2011; Davenport & Harris, 2007). Advances in knowledge modeling and representation, data mining, and analytics are creating a foundation for new models of knowledge development and analysis (Markoff, 2011). Perhaps nowhere are these new models more needed than in higher education.

Institutions of higher education generate enormous amounts of data on a daily basis but currently approach this enterprise from mostly a reporting and archival perspective. This is about to change and change radically. Today in higher education, analytics are most often used, if they are used at all, to guide administrative tasks, for example, in student recruitment and capital campaigns. As calls for academic accountability in such areas as degree completion and student success become increasingly strident, however, analytics are quickly being applied to teaching and learning. When applied in these areas, they are most often called *learning analytics*, and to gain some measure of how important learning analytics are very rapidly becoming, consider that they are a major priority for the Gates Foundation's U.S. funding, one of five key areas targeted by the Next Generation Learning Challenges initiative (see www .nextgenlearning.org). Learning analytics were also highlighted as one of six technologies likely to significantly affect higher education in the next 3 years in the 2013 *Horizon Report* (Johnson, Adams Becker, Cummins, Estrada, Freeman, & Ludgate, 2013), and are the basis for the EDUCAUSE Learning Initiative's new Seeking Evidence of Impact program (Brown & Diaz, 2011).

E-learning leaders must acquaint themselves with learning analytics. At the First International Conference on Learning Analytics and Knowledge, *learning analytics* was defined as "the measurement, collection, analysis and reporting of data about learners and their contexts, for purposes of understanding and optimising learning and the environments in which it occurs" (Long & Siemens, 2011, p. 32). Campbell, DeBlois, and Oblinger (2007) write, "Analytics marries large data sets, statistical techniques, and predictive modeling. It could be thought of as the practice of mining institutional data to produce 'actionable intelligence'" (p. 42).

Learning analytics are a particularly appropriate tool in e-learning leadership simply because online environments produce vast amounts of data that could be used to enhance learning when explored at the leadership level. To date, e-learning analytics have focused primarily on using learner characteristics to identify students generally at risk for failure who can then be provided with extra support (Johnson, Smith, Willis, Levine, & Haywood, 2011). However, one need only consider the data produced by LMSs to realize that all sorts of data are being commonly generated that could yield a variety of actionable intelligence. Morris, Finnegan, and Wu (2005), for example, found significant differences in time-on-task related participation in an LMS between students who withdrew from online classes and those who successfully completed them. This sort of analysis goes well beyond the gross identification of at-risk students from learner characteristics, leading many e-learning educators to call for reporting tools that can flag students as soon as they become at risk (Macfadyen & Dawson, 2010). Indeed, commercial applications that purport to do so are already emerging.

This sort of analysis is also clearly context dependent. E-learning leaders who would enhance learning effectiveness must become comfortable collecting, analyzing, and using data to make informed improvements in teaching and learning. Using learning analytics requires one to think carefully about what questions most need answering and what data are likely to produce meaningful answers. One way to guide such thinking involves conceiving of the e-learning process in terms of its inputs, processes, and outcomes (see Figure 5.2), and being sure to ask questions that identify and collect data associated with each of these areas. For example, the question, Does the use of video conferencing enhance learning in online courses? is not specific enough to produce useful answers, whereas, Does the use of video conferencing to support interactions between instructors and students in entry-level freshman courses enhance students' learning of important course concepts? is more likely to do so.

Inputs to e-learning are those factors that precede teaching and learning online but contribute to its success and its outcomes. E-learning processes are

Figure 5.2 Three Elements in the e-Learning Process.

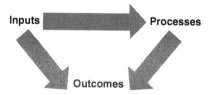

the interactions through which teaching and learning proceed online. These clearly affect learning outcomes, which are the desired knowledge, skills, and attitudes students should take away from a course. Because each of the three parts of the e-learning process is clearly important, and specifically because outcomes alone, especially gross outcomes, don't provide the information needed to improve teaching and learning, an effort should be made to specify aspects of each element and collect corresponding data.

In the following sections, each of the elements in the e-learning process and particular data sources related to them are discussed.

Inputs to e-Learning

Multiple inputs to online learning can have significant impacts on learning effectiveness. Three of these, faculty and faculty development, students and student services, and technology environments and supports, are addressed in other chapters and are not dwelled on here. It should be noted, however, that these are clearly areas e-learning leaders should pay attention to and that data on all these sorts of inputs need to be collected on an ongoing basis. In addition, leaders should develop ways of making such data useful so that analyses of the relationships among inputs, e-learning processes, and learning outcomes can be carried out.

For example, learner characteristics such as technology skills and experience (Bernard, Brauer, Abrami, & Surkes, 2004; Dupin-Bryant, 2004; Maki & Maki, 2002; Pillay, Irving, & McCrindle, 2006), good attitudes toward computers and online learning (Pillay et al., 2006), technology self-efficacy (Bernard, Brauer et al., 2004; Osborn, 2001), GPA (Bernard, Brauer et al., 2004; Cheung & Kan, 2002; Dupin-Bryant, 2004; Willging & Johnson, 2004; Wojciechowski & Palmer, 2005), self-motivation (Waschulle, 2005), self-directedness (Bernard, Abrami et al., 2004), and internal locus of control (Parker, 2003; Wang & Newlin, 2000) have been shown to affect learning online. As these characteristics can be indicators of risk and as many of them can be remediated, they can be important flags for early intervention of which e-learning leaders should be aware. In any case, such data should be collected and reviewed.

Research demonstrates that the perceived interactivity (Fasse, Humbert, & Rappold, 2009; Lenrow, 2009) and utility (Meyer, Bruwelheide, & Poulin, 2006) of courses and faculty responsiveness (Lenrow, 2009; Shelton, 2009) are good predictors of course completion. The strongest predictor of student success, however, seems to be the perceived presence of the instructor and peers (Boston et al., 2009; Liu, Gomez, & Yen, 2009; Meyer et al., 2006), which is discussed in the section on the CoI framework.

Student supports, such as access to online orientation programs (Lenrow, 2009; Wojciechowski & Palmer, 2005), peer mentoring (Bogle, 2008; Boles,

Cass, Levin, Schroeder, & Smith, 2010) and freshman interest groups (Rovai, 2003), computers and good Internet connections (Osborne, 2001; Waschull, 2005), and personal support (Boles et al., 2010; Chyung, 2001; Frid, 2001) can have a significant impact on student success with e-learning. E-learning leaders should make sure as many of these variables as possible are collected, even when they aren't sure how they might use them, because they might become important for future analyses. As Chuck Dziuban (2011) reminds us, "uncollected data cannot be analyzed" (p. 48).

Another clearly influential input to e-learning is the design of online courses. Several rubrics have been developed to evaluate online course design. Two of the most commonly used are California State University, Chico's Rubric for Online Instruction (2011–2012) and the Quality Matters (QM) Rubric Standards (Quality Matters, 2011). Rubrics such as these can be used by e-learning leaders to establish standards for quality in course design across a program, college, or institution.

Chico State *Rubric for Online Instruction*

Chico State developed its Rubric for Online Instruction (Committee for Online Instruction, 2003) as a self-evaluation tool to help designers and instructors developing or redesigning courses. The rubric explicitly identifies three levels of achievement related to standards in six categories: learner support and resources, online organization and design, institutional design and delivery, assessment and evaluation of student learning, innovative teaching with technology, and faculty use of student feedback. The rubric provides clear guidelines for elements that need to be included in high-quality online courses, but the three achievement levels are somewhat subjective, hence difficult to quantify, and the rubric mixes inputs and processes not only across categories but within them. However, it does provide data on course design that could be transformed into numerical information and it has the advantage of being a-theoretical. The Chico State rubric was also specifically designed for self-evaluation, thus leaders can share it with course developers and support their use of it without seeming to impose top-down standards.

Quality Matters Rubric Standards

On the other hand, Quality Matters employs a faculty-oriented but external peer review process designed to ensure quality in online and blended courses. It is centered on a rubric, originally developed through a Fund for the Improvement of Postsecondary Education grant to MarylandOnline, but is continually updated, the latest in 2011. The rubric is based on instructional design principles (Quality Matters, 2005) and is organized in eight categories: course overview and introduction, learner objectives, assessment and measurement, instructional materials, learner interaction and engagement, course technology, learner support, and accessibility (see Appendix A). An important aspect of the QM review process is that the review, while external, is conducted by faculty and instructional designers who have been through the process and is conceived as ongoing review and revision, making it less onerous to faculty and course designers.

Forty-one individual standards with ratings of 1, 2, or 3 points are contained in these eight categories; 21 standards have a rating of 3 points. A course must meet all these standards to obtain the QM level of quality course design. Eight of the 3-point standards are tied to the explicit provision of module level objectives. Three trained reviewers analyze the course site and rate each standard as existing, or not, at an 85% level or higher. In doing so, they refer to the QM Instructor Worksheet, which provides them with information about the course that may not be immediately evident. If the reviewer believes the standard exists at the 85% level, the full point value is awarded. A standard that isn't met at the 85% level gets no points.

Two of the three reviewers must rate a standard as being met for that standard to be identified as met in the course review. The three reviews are combined to determine the level at which the course has been rated, and the areas in need of revision are presented to the instructor. A major strength of the QM process is that comments are provided by the reviewers for each standard that is not met, which then guide the instructor during course redesign. Changes are made to the design based on the identified needs, and a second review is performed to ensure that all identified changes have been made.

Little research to date has explored links between QM review/redesign and learning outcomes. Preliminary research by Legon, Runyon, and Aman (2007) found higher grades and greater student interaction with course materials after redesign of a large enrollment undergraduate course. Swan, Matthews, Bogle, Welch-Boles, and Day (2012) similarly found higher overall course grades as well as higher grades on two major course assignments after a QM review and redesign of a graduate course in educational research methods.

Although the QM rubric is clearly objectivist in nature, as seen in the importance of module level objectives to achieving a successful review, what is particularly useful about it is that the review process is standardized, scoring is quite clear cut (standards are either met or not), and the review results in a numerical score. Currently, over 300 colleges and universities in 44 states are QM subscribers, including 11 statewide systems and several large consortia. Thus, e-learning leaders can improve the quality of courses at their institutions and achieve public recognition for doing so by participating in the QM consortium.

Assessing Learning Processes in e-Learning Environments

There are many ways to assess learning processes in online courses. Because most online learning happens in LMSs, such things as online discussions, instructor feedback, and online activities of instructors and students can be accessed quite easily. At least three sorts of learning processes can be categorized or measured using LMS reports and archived courses: pedagogical approaches, interactions, and forms of assessment. E-learning leaders should think carefully about which of these, and which aspects of these, are most important in their institutional context.

Pedagogical approaches can be categorized as objectivist versus constructivist, formal versus informal, low touch versus high touch, and so on, and their effects studied. Ben Arbaugh (Arbaugh, Bangert, & Cleveland-Innes, 2010), for example, has found pedagogical differences between what he identifies as hard and soft disciplines in business education. Aviv, Erlich, Ravid and Geva (2003) compared structured and unstructured online discussions and found higher levels of critical thinking in the structured discussion. Shea, Pickett, and Pelz (2003) found strong correlations between teaching behaviors and perceived learning across a variety of courses and institutions involved in online learning through the State University of New York Learning Network. Other pedagogical approaches that might be identified include the use of instructional strategies such as collaborative (Benbunan-Fich & Hiltz, 1999) or problem-based learning (Oliver & Omari, 1999), or the incorporation of technologies into instruction (Ice, Curtis, Phillips, & Wells, 2007).

Michael Grahame Moore (1989) identified three types of interactions that take place online: learner-instructor interactions, learner-content interactions, and learner-learner interactions. Hillman, Willis, and Gunawardena (1994) added interactions with interfaces to these three. There are many ways to measure interactions among participants in online courses, many of which can be accessed through LMS reporting functions. Research has shown that interactions with instructors (Jiang & Ting, 2000; Picciano, 1998; Richardson & Ting, 1999; Swan, 2001) and interactions among classmates (Jiang & Ting, 2000; Picciano, 1998, 2002; Swan, 2001) enhance perceived and actual learning in online courses. Indeed the Chico State Rubric for Online Instruction (Committee for Online Instruction, 2003) includes items focused on both these factors.

Assessment itself is another sort of learning process. Besides the sorts of outcomes that are measured, the importance of which cannot be exaggerated, what is assessed and how it is assessed also affects learning processes and general course outcomes (Swan, Shen, & Hiltz, 2006). Hawisher and Pemberton

(1997) related the success of the online courses they reviewed to the value instructors placed on discussion. Likewise, Jiang and Ting (2000) reported correlations between perceived learning in online courses and the percent of course grades based on discussion. Perhaps more important, researchers have shown that how online activities are assessed significantly affects student behaviors (Swan, Schenker, Arnold, & Kuo, 2007).

There are other ways of exploring online learning processes, social network analysis (Haythornthwaite, 2002), for example, or content analyses (Shea & Bidjerano, 2010), but what such methods and those previously mentioned have in common is that they all take an objectivist or quasi-objectivist stance. That is, they approach the learning process from the outside looking in. If one accepts the constructivist perspective, however, learning is uniquely individual and can therefore best be explored through the perspectives of individual learners. One instrument that does just that is the CoI survey, which also has the advantage of being grounded in one of the most widely accepted theoretical models of learning in online and blended environments.

CoI Survey

In 2008 researchers working with the CoI framework developed a survey (Swan et al., 2008) designed to measure student perceptions of the extent to which each of the presences (teaching presence, social presence, and cognitive presence) is expressed in online courses. The survey consists of 34 items (13 teaching presence, 9 social presence, and 12 cognitive presence) that ask students to rate their agreement on a 5-point Likert scale (1 = *strongly disagree* to 5 = *strongly agree*) with statements related to each of the presences (see Appendix B). It should be noted that assessing the extent to which communities of inquiry have developed in online courses through the eyes of students participating in them is very appropriate from a constructivist perspective. The CoI survey also provides a way to collect data on online learning processes from the very people with an intimate knowledge of them.

The CoI survey was validated through a confirmatory factor analysis of survey responses from 287 students at four institutions of higher education in the United States and Canada (Arbaugh et al., 2008). The results validate the survey and the CoI model itself.

The validated survey provides a quantitative measure of learning processes that can be used to assess the effectiveness of technological and pedagogical innovations in online courses across time and institutions. It has been used to further explore the CoI framework and the interactive effects of all three presences (Garrison, Cleveland-Innes, & Fung, 2010; Shea & Bidjerano, 2010) with some meaningful results. For example, researchers have begun linking perceptions of the presences to course outcomes (Arbaugh, 2010).

Boston and colleagues linked 21% of the variance in program retention to two social presence survey items (Boston et al., 2009).

The survey has also been used to explore the effects of particular technologies or pedagogical strategies on learning processes. For example, researchers have shown that the use of audio for instructor feedback (Ice et al., 2007) and mini presentations (Dringus, Snyder, & Terrell, 2010) enhance the development of all three presences, the use of video can enhance teaching presence (Archibald, 2010), the use of digital storytelling can enhance social presence (Lowenthal & Dunlap, 2010), and the forms of online discussion used in online classes influence the development of cognitive presence (Richardson & Ice, 2010). Researchers have even found that the choice of an LMS can influence the development of communities of inquiry (Rubin, Fernandes, Averginou, & Moore, 2010).

The CoI survey can also be used by e-learning leaders to assess the quality of learning processes in online courses. It not only provides quantitative measures of the overall CoI development and the development of each of the presences, but the individual survey items point to areas of strength and weakness in particular courses. For example, at the University of Illinois Springfield, faculty in the Teacher Leadership program are using a combination of an initial QM revision and ongoing iterative revisions to course implementation based on CoI scores to improve the design and delivery of their fully online core courses. Preliminary findings show significant improvements in course outcomes in the first course to undergo this review and revision process (Swan et al., 2012). Indeed, several e-learning programs have adopted it as their end-of-course survey precisely because it can provide actionable data. One such institution to do so is the American Public University System (Boston et al., 2009), where e-learning leaders are using it to pinpoint areas that might be changed to enhance student retention.

e-Learning Outcomes

Learning outcomes are, of course, what learning analytics measure most everything against. A large part of the point of keeping careful data on e-learning inputs and processes is to explore how these affect learning outcomes. With the escalating calls for greater accountability in higher education, and the recent scrutiny placed on e-learning in particular, learning outcomes are in the spotlight, and e-learning leaders need take charge of the kinds of outcome data their institutions collect. Learning outcomes alone, however, will not produce actionable intelligence. About six sorts of outcomes measures are commonly used to assess learning effectiveness: satisfaction, retention, course grades/success, achievement, proficiencies, and performance.

Some of these, such as learner satisfaction and retention, are discussed in other chapters of this book. Suffice it to say with regard to both these measures, that while these are the easiest metrics to obtain, they are also the easiest to misinterpret or misrepresent. It is very important to define in detail what exactly is being measured. A common measure of retention, for example, is course completion, or the percentage of students enrolled as of a certain date who are still enrolled at the end of the semester regardless of their grades (Bloemer, 2009; Shelton, 2009; Willging & Johnson, 2004). However, some institutions count students still enrolled at the end of the semester except those with failing (F) grades (Fasse et al., 2009; Lenrow, 2009; Nash, 2005; Twig, 2003) and some institutions count students earning a C or better (Bloemer, 2009). Moreover, institutions vary on the date students are considered enrolled, and semesters vary from 5 to 16 weeks, making enrollment after the tenth working day, for example, a somewhat slippery concept. Another measure of retention is semester to semester enrollment (Boston et al., 2009; Chyung, 2001; Meyer et al., 2006), but again, there is no common agreement on a definition of enrollment. And so it goes. It is therefore incumbent on e-learning leaders to carefully consider what precise measures they will use and explicitly define them. Such considerations should probably take into consideration the audience and how you will use the data you collect.

Another very commonly used source of outcome data is overall course grades (Arbaugh, 2000; Cavanaugh, 2001; Means et al., 2009). Overall course grades, however, are not particularly useful for anything other than within course comparisons because they can vary widely between courses, programs, disciplines, and institutions, especially in higher education. A similar, but much more useful measure is the percentage of student success, which refers to the number of students who were enrolled in the beginning of a course and who remain enrolled and obtained a grade of C or better at the undergraduate level, or B or better at the graduate level (Bloemer, 2009; Clark, Holstrom, & Millacci, 2009; Dziuban, Moskal, & Dziuban, 2000; Roblyer & Marshall, 2002–2003; Wojciechowski & Palmer, 2005). A course with a grade of C or B or better can usually be transferred to other institutions, indicating common acceptability while avoiding the trap of grade variations between programs, disciplines, or institutions.

One of the better outcome measures for individual courses and programs is achievement, which refers to whether students achieve the major goals set for them (Blackley & Curran-Smith, 1998; Johnson et al., 2000; Maki et al., 2000; Picciano, 2002). One good way to identify such goals is to focus on what Wiggins and McTighe (2006) call "enduring understandings" (p. 17).

Enduring understandings are the big ideas that learners should remember five years after they finish a course or program, if not for the rest of their lives. The authors distinguish enduring understandings from things that are important to know and to be able to do and things worth being familiar with (see Figure 5.3).

E-learning leaders can and should work with their faculties to identify enduring understandings and to develop ways of assessing their acquisition. This is particularly important at the program level where faculty must map the development of big ideas across program courses. It is important to note that Wiggins and McTighe (2006) also maintain that enduring understandings are often quite complex and so require complex assessment. Sometimes this can be achieved with comprehensive testing, such as for the goal that students develop a basic knowledge of a discipline. However, more often than not, assessing the development of enduring understandings requires problem-based or project-based assessments that explore students' abilities to apply what they have learned.

Proficiencies are the knowledge, skills, and attitudes deemed essential for particular disciplines. Most professions use certification exams to test proficiencies, and these are a good means for assessing the learning effectiveness of one's own programs relative to a national standard (Nesler & Lettus, 1995). While proficiency tests are not common in the sciences or humanities, the growing calls for increased accountability and increased standardization of outcomes in higher education suggest that proficiency or certification measures in these areas may be on the horizon. E-learning leaders should at least keep abreast of certification developments and possibly take a proactive stance concerning them by empowering their faculties to develop certification standards.

Figure 5.3 Enduring Understandings.

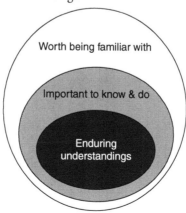

Performance is in some sense the gold standard of learning outcomes. It refers to students' success after graduation in obtaining or performing in a position, or in some cases being admitted to graduate programs. Performance is clearly a difficult outcome to measure because it requires keeping track of students after they graduate, but it can be done. In a study of community health nursing students, for example, Blackley and Curran-Smith (1998) not only found that distant students were able to meet their course objectives as well as resident students, but that the distant students performed equivalently in the field. Similarly, Nesler and Lettus (1995) reported higher ratings on clinical competence among nurses graduating from an online program than nurses who were traditionally prepared. Moreover, there are increasingly strident calls for just these sorts of measures to justify the high cost of higher education, especially regarding e-learning. Performance measures are for this very reason worth considering, especially in professional colleges where certifications are common.

Conclusions and Recommendations

This chapter explores what e-learning leaders need to know about learning effectiveness. This final section reviews the major points and their implications for e-learning leadership, and offers a few recommendations concerning how e-learning leaders might use that knowledge to ensure online learning effectiveness.

The first thing such leaders need to recognize is that online learning is different from traditional learning, and the online environment has different affordances and constraints than the face-to-face classroom. Constructivist approaches seem particularly well suited for e-learning, but it is clearly important that e-learning leaders stay conversant with contemporary learning theory, online learning research, and best practices in the field, as it is in constant flux. Interestingly, among the seven skills of K–12 leaders identified in Waters, Marzano, and McNulty's (2003) meta-analysis as accounting for at least 9% of the variance in student achievement was knowledge of current educational theories and practices and the sharing of that knowledge with faculty. The authors also uncovered the importance of leaders' being able to communicate their pedagogical vision and act as agents of change in their units or institutions and the importance of their advocating for it with the general public.

Second, e-learning leaders need to make themselves particularly knowledgeable about their own unique e-learning contexts, not just through immersing themselves in the culture of their institution but through the ongoing collection and analysis of empirical data on the inputs, processes, and outcomes of e-learning at their institution. In regard to inputs, e-learning leaders should provide faculty with access to instructional design support and work to develop common design standards. Concerning processes, e-learning leaders should encourage faculty, especially early adopters, to share their techniques and strategies for enhancing learning with each other. Moreover, they should involve faculty in developing output measures to assess the effectiveness of any changes made. Again, among the leadership skills identified as particularly important in enhancing student success in K–12 schools (Waters et al., 2003) were situational awareness, the ongoing monitoring of the impact of school practices on student learning, and the involvement of faculty in important decisions.

Although this chapter does not cover faculty development, faculty or student support, or optimal uses of technology, which are covered in other chapters of this book, it is important that e-learning leaders not lose sight of the critical importance of all of these in e-learning effectiveness. Faculty must be prepared to teach online and be supported in their work; students must be oriented to the challenges and rewards of online learning, and their efforts should be supported on an ongoing basis; technologies used must support pedagogical goals, function properly, and be accessible and transparent to student users. E-learning leaders must attend to each of these issues if they want to enhance learning effectiveness.

References

Anderson, T., Rourke, L., Garrison, D. R., & Archer, W. (2001). Assessing teaching presence in a computer conferencing context. *Journal of Asynchronous Learning Networks, 5*(2), 1–17.

Arbaugh, J. B. (2000). Virtual classroom versus physical classroom: An exploratory study of class discussion patterns and student learning in an asynchronous Internet-based MBA course. *Journal of Management Education, 24*(2), 213–233.

Arbaugh, J. B., Bangert, A., & Cleveland-Innes, M. (2010). Subject matter effects and the Community of Inquiry (CoI) framework. *The Internet and Higher Education, 13*(1–2), 37–44.

Arbaugh, J. B., Cleveland-Innes, M., Diaz, S., Garrison, D. R., Ice, P., Richardson, J. C., . . . Swan, K. (2008). Developing a community of inquiry instrument: Testing a measure of the community of inquiry framework using a multi-institutional sample. *The Internet and Higher Education, 11*(3/4), 133–136.

Archibald, D. (2010). Fostering the development of cognitive presence: Initial findings using the community of inquiry instrument. *Internet and Higher Education, 13*(1/2), 73–74.

Aviv, R., Erlich, Z., Ravid, G., & Geva, A. (2003). Network analysis of knowledge construction in asynchronous learning networks. *Journal of Asynchronous Learning Networks, 7*(3), 1–23.

Benbunan-Fich, R., & Hiltz, S. R. (1999). Impact of asynchronous learning networks on individual and group problem solving: A field experiment. *Group Decision and Negotiation, 8,* 409–426.

Bernard, R. M., Abrami, P. C., Borokhovski, E., Wade, C. A., Tamim, R. M., Surkes, M. A., & Bethel, E. C. (2009). A meta-analysis of three types of interaction treatments in distance education. *Review of Educational Research, 79*(3), 1243–1289.

Bernard, R. M., Abrami, P. C., Lou, Y., Borokhovski, E., Wade, A., Wozney, L., Wallet, P. A., Fiset, M., & Huang, B. (2004). How does distance education compare with classroom instruction? A meta-analysis of the empirical literature. *Review of Educational Research, 74*(3), 379–439.

Bernard, R., Brauer, A., Abrami, P., & Surkes, M. (2004). The development of a questionnaire for predicting online learning achievement. *Distance Education, 25*(1), 44–47.

Blackley, J. A., & Curran-Smith, J. (1998). Teaching community health nursing by distance methods: Development, process, and evaluation. *Journal of Continuing Education for Nurses, 29*(4), 148–153.

Bloemer, B. (2009). The UIS model for online success. *Journal of Asynchronous Learning Networks, 13*(3), 57–61.

Bogle, L. R. (2008). *Analysis of the effectiveness of the peer mentoring program in reducing the level of students not completing a course in Illinois community colleges.* Springfield: University of Illinois Springfield.

Boles, E., Cass, B., Levin, C., Schroeder, R., & Smith, S. (2010). Sustaining students: Retention strategies in an online program. *EDUCAUSE Quarterly, 33*(4). Retrieved from http://www.editlib.org/p/109182/

Boston, W., Diaz, S. R., Gibson, A. M., Ice, P., Richardson, J., & Swan, K. (2009). An exploration of the relationship between indicators of the community of inquiry framework and retention in online programs. *Journal of Asynchronous Learning Networks, 13*(3), 67–83.

Bransford, J. D, Brown, A. L., & Cocking, R. R. (2000). *How people learn: Brain, mind, experience, and school.* Washington, DC: National Academy Press.

Brown, J. S., Collins, A., & Duguid, S. (1989). Situated cognition and the culture of learning. *Educational Researcher, 18*(1), 32–42.

Brown, M. B., & Diaz, B. (2011). Seeking evidence of impact: Opportunities and needs. *EDUCAUSE Review, 46*(5), 41–54.

Brynjolfsson, E., Hitt, L. M., & Kim, H. H. (2011). *Strength in numbers: How does data-driven decision making affect firm performance?* Retrieved from http://papers.ssrn.com/sol3/papers.cfm?abstract_id=1819486#

Bush, V. (1945). As we may think. *Atlantic Monthly, 176,* 101–108. Retrieved from http://www.theatlantic.com/magazine/archive/1945/07/as-we-may-think/303881/

California State University, Chico. (2011–2012). *Rubric for online instruction.* Chico, CA: Author.

Campbell, J. P., DeBlois, P. B., & Oblinger, D. G. (2007). Academic analytics: A new tool for a new era. *EDUCAUSE Review, 42*(4), 40–57. Retrieved from http://www.educause.edu/library/erm0742

Cavanaugh, C. S. (2001). The effectiveness of interactive distance education technologies in K–12 learning: A meta-analysis. *International Journal of Educational Telecommunications, 7*(1), 73–88.

Cavanaugh, C. S. (2013). Student achievement in elementary and high school. In M. G. Moore (Ed.), *The handbook of distance education* (3rd ed., pp. 170–183). New York, NY: Routledge.

Chen, P. D., Guidry, K. R., & Lambert, A. D. (2009, April). *Engaging online learners: A quantitative study of postsecondary student engagement in the online learning environment.* Paper presented at the 2009 American Educational Research Association Annual Conference, San Diego, CA.

Cheung, L., & Kan, A. (2002). Evaluation of factors related to student performance in a distance learning business communication course. *Journal of Education for Business, 77*(5), 257–263.

Chyung, S. Y. (2001). Systematic and systemic approaches to reducing attrition rates in online higher education. *American Journal of Distance Education, 13*(3), 36–49.

Clark, M., Holstrom, L., & Millacci, A. M. (2009). University of Cincinnati: Case study of online student success. *Journal of Asynchronous Learning Networks, 13*(3), 49–55.

Committee for Online Instruction. (2003). *Rubric for online instruction.* Retrieved from California State University website: http://www.csuchico.edu/celt/roi/index.shtml

Davenport, T. H., & Harris, J. G. (2007). *Competing on analytics: The new science of winning.* Cambridge, MA: Harvard Business Press.

Dringus, L., Snyder, M. M., & Terrell, S. R. (2010). Facilitating discourse and enhancing teaching presence: Using mini-audio presentations in online forums. *Internet and Higher Education, 13*(1/2), 75–77.

Duffy, T. M., & Jonassen, D. H. (1992). *Constructivism and the technology of instruction: A conversation.* Hillsdale, NJ: Erlbaum.

Dupin-Bryant, P. (2004). Pre-entry variables related to retention in online distance courses. *American Journal of Distance Education, 18*(4), 199–206.

Dziuban, C. (2011). Impact in a transformational environment. *EDUCAUSE Review, 46*(5), 48.

Dziuban, C. D., Moskal, P. D., & Dziuban, E. K. (2000). Reactive behavior patterns go online. *Journal of Staff, Program, & Organization Development, 17*(3), 171–182.

Fallah, M. H., & Ubell, R. (2000). Blind scores in a graduate test: Conventional compared with web-based outcomes. *ALN Magazine, 4*(2).

Fasse, R., Humbert, J., & Rappold, R. (2009). Rochester Institute of Technology: Analyzing student success. *Journal of Asynchronous Learning Networks, 13*(3), 37–48.

Frid, S. (2001). Supporting primary students' on-line learning in a virtual enrichment program. *Research in Education, 66*, 9–27.

Garrison, D. R., Anderson, T., & Archer, W. (1999). Critical inquiry in a text-based environment: Computer conferencing in higher education. *The Internet and Higher Education, 2*(2/3), 87–105.

Garrison, D. R., & Arbaugh, J. B. (2007). Researching the community of inquiry framework: Review, issues, and future directions. *Internet and Higher Education, 10*(3), 157–172.

Garrison, D. R., & Cleveland-Innes, M. (2005). Facilitating cognitive presence in online learning: Interaction is not enough. *American Journal of Distance Education, 19*(3), 133–148.

Garrison, D. R., Cleveland-Innes, M., & Fung, T. S. (2010). Exploring relationships among teaching, cognitive and social presence: Student perceptions of the community of inquiry framework. *The Internet and Higher Education, 13*(1/2), 31–36.

Hawisher, G. E., & Pemberton, M. A. (1997). Writing across the curriculum encounters asynchronous learning networks or WAC meets up with ALN. *Journal of Asynchronous Learning Networks, 1*(1), 57–72.

Haythornthwaite, C. (2002). Building social networks via computer networks: Creating and sustaining distributed learning communities. In K. A. Renninger & W. Shumar (Eds.), *Building virtual communities: Learning and change in cyberspace*. Cambridge, UK: Cambridge University Press.

Hillman, D. C., Willis, D. J., & Gunawardena, C. N. (1994). Learner-interface interaction in distance education: An extension of contemporary models and strategies for practitioners. *American Journal of Distance Education, 8*(2), 30–42.

Ice, P., Curtis, R., Phillips, P., & Wells, J. (2007). Using asynchronous audio feedback to enhance teaching presence and students' sense of community. *Journal of Asynchronous Learning Networks, 11*(2), 3–25.

Jenkins, H. (2006). *Convergence culture: Where old and new media collide*. New York, NY: New York University Press.

Jiang, M., & Ting, E. (2000). A study of factors influencing students' perceived learning in a web-based course environment. *International Journal of Educational Telecommunications, 6*(4), 317–338.

Johnson, L., Adams Becker, S., Cummins, M., Estrada, V., Freeman, A., & Ludgate, H. (2013). *NMC horizon report: 2013 higher education edition*. Austin, TX: New Media Consortium.

Johnson, L., Smith, R., Willis, H., Levine, A., & Haywood, K. (2011). *The 2011 horizon report*. Austin, TX: New Media Consortium.

Johnson, S. D., Aragon, S. R., Shaik, N., & Palma-Rivas, N. (2000). Comparative analysis of learner satisfaction and learning outcomes in online and face-to-face learning environments. *Journal of Interactive Learning Research, 11*(1) 29–49.

Kanuka, H., & Anderson, T. (1998). Online social interchange, discord, and knowledge construction. *Journal of Distance Education, 13*(1), 57–75.

Legon, R., Runyon, J., & Aman, R. (2007, October). *The impact of "Quality Matters" standards on courses: Research opportunities and results*. Paper presented at the 13th International Sloan-C Conference on Online Learning, Orlando, FL.

Lenrow, J. (2009). Peirce College and student success. *Journal of Asynchronous Learning Networks, 13*(3), 23–27.

Liu, S. J., Gomez, J., & Yen, C. (2009). Community college online course retention and final grade: Predictability of social presence. *Journal of Interactive Learning, 8*(2), 165–183.

Long, P., & Siemens, G. (2011). Penetrating the fog: Analytics in learning and education. *EDUCAUSE Review, 46*(5), 31–40.

Lowenthal, P. R., & Dunlap, J. C. (2010). From pixel on a screen to real person in your students' lives: Establishing social presence using digital storytelling. *Internet and Higher Education, 13*(1/2), 70-72.

Luebeck, J. L., & Bice, L. R. (2005). Online discussion as a mechanism of conceptual change among mathematics and science teachers. *Journal of Distance Education, 20*(2), 21–39.

Macfadyen, L. P., & Dawson, S. (2010). Mining LMS data to develop an "early warning system" for educators: A proof of concept. *Computers & Education, 54*(2), 588–599.

Maki, R. H., Maki, W. S., Patterson, M., & Whittaker, P. D. (2000). Evaluation of a web-based introductory psychology course. *Behavior Research Methods, Instruments, & Computers, 32*, 230–239.

Maki, W., & Maki, R. (2002). Multimedia comprehension skill predicts differential outcomes in web-based and lecture courses. *Journal of Experimental Psychology, 8*(2), 85–98.

Markoff, J. (2011, October 10). Government aims to build an "eye in the sky." *New York Times.* Retrieved from http://www.nytimes.com/2011/10/11/science/11predict.html?pagewanted=all&_r=0

Means, B., Toyama, Y., Murphy, R., Bakia, M., & Jones, K. (2009). *Evaluation of evidence-based practices in online learning: A meta-analysis and review of online learning studies.* Washington, DC: U.S. Department of Education.

Meyer, K. A. (2003). Face-to-face versus threaded discussions: The role of time and higher-order thinking. *Journal of Asynchronous Learning Networks, 7*(3), 55–65.

Meyer, K. A., Bruwelheide, J., & Poulin, R. (2006). Why they stayed: Near-perfect retention in an online certification program in library media. *Journal of Asynchronous Learning Networks, 10*(4), 100–115.

Moore, M. G. (1989). Three types of interaction. *American Journal of Distance Education, 3*(2), 1–6.

Morris, L. V., Finnegan, C., & Wu, S-S. (2005). Tracking student behavior, persistence, and achievement in online courses. *The Internet and Higher Education, 8*(3), 221–231.

Murphy, E. (2004). Identifying and measuring ill-structured problem formulation and resolution in online asynchronous discussions. *Canadian Journal of Learning and Technology, 30*(1), 5–20.

Nash, R. D. (2005). Course completion rates among distance learners: Identifying possible methods to improve retention. *Online Journal of Distance Learning Administration, 8*(4). Retrieved from http://www.westga.edu/~distance/ojdla/winter84/nash84.htm

National Survey of Student Engagement. (2009). *Assessment for improvement: Tracking student engagement over time—Annual results 2009.* Bloomington: Indiana University Center for Postsecondary Research.

Nesler, M. S., & Lettus, M. K. (1995, August). *A follow-up study of external degree graduates from Florida.* Paper presented at the 103rd Annual Convention of the American Psychological Association, New York, NY.

Oliver, R., & Omari, A. (1999). Using online technologies to support problem-based learning: Learners' responses and perceptions. *Australian Journal of Educational Technology, 15*(1), 58–79.

Osborn, V. (2001). Identifying at-risk students in videoconferencing and web-based distance education. *American Journal of Distance Education, 15*(1), 41–54.

Parker, A. (2003). Identifying predictors of academic persistence in distance education. *USDLA Journal, 17*(1). Retrieved from http://www.usdla.org/html/journal/JAN03_Issue/index.html

Parker, D., & Gemino, A. (2001). Inside online learning: Comparing conceptual and technique learning performance in place-based and ALN formats. *Journal of Asynchronous Learning Networks, 5*(2), 64–74.

Piaget, J. (1957). *Construction of reality in the child*. London, UK: Routledge.

Picciano, A. (1998). Developing an asynchronous course model at a large, urban university. *Journal of Asynchronous Learning Networks, 2*(1), 3–19.

Picciano, A. G. (2002). Beyond student perceptions: Issues of interaction, presence, and performance in an online course. *Journal of Asynchronous Learning Networks, 6*(1), 21–40.

Pillay, H., Irving, K., & McCrindle, A. (2006). Developing a diagnostic tool for assessing tertiary students' readiness for online learning. *International Journal of Learning Technology, 2*(1), 92–104.

Quality Matters. (2005). *Research literature and standards sets support for quality matters review standards*. Retrieved from https://www.qualitymatters.org/files/Matrix of Research Standards FY0506_0.pdf

Quality Matters. (2011). *Quality Matters rubric standards 2011–2013 edition*. Retrieved from http://www.qmprogram.org/files/QM_Standards_2011-2013.pdf

Richardson, J. C., & Ice, P. (2010). Investigating students' level of critical thinking across instructional strategies in online discussions. *Internet and Higher Education, 13*(1/2), 52–59.

Richardson, J. C., & Swan, K. (2003). Examining social presence in online courses in relation to students' perceived learning and satisfaction. *Journal of Asynchronous Learning Networks, 7*(1), 68–88.

Richardson J., & Ting, E. (1999). *Making the most of interaction: What instructors do that most affect students' perceptions of their learning*. Paper presented at the Fifth International Conference on Asynchronous Learning, College Park, MD.

Roblyer, M. D., & Marshall, J. C. (2002–2003). Predicting success of virtual high school students: Preliminary results from an educational success prediction instrument. *Journal of Research on Technology in Education, 35*(2), 241–255.

Rovai, A. P. (2002). A preliminary look at structural differences in sense of classroom community between higher education traditional and ALN courses. *Journal of Asynchronous Learning Networks, 6*(1), 41–56.

Rovai, A. P. (2003). In search of higher persistence rates in distance education online programs. *The Internet and Higher Education, 6*, 1–16.

Rubin, B., Fernandes, R., Averginou, M. D., & Moore, J. (2010). The effect of learning management systems on student and faculty outcomes. *Internet and Higher Education, 13*(1/2), 82–83.

Seaman, J. (2009). *Online learning as a strategic asset; Volume II: The paradox of faculty voices: Views and experiences with online learning.* Washington, DC: Association of Public and Land-grant Universities. Retrieved from http://www.aplu.org/document.doc?id=1879

Shea, P. (2006). A study of students' sense of learning community in online environments. *Journal of Asynchronous Learning Networks, 10*(1), 35–44.

Shea, P., & Bidjerano, T. (2008, March). *Community of inquiry as a theoretical framework to foster "epistemic engagement" and "cognitive presence" in online education.* Paper presented at the annual meeting of the American Educational Research Association, New York, NY.

Shea, P., & Bidjerano, T. (2010). Learning presence: Towards a theory of self-efficacy, self-regulation, and the development of a communities of inquiry in online and blended learning environments. *Computers & Education, 55*(4), 1721–1731.

Shea, P., Li, C., Swan K., & Pickett, A. (2005). Developing learning community in online asynchronous college courses: The role of teaching presence. *Journal of Asynchronous Learning Networks, 9*(4), 35–44.

Shea, P. J., Pickett, A. M., & Pelz, W. E. (2003). A follow-up investigation of "teaching presence" in the SUNY Learning Network. *Journal of Asynchronous Learning Networks, 7*(2), 61–80.

Shelton, K. (2009). Does strong faculty support equal consistent course completion? It has for Dallas Baptist University. *Journal of Asynchronous Learning Networks, 13*(3), 63–66.

Swan, K. (2001). Virtual interactivity: Design factors affecting student satisfaction and perceived learning in asynchronous online courses. *Distance Education, 22*(2), 306–331.

Swan, K. (2002). Building communities in online courses: The importance of interaction. *Education, Communication and Information, 2*(1), 23–49.

Swan, K., Garrison, D. R., & Richardson, J. C. (2009). A constructivist approach to online learning: The community of inquiry framework. In C. R. Payne (Ed.), *Information technology and constructivism in higher education: Progressive learning frameworks* (pp. 43–57). Hershey, PA: IGI Global.

Swan, K., Matthews, D., Bogle, L., Welch-Boles, E., & Day, S. (2012). Linking online course design and implementation to learning outcomes: A design experiment. *The Internet and Higher Education, 15*(2), 81–88.

Swan, K., Richardson, J. C., Ice, P., Garrison, D. R., Cleveland-Innes, M., & Arbaugh, J. B. (2008). Validating a measurement tool of presence in online communities of inquiry. *e-Mentor, 2*(24). Retrieved from http://www.e-mentor.edu.pl/artykul_v2.php?numer=24&id=543

Swan, K., Schenker, J., Arnold, S., & Kuo, C-L. (2007). Shaping online discussion: Assessment matters. *e-Mentor, 1*(18), 78–82.

Swan, K., Shea, P., Fredericksen, E., Pickett, A., Pelz, W., & Maher, G. (2000). Building knowledge building communities: Consistency, contact and communication in the virtual classroom. *Journal of Educational Computing Research, 23*(4), 389–413.

Swan, K., Shen, J., & Hiltz, R. (2006). Assessment and collaboration in online learning. *Journal of Asynchronous Learning Networks, 10*(1), 45–62.

Swan, K., & Shih, L-F. (2005). On the nature and development of social presence in online course discussions. *Journal of Asynchronous Learning Networks, 9*(3), 115–136.

Tu, C-H. (2000). On-line learning migration: From social learning theory to social presence theory in CMC environment. *Journal of Network and Computer Applications, 23*(1), 27–37.

Tu, C-H., & McIsaac, M. (2002). The relationship of social presence and interaction in online classes. *American Journal of Distance Education, 16*(3), 131–150.

Twigg, C. (2001). *Innovations in online learning: Moving beyond no significant difference.* Troy, NY: Center for Academic Transformation, Rensselaer Polytechnic Institute. Retrieved from http://www.thencat.org/Monographs/Mono4.pdf

Twig, C. A. (2003). Improving quality and reducing cost: Designs for effective learning. *Change, 33*(4), 23–29.

Vaughan, N., & Garrison, D. R. (2006). How blended learning can support a faculty development community of inquiry. *Journal of Asynchronous Learning Networks, 10*(4), 139–152.

Vygotsky, L. S. (1978). *Mind in society.* Cambridge, MA: Harvard University Press.

Wang, A., & Newlin, M. (2000). Characteristics of students who enroll and succeed in web-based classes. *Journal of Educational Psychology, 92*(1), 137–143.

Wang, Y-M., & Chang, V. D-T. (2008). Essential elements in designing online discussions to promote cognitive presence—a practical experience. *Journal of Asynchronous Learning Networks, 12*(3/4), 157–177.

Waschull, S. (2005). Predicting success in online psychology courses: Self-discipline and motivation. *Teaching of Psychology, 32*(3), 190–192.

Waters, T., Marzano, R. J., & McNulty, B. (2003). *Balanced leadership: What 30 years of research tells us about the effect of leadership on student achievement.* Aurora, CO: Mid-Continent Regional Educational Lab.

Wiggins, G., & McTighe, J. (2006). *Understanding by design* (2nd ed.). Upper Saddle River, NJ: Pearson.

Willging, P., & Johnson, S. (2004). Factors that influence students' decisions to drop out of online courses. *Journal of Asynchronous Learning Networks, 8*(4), 23–31.

Wojciechowski, A., & Palmer, L. (2005). Individual student characteristics: Can any be predictors of success in online classes? *Online Journal of Distance Learning Administration, 8*(2). Retrieved from http://www.westga.edu/~distance/ojdla/summer82/wojciechowski82.htm

Wu, D., & Hiltz, S. R. (2004). Predicting learning from asynchronous online discussions. *Journal of Asynchronous Learning Networks, 8*(2), 139–152.

APPENDIX A

Quality Matters Rubric Standards 2011–2013 Edition With Assigned Point Values

Standards		Points
Course Overview and Introduction	1.1 Instructions make clear how to get started and where to find various course components.	3
	1.2 Students are introduced to the purpose and structure of the course.	3
	1.3 Etiquette expectations (sometimes called "netiquette") for online discussions, e-mail, and other forms of communication are stated clearly.	2
	1.4 Course and/or institutional policies with which the student is expected to comply are clearly stated, or a link to current policies is provided.	2
	1.5 Prerequisite knowledge in the discipline and/or any required competencies are clearly stated.	1
	1.6 Minimum technical skills expected of the student are clearly stated.	1
	1.7 The self-introduction by the instructor is appropriate and available online.	1
	1.8 Students are asked to introduce themselves to the class.	1
Learning Objectives (Competencies)	2.1 The course learning objectives describe outcomes that are measurable.	3
	2.2 The module/unit learning objectives describe outcomes that are measurable and consistent with the course-level objectives.	3
	2.3 All learning objectives are stated clearly and written from the students' perspective.	3
	2.4 Instructions to students on how to meet the learning objectives are adequate and stated clearly.	3
	2.5 The learning objectives are appropriately designed for the level of the course.	3

(Continues)

Standards		Points
Assessment and Measurement	3.1 The types of assessments selected measure the stated learning objectives and are consistent with course activities and resources.	3
	3.2 The course grading policy is stated clearly.	3
	3.3 Specific and descriptive criteria are provided for the evaluation of students' work and participation and are tied to the course grading policy.	3
	3.4 The assessment instruments selected are sequenced, varied, and appropriate to the student work being assessed.	2
	3.5 Students have multiple opportunities to measure their own learning progress.	2
Instructional Materials	4.1 The instructional materials contribute to the achievement of the stated course and module/unit learning objectives.	3
	4.2 The purpose of instructional materials and how the materials are to be used for learning activities are clearly explained.	3
	4.3 All resources and materials used in the course are appropriately cited.	2
	4.4 The instructional materials are current.	2
	4.5 The instructional materials present a variety of perspectives on the course content.	1
	4.6 The distinction between required and optional materials is clearly explained.	1
Learner Interaction and Engagement	5.1 The learning activities promote the achievement of the stated learning objectives.	3
	5.2 Learning activities provide opportunities for interaction that support active learning.	3
	5.3 The instructor's plan for classroom response time and feedback on assignments is clearly stated.	3
	5.4 The requirements for student interaction are clearly articulated.	2

Standards		Points
Course Technology	6.1 The tools and media support the course learning objectives.	3
	6.2 Course tools and media support student engagement and guide the student to become an active learner.	3
	6.3 Navigation throughout the online components of the course is logical, consistent, and efficient.	3
	6.4 Students can readily access the technologies required in the course.	2
	6.5 The course technologies are current.	1
Learner Support	7.1 The course instructions articulate or link to a clear description of the technical support offered and how to access it.	3
	7.2 Course instructions articulate or link to the institution's accessibility policies and services.	3
	7.3 Course instructions articulate or link to an explanation of how the institution's academic support services and resources can help students succeed in the course and how students can access the services.	2
	7.4 Course instructions articulate or link to an explanation of *how* the institution's student support services can help students succeed and how students can access the services.	1
Accessibility	8.1 The course employs accessible technologies and provides guidance on how to obtain accommodation.	3
	8.2 The course contains equivalent alternatives to auditory and visual content.	2
	8.3 The course design facilitates readability and minimizes distractions.	2
	8.4 The course design accommodates the use of assistive technologies.	2

From Quality Matters (2011). Copyright 2011 by MarylandOnline. Adapted with permission.

APPENDIX B

Community of Inquiry Survey

The following statements relate to your perceptions of **Teaching Presence**: the design of this course and your instructor's facilitation of discussion and direct instruction within it. Please indicate your agreement or disagreement with each statement.

#	Statement
1	The instructor clearly communicated important course topics.
2	The instructor clearly communicated important course goals.
3	The instructor provided clear instructions on how to participate in course learning activities.
4	The instructor clearly communicated important due dates/time frames for learning activities.
5	The instructor was helpful in identifying areas of agreement and disagreement on course topics that helped me to learn.
6	The instructor was helpful in guiding the class toward understanding course topics in a way that helped me clarify my thinking.
7	The instructor helped to keep course participants engaged and participating in productive dialogue.
8	The instructor helped keep the course participants on task in a way that helped me to learn.
9	The instructor encouraged course participants to explore new concepts in this course.
10	Instructor actions reinforced the development of a sense of community among course participants.
11	The instructor helped to focus discussion on relevant issues in a way that helped me to learn.
12	The instructor provided feedback that helped me understand my strengths and weaknesses relative to the course's goals and objectives.
13	The instructor provided feedback in a timely fashion.

The following statements refer to your perceptions of **Social Presence**: the degree to which you feel socially and emotionally connected with others in this course. Please indicate your agreement or disagreement with each statement.

#	Statement
14	Getting to know other course participants gave me a sense of belonging in the course.

15	I was able to form distinct impressions of some course participants.
16	Online or web-based communication is an excellent medium for social interaction.
17	I felt comfortable conversing through the online medium.
18	I felt comfortable participating in the course discussions.
19	I felt comfortable interacting with other course participants.
20	I felt comfortable disagreeing with other course participants while still maintaining a sense of trust.
21	I felt that my point of view was acknowledged by other course participants.
22	Online discussions help me to develop a sense of collaboration.

The following statements relate to your perceptions of **Cognitive Presence**: the extent to which you were able to develop a good understanding of course topics. Please indicate your agreement or disagreement with each statement.

#	Statement
23	Problems posed increased my interest in course issues.
24	Course activities piqued my curiosity.
25	I felt motivated to explore content related questions.
26	I utilized a variety of information sources to explore problems posed in this course.
27	Brainstorming and finding relevant information helped me resolve content-related questions.
28	Online discussions were valuable in helping me appreciate different perspectives.
29	Combining new information helped me answer questions raised in course activities.
30	Learning activities helped me construct explanations/solutions.
31	Reflection on course content and discussions helped me understand fundamental concepts in this class.
32	I can describe ways to test and apply the knowledge created in this course.
33	I have developed solutions to course problems that can be applied in practice.
34	I can apply the knowledge created in this course to my work or other non-class related activities.

The complete survey is available from http://communitiesofinquiry.com/methodology

6

SUPPORTING FACULTY SUCCESS IN ONLINE LEARNING

Requirements for Individual and Institutional Leadership

Lawrence C. Ragan and Raymond Schroeder

As online learning activities continue to grow and expand, attention has increasingly shifted to the role of the instructor in the online teaching and learning process. This attention is desired and warranted as it provides an opportunity to examine and consider the role and impact of the online instructor on learner success within this new teaching context. It also has fostered an increased focus on how to prepare and support instructors in this new environment. For institutional leaders, two domains of supporting faculty success in online learning require consideration: development and preparation of the individual online instructor and institutional-level faculty services to ensure teaching success.

To a large degree, individuals teaching in today's online classrooms have had little or no personal online experience in an online learning environment. Their repertoire of teaching skills and competencies are limited to their face-to-face classroom experiences. Helping these individuals make the transition to a learning system that assumes the separation of instructor and learner by time and/or distance requires careful design and implementation. As the number of online instructors increases, additional support needs for continual improvement also require an institutional response. This may involve technical support, pedagogical or logistical support, or new administrative policies and procedures.

The required online teaching skills are also developmentally oriented, requiring basic survival skills for the novice, and more sophisticated and complex skills for the experienced instructor (Ko & Rossen, 2010; Smith, R.,

2008; Varvel, 2007). How these skills and competencies are addressed is contextualized to the culture, practices, and administrative structure of the online initiative in the institution. The challenge for the institution is to understand and address the needs of the online instructor and create the appropriate programs and support services and policies that help develop the competencies necessary for online teaching success.

This chapter explores these two domains as separate but related leadership issues. The preparation of the individual instructor with the skills and competencies necessary to succeed online will be defined through 10 themes that together encompass good practice in professional development in this area. In addition, the role of the institution in providing adequate support services and systems are explored. Both of these domains call for institutional vision and leadership to identify and provide the core professional development services and ongoing faculty support. This chapter focuses primarily on the preparation of the instructor with online teaching competencies. To illustrate how these two concepts interact in an institutional environment, a case study from the University of Illinois Springfield illustrates one institutional response to leadership in faculty development.

Overview

Since online education as an instructional learning system began in earnest in the mid-1990s, concerns have been expressed regarding a wide range of issues related to its effectiveness and viability (Grineski, 2002; Russell, 2001; Twigg, 2001). The scrutiny was welcome as it enabled online practitioners to focus on those areas seen as critical to teaching and learning effectiveness. An examination of the quality of online course design, academic integrity, student support, and overall systems performance prompted a variety of panel debates, research studies, and theoretical models. This examination has led to an improved learning environment for instructor and student. It is likely and necessary that this research continue and expand to inform the practice and refine online learning.

During the first 10 years of online course design, development, and delivery, the role of the online instructor within this emerging educational ecosystem was only tangentially considered (Boettcher & Conrad, 2002; Dillon & Walsh, 2002; Ragan, 2007). Early approaches to online instructor preparation were part and parcel of the instructional design process. That is, as instructors designed and crafted the online learning space, frequently with the support of instructional design staff, they became intimately familiar with the pace and flow of the course and required little or no additional preparation for teaching the course. This approach did leave gaps in online instructor preparation, such as understanding the needs of adult learners and the administrative tasks necessary to launch and bring the course to successful completion.

As the number of online learning course offerings expanded (Allen & Seaman, 2004, 2005, 2007, 2008, 2010, 2011), however, more and more individuals who had little or no familiarity with online teaching were engaged to instruct additional sections of preconstructed online courses that the new instructor had no personal role in developing. A need emerged for professional development for these new recruits that addressed a range of skills and competencies to adequately prepare for online teaching success.

Many institutions entering the online learning arena in the mid-1990s through the middle of the first decade in the twenty-first century initially focused their resources and energy on course design and development and construction of the technical infrastructure, financial models, student services, and marketing of their online programs. These efforts were placing a tremendous demand and strain on traditional systems and services originally constructed to serve a resident-based student population. The role and responsibilities of the instructor in this rapidly evolving learning system were not well understood, and online teaching expectations were not communicated. The mantra of "good teaching is good teaching" prevailed (Ragan, 2000). Instructors were encouraged to consider what they did well in the classroom and apply it to their online courses. Although this approach stressed the importance of pedagogy, it failed to identify the unique challenges of teaching online as well as embrace the new instructional possibilities of the medium.

One reason this approach worked initially was because many of the early online instructors demonstrated characteristics associated with early adopters, such as being self-managed and self-directed. Through sheer determination and will, they did what they needed to do to successfully complete the instruction of the online course. As their own trial and error led to better online teaching, new methodologies, strategies, and techniques emerged that enveloped the old mantra of good teaching and identified effective online teaching techniques that took advantage of the new medium. Many institutions, such as the State University of New York (Pickett, 2011) and the University of Central Florida, did develop early faculty development programs well suited to serving the professional development needs of the online instructor.

The articulation of these new instructional techniques and skills began to aggregate into lists of best practices for effective online instruction (American Distance Education Consortium, 2003; Chickering & Ehrmann, 1996; Smith, 2005). Individuals shared their specific strategies and techniques for instructional effectiveness first in their disciplines and then in the broader scope of their institution's overall online distance education initiative. Translating these strategies into specific skills and competencies for online teaching success is a continual process informed by research and practice (Bigatel, Ragan, Kennan, May, & Redmond, 2012; Pelz, 2004; Thach & Murphy, 1995; Varvel, 2007). Today, institutional leaders of online distance education initiatives need to proactively address the needs of the individual instructor and the larger institutional context where instruction takes place to fully realize the potential of online learning.

Faculty Capacity Issues and an Increasingly Diverse Instructor Profile

The exponential growth in demand for online learning creates an institutional challenge of ensuring adequate instructor capacity, that is, the number of instructors necessary to teach online. Institutions tend to use one of several ways to deal with the problem of scale, such as increasing the student-instructor ratio, increasing the instructor's course load, or using a team approach in which a small group of faculty members develop a course that is then taught by a cadre of part-time or adjunct instructors.

While each of these strategies can contribute to meeting the demand for more and more online offerings, they also present the additional issue of instructional quality. Whatever approach or mix of approaches may be used, the institution will ultimately need to identify and prepare many more course instructors, some of whom may be making the transition from the face-to-face classroom, and others as adjuncts who may have little or no classroom teaching experience. Although the professional background and working context of the traditional and the adjunct online instructor may be very different, the core skill sets and competencies for online teaching success remain largely the same.

Mirroring the diversity in the online student population, there is an increased range of background, academic, and work experiences of individuals engaged in the instruction of online courses. Since the online environment eliminates the traditional requirement for instructors to be physically located at or near the home institution, instructors in online courses can be drawn from the national workplace or other academic institutions. We can also envision that over time a cadre of professional online instructors—individuals who have made a career of teaching in multiple online institutions—may emerge who teach simultaneously at multiple institutions. These individuals may be situated locally, regionally, nationally, or internationally. Regardless of where they reside, the need for adequate preparation prior to teaching online and subsequent methods of faculty support is crucial.

This profile diversity of the online instructors creates new challenges for institutions in terms of recruitment, enculturation to the academy, and ongoing professional development. An online instructor in the institution may have professional requirements that include departmental or institutional committee assignments, research, publications, face-to-face teaching, grant writing, and outreach activities including community service. An online instructor external to the institution may be faced with additional challenges of managing and balancing professional responsibilities with an online teaching load. Availability to participate in professional development programs during typical hours of the workday may be limited or nonexistent. In both cases, the personal life of today's instructor is a complex arrangement of family, civic, and social responsibilities. The configuration of life demands coupled with teaching an online course can put stress on even the most grounded and well-organized individual.

Leaders of online learning programs need to carefully consider the processes, systems, and services that will be used to prepare this diverse population for online teaching success. Whether the professional development services are provided by an instructional designer in the academic department, other departmental staff, or by an institutionally sponsored faculty development unit, these individuals need a clear, efficient, and effective means of obtaining, maintaining, and improving their online teaching skills. Additionally, serving the ongoing development needs of all online instructors also demands a coordinated and well-resourced response.

Part of the challenge of meeting these diverse professional development needs is understanding their institutional context. Clearly articulating the relationship between the academic department and the online delivery system is critical to efficient operation and the reduction of confusion regarding reporting lines and accountability. With the online instructor serving as the primary interface between the learners and their institution, the adequate preparation and attention to their continual growth is not only necessary, it is essential. The investment of resources to adequately prepare the online instructor can be directly or indirectly related to student satisfaction and retention.

In this context, institutional leaders need to consider strategies and methods to support the transition of the online instructor from the face-to-face to online classroom. One approach is to consider the most difficult transitional points for instructors in this process. Instead of suggesting that the online instructor convert from the face-to-face classroom to online learning, developers of faculty preparation and support programs should consider addressing the primary differences between the two teaching formats. Preparing the online instructor to recognize and manage these differences provides the foundation for a successful teaching and learning online experience.

The adjustments the instructor has to make to be successful in the online classroom require a reconceptualization of the basic assumptions and practices of the teaching and learning process. Layered over this shift in pedagogical thinking is a technological interface that can impede or encourage the teaching and learning experience. From the basics of establishing a teaching personality and maintaining regular visibility in the online classroom to understanding the nuances of academic integrity issues, the online instructor must manage a new learning space with sometimes still emerging standards of practice. How these dimensions vary in complexity, scope, and applicability is based on institutional context, including history, infrastructure, and mission.

Ten Essential Dimensions of Faculty Preparation

The transition from a face-to-face classroom to online teaching may appear to be simply a move from the physical to the virtual learning space. In practice, however, the adjustment has conceptual and emotional implications, as well as a need for new and specific skill set development. When teaching online, especially in situations where the learners will never experience any on-campus aspect of their education in a traditional, physical campus environment, the faculty member is the critical link between the learner and the educational institution. A poorly prepared online educator can irreparably damage the learning path for the online learner leading to frustration and student failure. It is also important that the instructor understand the needs of the distant learner, which can be significantly different from a traditional campus-based student. When a learner has a poor online educational experience it can close the door to future formal learning, and that door may not open again. Conversely, a competent and confident online educator may positively affect the learning path and life of a learner he or she may never meet face-to-face and help foster a lifelong learning relationship between the learner and the institution.

Although the mantra of good teaching is good teaching holds true as a general philosophy in any delivery format, it is not adequate to highlight the changes during the transition from the face-to-face to the online classroom. The core tenets of understanding learner characteristics, clearly communicating learning outcomes, and establishing clear grading and assessment standards remain good principles of quality instruction. However, two forces converge in the online classroom that have an impact on the role of the educator as never before: a reexamination of the teaching and learning process and the role of the instructor, and an increasingly sophisticated technology infrastructure. Technology-enabled communications systems have redefined teacher and learner access to information; the type, style, and frequency of interactions between class participants; and the ability to deliver instruction in a distributed fashion to a global audience. Coupled with these technology enhancements is a reconceptualization of what constitutes the teaching and learning process (Moore & Kearsley, 2011; O'Neil, 2006). This convergence has created a dynamic that can no longer be ignored by either the faculty member or the institution. What it means to teach in today's online classroom is dramatically different from the face-to-face classrooms of 20 years ago (Bawane & Spector, 2009; Phillips, 2008; Seaman, 2009).

Multiple dimensions have emerged from experience and research as areas to consider when assisting faculty transitioning from a face-to-face to an online delivery system. Although there are multiple ways to arrange these topics, these 10 themes encompass the primary areas for consideration. Additionally these themes present challenges for individual as well as institutional leadership and provide a framework for considering faculty preparation initiatives, faculty support services, and institutional policy. The presentation of these dimensions does imply a priority in order of difficulty based on experience. A case study from the University of Illinois Springfield follows and exemplifies the principles of institutional leadership as a response to the design, development, and delivery of an online program.

1. Establishing and Maintaining Teaching Presence

One of the most difficult concepts to internalize when making the transition from the face-to-face to online classroom is an understanding of how to establish and maintain teaching presence (Garrison, Anderson, & Archer, 1999). In the face-to-face classroom, presence is established in a physical dimension. In the online classroom, teaching presence takes on a new and virtual meaning. Teaching presence online is less about being in the same time zone or same geographic space and more about being active, visible, and engaged while providing the instructional leadership necessary to conduct the online class.

Without previous online teaching or learning experience to draw upon, many novice instructors struggle to grasp their role in the online classroom. In the face-to-face classroom, the physical dimension of that experience contributes largely to teaching presence. In the absence of that physical dimension in the online classroom, understanding and embracing teaching presence may require a shift of beliefs on the role of instructor. In essence, online instructors need to be more intentional in their efforts to establish and maintain teaching presence. This shift does not come easily to many as instructors revert to the methods they observed and practiced in their face-to-face educational experiences. Faculty development activities that encourage the online instructor to understand teaching presence in the online classroom is a critical step toward online teaching success.

2. The Changing Classroom Dynamics

Although online learning can take various shapes and forms, a fundamental shift of classroom dynamics occurs when moving from the face-to-face to online experience. The very concept of a classroom must be reconsidered from a specific location where course participants gather to a learning environment where class participants never meet. The type and frequency of interactions change online, and new boundaries for classroom behavior may need to be established.

The ability to effectively educate geographically dispersed learners who are located in multiple time zones changes the nature of interactions between course participants. The nature of this change is often more difficult to imagine for novice online faculty who have had only face-to-face experiences and prompt such questions as, What is it like to interact with students in a meaningful way when you may be separated by one, two, or even five time zones? How do I conduct "class" each day? How will we build a learning community when we're not even in the same town? How will the learners know I am the instructor? These are among the common and valid questions when considering this transition to the online classroom.

Until one experiences the unique dynamics of engaging with course participants in an online classroom, it is difficult to conceptualize the shift in classroom dynamics. The pleasure of receiving the first posting to a discussion forum or getting to know the online learner in more personal and meaningful ways is hard to describe until experienced. These changing dynamics, some positive and others not so positive, are best appreciated through direct experience. Participating in an introductory activity with their peers in an online class can lead learners to a better appreciation of the methods that can be used to create an active online learning community. Encouraging or even requiring the novice online instructor to participate as a student in an online learning experience can greatly enhance his or her ability to manage and master the changing dynamics of the online classroom.

3. Time and Workload Management

Real or perceived, research and practice bear out that teaching online can require more time than teaching face-to-face (Allen & Seaman, 2010; Lazarus, 2003). It is generally accepted that the online classroom will require an additional 10% to 15% of faculty members' time to successfully complete the course. This simple reality has been a barrier, and in many cases the excuse, for faculty not to consider the transition. The increased time demands can present a formidable barrier to a successful online teaching experience. Attempting to analyze where the additional time is spent in the online classroom is in the end probably not as critical as providing faculty with the core skills and time management strategies they need to survive in the online classroom.

Today, many best practices for effective time management have been identified and can be included in online instructor preparation programs. Techniques that enable better organizational skills, structuring and scheduling course activity time frames, and the of use social networking systems as part of class communication can be used to help control and manage online instructional time. Over a period of offerings, many online instructors have developed their own strategies for gaining efficiencies when teaching online. Many of these strategies—for example, the use of weekly discussion forum summaries or creating a course operation checklist and grading rubrics—can be shared with novice online instructors as a way to become more efficient when teaching online.

4. New Learner Characteristics

The access to an education enabled by online learning ensures a richness of learner diversity as never before. Individuals across the globe can participate as equals in the online classroom. Barriers of language, race, gender, and other visible signs of differences can be neutralized in class discussions, team projects, and other class interactions. This potential diversity of learners can also challenge faculty members to reconsider what they know and believe of the students in their class.

Of particular interest in online learning is the trend of adult learners returning for either first-time college studies or advanced postgraduate efforts (Moore & Kearsley, 2011). These individuals bring with them a unique set of work and life experiences and learning goals that can greatly influence the pace, relevancy, and tone of the online classroom. How to best address the needs of all students begins with a thorough appreciation of the diversity represented in the online classroom.

5. Teaching Via a Technology Interface

It may appear obvious that technology presents an aspect that needs to be addressed as faculty move from the face-to-face to online classroom. The nature of the pressure that technology places on the novice online educator can easily be underestimated. Gaining the necessary technology skills to manage an online course requires an appreciation of the evolution of technical competence. The specific technological skill sets required to survive a first or even third online course offering can be very different from those developed after five or more offerings. As the initial challenges of simply logging in and accessing the course content are conquered, the more rewarding and sophisticated methods of using technology to support strategies such as team building and group exercises may be addressed.

When providing faculty with technical training in the learning management system and related tools, it is easy to assume that all technical capabilities should be explored and taught. It is easy to overwhelm novice instructors with a multitude of system features when all they really require are the basics. Most learning management systems are complex, data-driven environments with hidden and often overwhelming levels of nuances. A mind-numbing number of boxes to be checked, switches to be flipped, and toggles to be set can easily confuse and alienate the novice user.

6. Online Teaching Quality Assurance

One of the general areas of concern for faculty making the transition to the online classroom is the question of quality of the teaching and learning process. It is difficult at times when teaching online to determine exactly what aspects of quality are in question. Many novice online educators are concerned that this new teaching experience may reflect poorly on their personal standards of teaching. Additionally, the level of comfort and familiarity in the face-to-face classroom enables faculty to gauge their performance against their perceived standards of teaching quality. In the online classroom the novice instructor may miss nonverbal cues of attention, understanding, and interaction. These markers of quality in the face-to-face classroom are not present in the online classroom, requiring new techniques and strategies to ensure teaching excellence.

Addressing the range of quality concerns and establishing metrics and communicating standards can alleviate many of these concerns. In the past 10 years, standards have been identified and are being validated nationally that establish benchmarks for excellence. One example of emerging standards is the rubric established by the Quality Matters (www.qmprogram.org/rubric) organization that defines priority-ranked standards in eight dimensions of online course design (Shattuck, 2007). Additionally, many online learning organizations, as well as individual academic units, have defined online teaching performance metrics that serve as a guide for quality online instruction.

7. Ensuring Accessibility

When creating an online course, consideration should be given to making sure the course learning environment is accessible to all learners. This includes the learning management system, the course content, systems supporting class interactions, external web-based resources, library resources, hardware or software, and purchased items such as texts or other materials.

Many individuals who face access challenges of one form or another benefit from the flexibility of online learning. Without the requirement of physical presence, the totally online classroom creates new opportunities for those with special needs, physical or otherwise. However, while online courses may feature media and interaction technologies that enrich the environment for many, those same features may also present access barriers for some populations, such as the hearing or visually impaired. A student with a physical disability in a face-to-face course may be assisted locally using services such as note takers or interpreters. However, in an online course where students are geographically dispersed, distance can present logistical challenges to providing such services; linking remote students with support resources local to them can enable their online learning success. Students with learning disabilities may require extra time to take tests and complete assignments. The online classroom can accommodate these students by careful consideration of the tasks, due dates, and timing of class events.

8. Understanding and Managing the Legalities of Online Education

In the face-to-face classroom, faculty are the managers and facilitators of the learning experience. Resources created or derived from class interactions, assignments, and group projects are bound, and somewhat limited, to that class experience. Rarely are questions raised of ownership, privacy, or intellectual property. What is developed within the confines of the class generally operate within those boundaries. There are exceptions, of course, where class projects may spawn new services, products, or even businesses, but these are rare.

The visibility, speed, and global reach of the online teaching and learning environment, creates new and difficult questions regarding the legalities of content acquisition and use, distribution, attribution, copyright, intellectual permissions, and academic integrity. In a space with unclear boundaries of ownership, content manipulation and academic freedom, faculty are often left perplexed and overwhelmed with the task of interpreting the legal ramifications of their class activities. Add to this dilemma content that is created, stored, and shared in a public forum or on corporate websites, and the options and implications are staggering.

To navigate this space effectively and efficiently, online instructors require guidance, advice, and in many cases, direct support to address the legalities of their online teaching activities. Where possible, support services such as a copyright clearance center can alleviate faculty workload and concern by seeking and securing copyright permissions on materials used in the online classroom. In some cases, legal guidance may be necessary to assist the online instructor in determining the appropriate steps to maintain compliance with accepted societal and institutional policies.

9. Course Construction/Delivery Team Processes

For many faculty the design, development, and delivery of an online course requires a new team-oriented approach unlike anything they may have experienced previously. Faculty may not be familiar with the multiple roles and responsibilities of instructional designers, multimedia developers, project managers, and student support staff. Previously, the individual instructor was responsible for most aspects, short perhaps of scheduling and room assignments, of creating and delivering a course. In many cases, for the first, second, or third delivery, the instructor may be creating and instructing the course simultaneously.

In the online teaching and learning environment the services of many others may be required to successfully construct, implement, and deliver the online classroom. Typically the online course is fully developed prior to delivery. This may require the services of a project manager to monitor the overall process, an instructional designer to ensure the implementation of sound pedagogical practices, multiple media developers to construct media or interactive learning objects, and a course implementer responsible for uploading and managing the course within the learning management system. In the online classroom, creating and instructing simultaneously is not encouraged nor viewed as a best practice.

10. Online Learning Systems Complexity

A successful online learning program is the result of a complex set of operations and services from a range of organizations and individuals within and external to the institution. These skills and services include knowledge and proficiency in such areas as pedagogy and andragogy, technology, and administrative tasks and systems to adequately support program delivery. Marketing staff may need to be included to adequately promote the course or program offering. A student and faculty help desk may need to be staffed with extended hours if serving audiences in different time zones.

Each domain, regardless of the level of impact, plays an essential role in contributing to the overall student online experience. Coordination and communication between and among these units is essential for successful deployment of the online learning experience. Institutional leaders need to consider and account for activity and adequate support in each of these domains.

From Personal to Institutional: Supporting Faculty Online Success

As educators at all levels consider the transition from the face-to-face to online classroom, they will need to consider their responses to these 10 critical transitional challenges. Those responses will be based on their views of the educational exchange between learner and instructor, their role as teacher in that exchange, and their ability to remain flexible, embrace change, and assume some level of risk throughout their online teaching experience. Establishing a strong network of peers and joining a community of practice to learn from and share stories of success and failures can greatly assist the online faculty through this period.

Institutional leaders must also consider the ramifications of developing and supporting an online learning system. This delivery format requires new ways of approaching the complexities and challenges presented by a relationship between institution and learner separated by time or geography. A thoughtful and comprehensive approach to providing faculty the support and systems that enable their success must be at the core of this delivery format. How each institution responds to these challenges, similar to the individual response of the faculty, will be based on a willingness to be flexible and to reconsider operational practices and relationships while respecting the history and culture of the institution.

Elements of Institutional Leadership

As is increasingly being recognized, the institution has a responsibility and duty to ensure that faculty members involved in online learning obtain and maintain the skills and competencies required for successful online teaching. It is also important that the institution create an environment in which online teaching is accepted so that faculty members see teaching online as a satisfying, recognized, and rewarding professional activity. In this section, we look at several strategies that online distance education leaders might consider as part of an institutional faculty support infrastructure.

Historical Context and Influencing Factors

Institutions of higher education are facing changes in the methods, systems, and formats used to provide their constituents with access to their learning experience. Unlike teacher preparation for elementary and secondary schools, those teaching at the university level traditionally have not had foundation courses in educational theory and practice. In many cases they have not received instructional methods and strategies classes or guidance in the integration of technology into the teaching and learning process. Rather, university faculty members are expected to have course work and degrees in their primary field of study. Historically, without the benefit of preparation in pedagogy, many university faculty teach the same way they were taught, mirroring the methods they experienced and creating a potential circle of mediocrity.

Relatively little emphasis was placed on university faculty development nationally. Many faculty members have recognized they may have deficiencies in knowing and applying the best pedagogy and latest research on effectiveness in teaching practices but are uncertain how to address these needs. That recognition has been known to contribute to a sense of insecurity, even defensiveness, about the way faculty members instruct.

In the tradition of the academy, many faculty members are hired with the expectation of conducting scholarly research and securing the funds to conduct their research. At times, teaching and supporting students have become secondary functions on the path to tenure and promotion. The implementation of online teaching initiatives has further exacerbated the concerns of faculty hired under one set of circumstances and finding themselves called to service under another. In some cases this shift in core responsibilities has resulted in a reluctance to adopt and embrace the new technologies and techniques associated with online learning. Conflict has resulted between administrations, which are motivated to move forward to attain increased enrollments, and faculty members, who feel defensive and unsupported in development opportunities to adapt to the new learning environment online.

Faculty organizations such as unions and structures such as the faculty senate identified these conflicting and changing expectations as points that require strong faculty support and representation. These bodies recognize that the rules have changed, driven in large part by changing demographics and economics. A generation of faculty members find themselves in the unenviable position of significantly changing what they do and how they do it to thrive in the evolving landscape of a new academy.

Some faculty members adapted early and became leaders of change. University leaders often found that an effective practice was to identify these faculty champions, early adopters of online learning who are also faculty opinion leaders, and celebrate their work as well as provide necessary support services to ensure their success. Providing these individuals with the opportunity to share their experiences broadly across campus proved effective in furthering the role of the online instructor. Providing financial incentives to faculty members, often in the form of summer stipends or course development grants, encouraged faculty to engage in developing the expertise and experience to teach successfully online. Providing ready assistance with the associated learning technologies along with sound pedagogy and instructional design is recognized as a good administrative practice that helps to ensure successful online classes with superior learning outcomes and students' high persistence.

Providing Professional Development

In an online distance education program, the institution must be prepared to provide support to two distinct groups of faculty: those who work on campus and live near campus, and those who live at a distance, like many of the program's students, and do not have ready access to campus-centric support services.

Strategies for providing professional development support for faculty who may be on or near campus and part of a resident-based program need to address the challenges faculty face of competing workload requirements, comfort level in the use of technology, and, in some cases, a shift in pedagogical style and approach. Faculty moving from the classroom to an online course may experience a type of culture shock because of their perceptions and beliefs of effective classroom pedagogy and class dynamics. Without firsthand experience of the pace, flow, and interactions of the online classroom, the first, second, or even third course offering can be a difficult, frustrating, and discouraging experience. Faculty may also not be aware of the often rich set of support resources available to them once the course is operational.

Approaches to providing support to adjunct/part-time instructors need to take into account the additional challenges faced by adjuncts who may not be locally available for participation in faculty preparation programs. Many of these instructors continue to maintain full-time employment and teach their online courses in the evenings or weekends. Participation in professional development events scheduled during the workday and potentially in a different time zone creates additional difficulties for these individuals. Creative techniques of designing asynchronous program offerings, access to recorded synchronous events, or blended programs can serve the needs of faculty far and near.

One approach to serving instructors making the transition to the online classroom is communicating that they are not expected to know how to teach in this new medium, but they are expected to develop these new skills with the institution's support. Not having received degrees via an online program, most faculty are willing to embrace the available services offered to ensuring their success. Desiring to serve their learners, these faculty are ready and willing participants for professional development programming.

Preparing Faculty to Teach Online

Clearly, teaching online requires a new set of skills and attitudes. Leadership in faculty preparation may involve a variety of organizational strategies. A faculty development program may be housed within an academic unit, and the preparation is specific to the needs and academic culture of a specific discipline. In cases where the distance education program develops and delivers programs with academic units across the institution, the faculty development resource may be housed centrally. In some cases, institutions may contract with external training and development organizations. Crafting an effective and cost-efficient faculty development program may include a creative mix of program offerings from some or all of these sources. The final structure can depend on a variety of institutional factors. The key for the distance education leader is to understand the environment and ensure that appropriate resources are available.

Institutional leaders must be cognizant of several factors influencing today's higher education landscape. The Internet has reduced barriers of time and location, not only for the learner but also the instructor. No longer bound by geography, online instructors may also be distributed throughout the world. This access to a new pool of instructional talent offers institutions additional methods to meet the increasing demand for instructors of online sections. It also presents a new set of challenges, which is needing to ensure these individuals are adequately prepared for online teaching success. Mandated professional development programs are one strategy institutions are using to ensure the quality of their online instructors. Finally, with the distribution of an online teaching pool, enculturation of these individuals to the academy and maintaining a community of practice require creative strategies.

An issue of frequent consideration for leaders of online learning programs is the requirement for faculty to complete a mandatory professional development plan prior to teaching online. Although the response to this issue is contextual to the culture and practice within every institution, the core issue of faculty possessing and demonstrating competency needs to be considered. Identifying and articulating the necessary skills and competencies, and requiring, at a minimum, demonstration of aptitude with these competencies should be addressed at the leadership level.

One approach to address the question of mandatory versus volunteer participation is moving to a competency assessment technique of assessing faculty readiness for teaching online. By requiring novice and experienced faculty alike to demonstrate their proficiency in teaching online, the requirement of completing a mandatory program is averted. Constructing and managing such a program can present some unique challenges for the professional development staff. For example, assessing the entry-level skills of the online instructor and then tracking progress toward mastery of the required skills and competencies requires data tracking and information management tools.

Communities of Practice

Communities of practice were first formalized at the dawn of the twenty-first century. Social learning researcher and author Étienne Wenger (2006) developed the concept originally for businesses and later for other organizations. In a community of practice, the administration takes a backseat, and others such as the online instructors and support staff meet (in person or online) to interact, collaborate, and articulate the vision, as well as address issues and concerns. In online learning this can mean that the university administration provides a level of support in terms of meeting location, refreshments, speaker funding, and so forth. The agenda and activities are managed by those in the community of practice who work in support of the initiative. In the case of online learning, these may include professors, professional staff, technical staff, graduate assistants, and interested online students. Collectively and in small groups the community members can initiate programs and recommend new policies and practices. Communities of practice are especially well applied to online learning because of the wide range of services, technologies, and disciplines involved in the online initiative.

Building a Community of Online Faculty Practitioners

Unlike the disciplined-based faculty communities that have emerged over the years, the need exists for faculty participation in a larger community of practice for online teaching and learning. Regardless of the academic domain of the instructor, the emerging pedagogical practices, strategies for managing the workload, and creative use of online technologies serve as a common foundation for sharing and learning. Institutional leadership would well serve the local and distant faculty development needs of participating online instructors by establishing and maintaining communities of practice in this rapidly changing and exciting method of instruction.

Other strategies for building faculty communities do not require extensive staff resources. Encouraging and supporting faculty participation in the online learning special interest group in their professional associations and organizations can greatly enhance individual practice. Likewise, encouraging and supporting research in their field of study and examining issues evolving from participation in online learning not only serves to incentivize tenure-track faculty to teach online but also serves the broader field of online learning. Providing incentive grants and special project funding concentrates energy and resources as well as provides visibility and recognition to the online instructor.

Managing Teaching Load and Rewards

Some faculty members have contended that teaching online takes significantly more time than teaching a traditional class on campus. Commonly, these statements grow out of individual perceptions and anecdotal reports, while empirical studies show mixed results dependent on many variables. Institutional leaders also need to recognize and address the issue of workload assignment and adjust teaching loads appropriately. One successful approach to addressing these concerns is to invite faculty leaders to meet with colleagues from other campuses where online learning is accepted and supported. Visiting those campuses or inviting trusted leaders to come to the campus may provide a way for frank and honest discussions between faculty members. A second approach is to assure the online faculty that a full range of support will be available to those who teach online. Clearly defining the range and methods of access to those services will alleviate faculty concern as they make the transition to the online teaching environment.

Avoiding Faculty Burnout

In this era of increasing demands on faculty, decreasing budgets, and changing priorities, burnout can occur on campus and online. Driving faculty members is the knowledge that financial emergencies have been declared in which tenure is no longer guaranteed. Sometimes called *financial exigency*, these conditions enable the administration to suspend tenure and locus of assignment to fully use faculty members to meet the needs of the university. As a result, faculty members may become concerned that their positions will be eliminated and filled with far less expensive adjunct teaching faculty members. Salaries received by adjunct faculty are generally lower than those who are on full-time faculty appointments. The master teacher approach is used at some universities in which a full-time faculty member leads a number of part-time faculty members in teaching multiple sections of a class. The master teacher serves as a mentor and expert for questions that arise in the classes. This strategy enables multiple sections of the same course to be delivered while ensuring quality because of the oversight of the master instructor.

Providing a Supportive Policy Environment

Early in the development of an online distance education initiative, it is not unusual for many things to be seen as exceptions to the rule rather than as common practice. Often, these exceptions are made on the front line, so a practice in one academic department may be quite different from the solution to the same problem in a different unit. As the distance education initiative takes root at the institutional level, however, it is important that common practices be established on the basis of well-considered institutional policies. For instance, faculty compensation for development and instruction of online courses should be consistent across academic units. Similarly, an institution-wide policy is needed regarding copyright and faculty control over the use of content developed for use in courses. The online distance education program leader plays a key role in identifying areas where practice is inconsistent and in bringing these issues to the policy table.

None of the practices, programs, and initiatives described here comes without the broader support of the institution. The institutional support of faculty members engaged in the online learning initiative is essential to online program success. Without strong, organized support at the institutional level, faculty interest is unlikely to be sustained. The next part of this chapter contains a case study provided as a model of institutional leadership of online instructor preparation and support. It examines the establishment of the online business program at the University of Illinois Springfield.

University of Illinois: An Approach to Faculty Engagement

In 1995 the University of Illinois installed a new president, James J. Stukel, who traveled the state to assess the expectations of citizens, businesses, and industry for the flagship land-grant university. He learned from major corporations, notably Motorola, John Deere, and Caterpillar, that access to online graduate degrees was a priority. The University of Michigan and Stanford University had already initiated online engineering programs that allowed career professionals to advance in their engineering education without leaving their jobs. In response to the needs specified by these large corporations, Stukel gave his new vice president for academic affairs, Sylvia Manning (who later became president of the Higher Learning Commission), the task of initiating support for and seeding new online programs on the three campuses of the university. Manning created the University of Illinois Online and named electrical engineering professor Burks Oakley as executive director. Oakley had received one of the early Alfred P. Sloan Foundation grants for Learning Outside the Classroom to support a circuit tutor program for his beginning electrical engineering students.

The University of Illinois Online program secured additional Sloan Foundation grant funds matched by local university funds to initiate online programs in a wide array of disciplines on the three campuses of the university. The Springfield campus also received funding to establish an Office of Technology-Enhanced Learning to provide support to faculty members who sought to either use Internet resources in their classes or deliver classes online. That unit eventually grew into a full-service faculty support unit, the Center for Online Learning, Research, and Service, which provided resources and support for faculty members in using the Internet for their three-part mission of teaching, scholarship, and service. Fourteen years after the original founding of the unit, the university as of this writing delivers 17 online degrees, many certificates, and 40% of its total credit hours online, with more than half the graduate credit hours in online classes. From its inception, the University of Illinois Springfield program has been in the mainstream of the academic structure.

But the University of Illinois Springfield approach was not common in the early days. Locating the online initiative in the extended education, continuing education, or professional studies area of the university was much more common. Online learning was seen as a natural extension of the outreach and correspondence programs at many universities. That was the case on the Chicago and Urbana campuses where online learning generally was supported through specialized units and colleges. A notable exception is the Illinois master of library and information science program, founded in the early 1990s and based at the Urbana campus, which continues to be one of the most highly regarded and successful online programs in the country. The University of Illinois Springfield was originally chartered as Sangamon State University in 1970. In the 1980s faculty members were granted collective bargaining and chose representation though a local chapter of the American Federation of Teachers/Illinois Federation of Teachers. In 1995 the campus merged with the University of Illinois system. The bargaining unit representation was made up of faculty members at all campuses of the university. As a result, collective bargaining ended at the Springfield campus. In 1997 Manning invited Ray Schroeder, a senior full professor who had previously served in governance leadership and briefly as president of the faculty union local before it was disbanded, to initiate an online learning initiative on the campus. By choosing a veteran faculty member with 20 years of experience in faculty leadership on the campus, a level of trust was established from the beginning of the initiative.

The first move was to establish a university unit dedicated to faculty support: the Office of Technology-Enhanced Learning. The mission of the unit was to ensure that faculty members had the resources they needed and all the pedagogical and technological support they desired to assist them in developing and delivering online classes and degree programs. Over time, the unit expanded to become the Center for Online Learning, Research, and Service. Its mission expanded to support the three-part mission of faculty members: teaching, scholarship, and service. Incentives were distributed to faculty members for the extra time and effort required to adapt on-campus classes for online delivery. A cohort of 10 faculty research fellows were selected and supported in conducting research, presentation, and publication related to online learning. While the service component is not fully implemented, it is anticipated that the campus will soon support one or more open online peer-reviewed academic journals.

Ongoing faculty development is offered through multiple venues. More than a dozen relatively intensive 8-week online classes are available for faculty to take, joining faculty members from other campuses across the state of Illinois in addressing topics ranging from orientation to advanced communication strategies in online classes. Weekly faculty development sessions are offered on the campus with simultaneous online streaming covering a wide variety of topics ranging from new interactive technologies to effective practices. More than 100 online 10-day workshops are offered to the faculty through the Sloan Consortium. Monthly interinstitutional online webinars on online learning are offered, and the community of practice sessions, which often include invited national speakers, are held four times a year.

The unit is significantly self-supporting with two thirds of its funding coming from a fraction of the online course fees, grants, and contracts. A minority of funding comes from state appropriations. In large part because of the success of this unit, the online initiative grew steadily without faculty objection. Now more than one third of course enrollments are in online classes and more than half of the graduate credit hours taken at the university are online. The student base is diversified, with online students from nearly every state and numerous countries. Without the early acceptance of faculty members, leveraged by a trust in the leadership of the initiative, this program was unlikely to have succeeded to the extent it has.

Concluding Thoughts

As the academy adjusts to the reality that online learning is becoming necessary for institutions of higher education to survive, faculty and administrators have begun to realize that inclusive and transparent discussions were key to establishing and maintaining trust in an institution. Faculty members are a critical component of the institution, and administrative leaders must recognize and consider the impact of institutional initiatives in online learning on faculty roles and responsibilities as well as culture and history. Conversely, faculty must understand and appreciate the fiscal realities of today's higher education systems including pressure from external political forces, alumni and boards of trustees, and students. If administrators of an institution fail to fully involve the faculty in the decision-making process through shared governance or open and transparent collective bargaining, they will fail to succeed in completing the transition from a twentieth-century university to a twenty-first-century university.

References

Allen, I. E., & Seaman, J. (2004). *Entering the mainstream: The quality and extent of online education in the United States, 2003 and 2004.* Retrieved from http://www.sloan-c.org/resources/entering_mainstream.pdf

Allen, I. E., & Seaman, J. (2005). *Growing by degrees: Online education in the United States, 2005.* Retrieved from http://sloanconsortium.org/publications/survey/growing_by_degrees_2005

Allen, I. E., & Seaman, J. (2007). *Online nation: Five years of growth in online learning.* Retrieved from http://www.sloan-c.org/publications/survey/pdf/online_nation.pdf

Allen, I. E., & Seaman, J. (2008). *Staying the course: Online education in the United States, 2008.* Retrieved from http://sloanconsortium.org/publications/survey/staying_course

Allen, I. E., & Seaman, J. (2010). *Learning on demand: Online education in the United States, 2009.* Retrieved from http://sloanconsortium.org/publications/survey/learning_on_demand_sr2010

Allen I. E., & Seaman, J. (2011). *Going the distance: Online education in the United States, 2011.* Retrieved from http://sloanconsortium.org/publications/survey/going_distance_2011

American Distance Education Consortium. (2003). *ADEC guiding principles for distance teaching and learning.* Retrieved from http://www.adec.edu/admin/papers/distance-teaching_principles.html

Bawane, J., & Spector, J. M. (2009). Prioritization of online instructor roles: Implications for competency-based teacher education program. *Distance Education, 30*(3), 383–397. doi: 10.1080/01587910903236536

Bigatel, P., Ragan, L., Kennan, S., May, J., & Redmond, B. (2012). The identification of competencies for online teaching success. *Journal of Asynchronous Learning Networks, 16*(1), 59–77.

Boettcher, J. V., & Conrad, R-M. (2002). Principles of technology and change to guide our journey to the web. In L. Foster, B. L. Bower, & L. W. Watson (Eds.), *Distance education: Teaching and learning in higher education* (pp. 167–172). Boston, MA: Pearson Custom Publishing.

Chickering, A. W., & Ehrmann, S. C. (1996). *Implementing the seven principles: Technology as lever.* Retrieved from http://www.tltgroup.org/programs/seven.html

Dillon, C. L., & Walsh, S. M. (2002). Faculty: The neglected resource in distance education. In L. Foster, B. L. Bower, & L. W. Watson (Eds.), *Distance education:*

Teaching and learning in higher education (pp. 275–283). Boston, MA: Pearson Custom Publishing.

Garrison, D. R., Anderson, T., & Archer, W. (1999). Critical inquiry in a text-based environment: Computer conferencing in higher education. *The Internet and Higher Education, 2*(2), 87–105.

Grineski, S. (2002). Questioning the role of technology in higher education: Why is this the road less travelled? In L. Foster, B. L. Bower, & L. W. Watson (Eds.), *Distance education: Teaching and learning in higher education* (pp. 34–41). Boston, MA: Pearson Custom Publishing.

Ko, S., & Rossen, S. (2001). Teaching online: An overview. In *Teaching online: A practical guide* (pp. 3–21). Boston, MA: Houghton Mifflin.

Lazarus, B. D. (2003). Teaching courses online: How much time does it take? *Journal of Asynchronous Learning Networks, 7*(3), 47–53.

Moore, M. G., & Kearsley, G. (2011). *Distance education: A systems view of online learning* (3rd ed.). Belmont, CA: Wadsworth.

O'Neil, T. D. (2006). *How distance education has changed teaching and the role of the instructor.* Retrieved from http://www.g-casa.com/download/ONeil_Distance_Education.pdf

Pelz, B. (2004). Three principles of effective online pedagogy. *Journal of Asynchronous Learning Network, 8*(3), 33–46.

Pickett, A. (2011). *SLN Faculty Development Program description.* Retrieved from http://wiki.sln.suny.edu/display/SLNED/SLN+Faculty+Development+Program+Description

Phillips, W. (2008). *A study of instructor persona in the online environment* (Doctoral dissertation). Available from ProQuest Digital Dissertations (AAT 3319267).

Ragan, L. C. (2000). Good teaching is good teaching: The relationship between guiding principles for distance and general education. *Journal of General Education, 49*(1), 10–22.

Ragan, L. C. (2007). The role of faculty in distance education: The same but different. *Journal of Veterinary Medical Education, 34*(3), 232–237.

Russell, T. L. (2001). *The no significant difference phenomenon* (5th ed.). Chicago, IL: International Distance Education Certification Center.

Seaman, J. (2009). *Online learning as a strategic asset: Volume II: The paradox of faculty voices: Views and experiences with online learning.* Washington, DC: Association of Public and Land-grant Universities. Retrieved from http://www.aplu.org/document.doc?id=1879

Shattuck, K. (2007). Quality Matters: Collaborative program planning at a state level. *Online Journal of Distance Learning Administration, 10*(3). Retrieved from http://www.westga.edu/~distance/ojdla/fall103/shattuck103.htm

Smith, R. (2008). *Virtual voices: Online teachers' perceptions of online teaching standards and competencies* (Doctoral dissertation). Available from ProQuest Digital Dissertations (AAT 3313841).

Smith, T. (2005). Fifty-one competencies for online instruction. *Journal of Educators Online, 2*(2). Retrieved from http://www.thejeo.com/Ted%20Smith%20Final.pdf

Thach, E. C., & Murphy, K. L. (1995). Competencies for distance education professionals. *Educational Technology Research and Development, 43*(1), 57–79.

Twigg, C. A. (2001). *Innovations in online learning: Moving beyond no significant difference.* Retrieved from http://www.thencat.org/Monographs/Innovations.html

Varvel, V. E. (2007). Master online teacher competencies. *Online Journal of Distance Learning Administration, 10*(1). Retrieved from http://www.westga.edu/~distance/ojdla/spring101/varvel101.htm

Wenger, E. (2006). *Communities of practice: A brief introduction.* Retrieved from http://www.ewenger.com/theory/

7

OPTIMIZING STUDENT SUCCESS THROUGH STUDENT SUPPORT SERVICES

Meg Benke and Gary Miller

Effective leadership in online education recognizes the central importance of optimizing student success. The Five Pillars of Quality Online Education developed by the Sloan Consortium distinguishes between learning effectiveness and student satisfaction. The Sloan pillars measure student satisfaction by the extent to which the students "are pleased with their experiences in learning online, including interaction with instructors and peers, learning outcomes that match expectations, services, and orientation," that "faculty/ learner interaction is timely and substantive," and that there are "adequate and fair systems to assess course learning objectives" (Sloan Consortium, 2009). Because distance students do not have as much ready access to the informal support mechanisms—including informal access to other students—found on many campuses, a successful distance education program must provide more formal support services. The pillar quality definition has evolved to go beyond student satisfaction to assessing the effectiveness of student services and other programmatic interventions related to student success.

This has implications for the leader's work at the organizational level and requires a holistic approach to understanding the learner. With the primary focus on the student, staff can then be mobilized for a student-centered learning environment that moves beyond program offerings to a model that ensures these offerings meet goals of enhancing student success. This chapter will explore this dimension of leadership by focusing on organizational initiatives

We would like to thank Craig Lamb, Empire State College; Karen Swan, University of Illinois Springfield; Kishia Brock, Rio Salado College; and particularly Jill Buban, Empire State College, for their contributions to this chapter.

and ongoing challenges related to the provision of student services to promote success and retention with distance students. Creating an institutional environment that is learner centered relies on the leadership and organizational perspectives of the institution and the field of distance learning. This chapter concludes with two case studies that provide evidence of forward-thinking leadership in online student services through the lens of a comprehensive adult-serving higher education institution and a community college.

Student Services Leadership and Organizational Perspectives

One important characteristic of distance education has not changed with the revolution in technology: the critical role of student services regarding distance students. Distance students develop very close relationships with their advisers, for instance, at a level that is beyond most relationships at traditional colleges. Advisers often serve as the students' main connection to the institution in a distance program. Other services that play an integral role in this environment include accessible student portals where students can access information such as registration forms, transcripts, financial aid, and graduation information; information regarding courses; and learner supports, such course tutoring services, writing support, and resources for conducting research at a distance. Services students require at traditional institutions need to be retooled to be provided in a distance format that can be easily understood and can be a valuable learning tool for distance learners; the services cannot simply be thought of as being transferable between environments. There are strong linkages between how students are supported in an online distance education program and improved efficiency in the delivery of the campus-based programs. Distance education student services have a strategic value that is not typically considered in a traditional environment.

Emerging National Quality Standards for Student Services

The necessity of and reliance on progressive, dependable student service programs in the distance learning environment must be a consideration in the overall structure of the online program. Planning online programs presents organizational challenges, which left unaddressed, may impede success (Otte & Benke, 2006). However, there are models for achieving organizational success, and several organizations have developed templates other institutions can use.

One example is the Sloan Consortium's scorecard, which includes adaptations of the 24 quality standards identified by the Institute for Higher

Education Policy (Phipps & Merisotis, 2000) and identifies 70 quality indicators that administrators of online programs can use to obtain measureable results. Several of these indicators specifically address student services, including the following:

- The program demonstrates a student-centered focus rather than trying to fit service to the online education student in on-campus student services.
- Students receive (or have access to) information about programs, including admission requirements, tuition and fees, books and supplies, technical and proctoring requirements, and student support services prior to admission and course registration.
- Throughout the duration of the course/program, students have access to appropriate technical assistance and technical support staff. (Sloan Consortium, 2011)

The standards can be used by a team from an institution to conduct a self-assessment, or they can be used by a consulting peer to assess in a peer review. In the student services area, the WICHE (Western Interstate Commission for Higher Education) Cooperative for Educational Technologies (WCET) leaders developed resources and services available on its website. In 1995 leaders in WCET drafted one of the earliest illustrations of approaches to assessment, *Principles of Good Practices for Electronically Offered Academic Degree and Certificate Programs* (Shea & Armitage, 1995). These guidelines are available for self-assessment and peer review.

The Institute for Higher Education Policy developed 24 benchmarks for Internet-delivered education in 2000 (Phipps & Merisotis). Narrowed into seven categories—institutional support, course development, teaching/learning, course structure, faculty support, student support, and evaluation and assessment—the benchmarks allow for student centeredness to be at the forefront of programmatic planning for online education. An example of a student support benchmark is, "Questions directed to student service personnel are answered accurately and quickly, with a structured system in place to address student complaints" (Phipps & Merisotis, 2000, p. 26).

Most definitions of *success* and *quality* in online education emphasize learner support services (Hartman, Dziuban, & Moskal, 2007; Moloney & Oakley, 2006) and benchmarking student outcomes, student retention, and student satisfaction (Abel, 2005; Schiffman, 2005). In addition, most regional accrediting agencies now have distance education standards, and most of these have a section on student support. Student services are now recognized as imperative to effective online delivery and should be considered comprehensively by the senior leadership of the institution (Bates, 2000; Green, 2010; Otte & Benke, 2006).

Many leaders of distance education programs also use benchmarking as an approach to the examination of online success and quality in the provision of services (Moloney & Oakley, 2006). The Sloan Consortium was founded partially to ensure that institutions it funded shared and learned from best and emerging practices. Large lead institutions such as Empire State College, the University of Maryland, University of Massachusetts Lowell, the University of Central Florida, and the University of Illinois Springfield regularly present and share best practices and offer collegial opportunities to benchmark in key areas such as academic advising, organization models for student services, technology to support learners, and so on. Community colleges have also been at the forefront of benchmarking best practices, with collaborations around the country such as with Rio Salado College, or institutions in New York State through the State University of New York Learning Network.

Specific Leadership Challenges in the Student Services Area

In distance education the student service unit should be led or directed in such a way to ensure that the knowledge student-services staff gain about students can be linked to other functions, including instructional design, faculty development, marketing, or the academic program. The student services unit needs a leadership level that is appropriately positioned so problem areas are quickly addressed in a proactive approach. One approach many colleges have established uses call centers or automated tracking that moves isolated problem solving to more sophisticated inquiry and program improvement measures through technology. A number of institutions are now using learning analytics to track patterns of student engagement and to be more responsive.

A second challenge in some more traditional institutions is when the online program is one independent unit, and a counterpart unit serves campus-based students. At times there may be policy implications but most are cultural and organizational. The policy implications sometimes stimulate the establishment of distinct perspectives to serve the student at a distance. For example, student appeals, student judiciary, or conduct policies generally need to be revised for them to work at a distance. The cultural or organizational perspectives may need greater attention. For instance, there may be an assumption that distance or off-campus students are not interested in community or alumni-type events, or the notice periods of such activities are so short that the distance student cannot participate. While numbers have not always been significant, administrators of most distance learning programs that are learner-centered figure ways to engage distance students in community and alumni events. Making sure that the distance student has the opportunity to apply or be recognized for campus or professional awards or has access to support services are important aspects of this challenge.

A third leadership challenge, particularly in smaller institutions where academic advising may be decentralized into traditional academic offices, is creating a balanced relationship between centralized distance learning services and the traditional academic office. As programs grow, there may also be a need to fund new positions in the traditional unit to handle integration.

Finally, a fourth organizational challenge may be the emergence of more open learning management systems and platforms. As programs move to using multiple systems and technologies for services, the distance learning program loses some of the centralized control that has allowed for monitoring and improvement of services. Learners could possibly become more isolated, and connecting them may be more difficult. On the other hand, these open learning environments create greater opportunities for cross-institutional and global interactions for learners. Institutions are already exploring virtual international experiences, service-learning projects around the world, and greater uses of independent study.

Sustainability Models for Student Services and Resource Issues

Most successful distance learning programs have made a significant investment in student services staff and other support resources, generally at a level higher than traditional institutions if we take away staff responsibilities and facilities for residential living. Especially if the institution works with adjunct distant faculty, comprehensive service supports must be available for students and the distant faculty. Three approaches can address the need to staff appropriately for this function.

1. An incremental approach would identify full-time equivalent enrollment milestones and add staff for services as enrollments grow. An alternative incremental approach is to add staff as new programs emerge.
2. Distance learning programs also usually lead in technology to support services; software to support students and faculty is now available through customer relationship management systems or other systems.
3. A third approach used by some newcomers to online education is to outsource the entire service function to a company for a fee rather than develop an independent system.

All these models can be viable, depending on the infrastructure already available at the institution, the growth strategy of the online distance education program, the business model of the online program, and the institution's long-term commitment.

Larger open institutions around the world have become particularly proficient in the delivery of student services and developing sustainable models. The Open University of the United Kingdom was the first of these institutions and continues to be a leader in the increasingly diverse international open university movement.

What Do Students Want?

How do institutions determine what student services are appropriate and effective for distance students? Distance educators actually have led the field of student services, creating the basis for the current focus of student services, learner-centered programs, and services. Since the foundation of distance education in correspondence study, and later, video or TV, strict attention has been paid to making sure learners had access not only to instruction but to the services they needed to succeed without physically attending classes at the campus. As distance education has evolved to being delivered completely online, its audience has grown and become more diverse. Today, online distance education serves underrepresented populations, adult learners, and military students nearby and quite distant from an institution's traditional classrooms. These nontraditional student populations have increased the need for student services to be delivered online at any time, and online education has allowed these services to be delivered more directly.

Many research studies have been conducted to identify the interests of distance learners in different services. Past studies suggest trends that students want access to one-on-one advising, or real-time advising, and clear information regarding curricular needs (Raphael, 2006). At Western Governors University, founded specifically to serve learners at a distance, the leadership points to one-on-one advising and access to a community of learners as essential to online learners' success.

In a study completed at New York Institute of Technology (LaPadula, 2003), students prioritized their interest in having the following additional online services: book clubs, newspaper, online peer support groups (25% to 38% reported interest); academic advising/career counseling (50% to 69% reported interest); technical assistance on how to complete research online (36% to 42%); and personal/mental health counseling (25% to 34%). Students expressed satisfaction with services such as the library, admissions, textbooks, technical assistance, prior learning assessment, academic advising, registration, and the student commons, all provided online.

Raphael (2006) conducted a study on distance learners' perceived need for student services and identified the following five: clear, complete, and timely information regarding curriculum requirements; an online bookstore that includes online textbook retrieval information and ordering; online payment and tracking of orders at the online bookstore; access to individual academic advising; and an online bookstore that clearly describes delivery methods. The bottom five perceived needs were orientation as a required course; distance learning student government; a website that links to other colleges' and universities' counseling sites; access to information about health and wellness programs; and access to self-help tools, online links, and information regarding locally based counseling services.

While students' perceived needs vary among these studies, a common theme is a student's perceived need for one-on-one advising, which also correlates with Raphael (2006) and LaPadula's (2003) surveys of students' perceived needs for support in online courses. Pullan (2011) also completed a study to determine the perceived needs of students, and the most important items were online access to the college catalog; clear, complete, and timely information regarding curriculum requirements; online payment and tracking of orders; access to real-time academic advisers; and an online bookstore that includes online textbook ordering. Again, this points to the high perceived need for academic advising. Rio Salado College and Empire State College, institutions noted in the case studies later in this chapter, offer online access to academic advising to all degree-seeking students.

Other similarities between the studies include students' desire for information regarding curriculum requirements, payment, and bookstore access. The least important items to students in Pullan's (2011) survey were a distance learning student government, a website that links to other colleges' and universities' counseling centers, an online information literacy workshop, an online writing lab, and access to online links and information regarding locally based counseling services.

Ludwig-Hardman and Dunlap (2003) identified the following needs for successful online learners through services: identity, individualization, and interpersonal interaction. As the field develops, and technology becomes more available to support students through automated services, student services leaders balance the provision of services that can be offered more efficiently through technology but also retain the personalization through portals or related tools. The distance student still requires interpersonal interaction from faculty and staff, perhaps some automated, and some reserved for person-to-person interaction.

Beyond Learner Perceptions: What Services Are Effective?

Higher education generally has become much more measurement oriented. In student services, the field has focused on creating efficiencies, targeting services where they are needed, and learning analytics. Online learning environments allow for more easily accessible, real-time student data.

A study interviewing leaders of successful online programs indicated the following techniques to assess quality control for student support services: ensuring student satisfaction, benchmarking student services against those of leading providers, and sharing the responsibility for quality with the academic units (Gopalakrishnan, 2011). A number of institutions have effectively used learning analytics, particularly in the student services areas (Campbell, DeBlois, & Oblinger, 2007). The American Military University, for example, uses the course management system and other indicators to promote student success and retention.

Services That Enhance Student Success and Retention

One area of keen inquiry is promoting the course and degree completion of distance students. Many distance learning programs were started as programs that expanded access for adult or other nontraditional learners possibly new to the higher education environment. This resulted in rates of completion that are at times lower than campus-based programs. Because distance learning is designed around access and often focused on working adults for whom education is one of several competing priorities, dropout rates tend to be higher than those of traditional on-campus programs (Allen & Seaman, 2007; Boston et al., 2009).

Promoting Community

Isolation is often a key reason given for lack of student persistence in online programs. Promoting community in online learning has long been discussed as a solution to the inherent isolation of the distant learner. It has been operationalized at a number of institutions that offer online community groups, such as the Electronic Peer Network at Excelsior College, the Speakeasy and Student Café at Washington State University's Extended Degree Program, and online student government at the Open University of the United Kingdom. Student success in online environments can be promoted by including other cocurricular activities that promote a sense of community

(LaPadula, 2003). A sense of community also helps student retention. Rovai (2002) reports that learners who have similar expectations and goals and a sense of belonging and connectedness rely on each other and interact with each other. He developed the classroom community scale, which has been used in his own work and by others (e.g., Shea, 2006) to compare students' perceptions of community in the online classroom and their perceived learning. Sadera, Robertson, Song, and Midon's (2009) study proved that a positive relationship exists between students' sense of community and their learning success in online courses.

Persistence

While there are no specific models of retention in online higher education programs, two models developed to explain persistence among traditional (Tinto, 1975) and nontraditional (Bean & Metzner, 1985; Metzner & Bean, 1987) face-to-face higher education students are often evoked in the literature on persistence in online environments. Tinto's (1987, 1998) integration model views persistence as determined by a series of causal factors related in a longitudinal process. In Tinto's model, learner characteristics affect commitment, which in turn affects academic performance and interactions with faculty and peers, which lead to the student's being more or less integrated into the academic and social systems of an institution. Academic and social integration, then, predict retention. A good deal of research involving traditional face-to-face students supports this model (Astin, 1984; Pascarella & Terenzini, 1980). However, others have found the model needs to be adapted for nontraditional students. Bean and Metzner (1985), for example, found that although academic integration definitely mattered, the most important influences on persistence were the perceived utility of courses being taken (academic integration) and the encouragement, not from faculty and peers in the institution, but of family, friends, and employers outside the institution (social integration).

Other Ways to Engage Students

The types of extra supports most likely to result in online learners' retention in courses and programs are suggested by another line of research that looks at the effects of online learning environments on student success. Taken altogether, this research seems to suggest that in the online environment, academic and social integration are interwoven. For example, research has shown that peer mentoring, the mentoring of current students by others who have completed a course, can significantly affect student success (Bogle,

2008; Boles, Cass, Levin, Schroeder, & Smith, 2010). Similarly, participation in online student learning communities (Rovai, 2003; Santovec, 2004), orientation programs (Lenrow, 2009; Wojciechowski & Palmer, 2005), and freshman interest groups (Rovai, 2003) have been shown to predict student persistence. Ongoing student support services (Chyung, 2001; Frid, 2001) and the use of specialized program coordinators to whom students can turn for help (Boles et al., 2010) have also proved effective in improving retention.

Promoting Community in Courses

In courses, research demonstrates that the perceived interactivity (Fosse, Humbert, & Rappold, 2009; Lenrow, 2009) and utility (Meyer, Bruwelheide, & Poulin, 2006) of courses and faculty responsiveness (Lenrow, 2009; Shelton, 2009) are good predictors of course completion. The strongest predictor of program retention, however, seems to be the perceived presence of the instructor and peers (Boston et al., 2009; Liu, Gomez, & Yen, 2009; Meyer et al., 2006). Findings related to interaction and social presence in course learning environments seem also to support the notion that Tinto's (1987) concepts of academic and social integration are collapsed into one construct in online learning.

Trends in Student Services

The effective distance learning student services leader actively watches various trends in student behavior and technology usage. Student services professionals recognize that communicative technologies such as Skype, texting, and social media sites offer many opportunities to offer student supports depending on any student's particular need. The level of support offered in these formats is on the forefront for many institution administrators as they better understand the changing needs of their student population.

Another emerging trend is the creation of *personalized learning environments*. Orientation, online open houses, congratulatory calls and e-mails, online first-year experience, on-campus venues, resource portals, peer mentoring programs, and data-driven decision making are all strategies that Drexel University uses with its online master of science in higher education program by integrating what it calls Online Human Touch services into its program (Betts & Lanza-Gladney, 2010). These strategies have been successful in creating personalized environments for graduate online students at Drexel. Undergraduate institutions such as Rio Salado College, Empire State College, and Western Governor's University are using similar strategies to create personalized learning environments in an effort to better serve students. Empire State College uses mentoring at a distance in which each student is assigned to a faculty mentor who works one-on-one with the student via e-mail and telephone conversations, and some via social networking, online chats, and video messaging. Western Governors University, another institution that serves students online, uses student mentors to provide students with personalized support. Rio Salado College offers all new students services through an outreach center that contacts every newly enrolled student by e-mail with a variety of resources that assist the student in being successful. Rio Salado also provides students with access to the Rio Student Lounge, an online facility that provides social engagement and a connection to the institution, both predictors of student success and retention.

Case Studies

The impact of leadership and innovation in student services can best be seen by looking at specific programs. We examine two cases in this chapter: Empire State College of the State University of New York and Rio Salado College in Arizona. Both institutions offer comprehensive online services but are in a constant process to update and improve. The Empire State College example demonstrates the importance of directly embedding student supports in the academic experience. The Rio Salado College example illustrates the movement to using learning analytics for program and services improvements.

Case Study One: Empire State College's Academic Support Services

Empire State College has served adult learners for 40 years from a distance. The distance learning unit serves 10,000 students online and is able to do so effectively through consistent evaluation and evolving practices in support services for students. The newer model rejects the notion that academic support should reside external to students' core academic experiences as inefficient in tight economic times. Academic support collaboration with faculty at all phases of a study (from design to implementation to revision) has proven to be much more effective in connecting students to assistance if and when it is needed. Point-in-time approaches are becoming the norm not just for online academic support areas but for blended and face-to-face approaches as well.

A peer tutor program has shown to be successful, but it remains an individualistic and external (to the course) distance-based support approach.

Students seeking a tutor often begin their tutoring relationship weeks or sometimes months after the first signs of course difficulties arise. Based on a supplemental instruction approach (www.umkc.edu/asm/si), the course assistant model that Empire State College has developed has shown much more student success on multiple levels. The data are still limited, but initial indications show that placing an embedded course assistant or tutor in an online course from the first day of the term increases students' willingness to seek assistance when they need help related to content or other factors and increases the frequency students in need use other support services such as coaching or library assistance. The course assistant is a known entity from the first day of the term since he or she is internal to the study, building a rapport with the students assigned to the section. The course assistant is also involved in other course activities (course discussions, responding to general student questions), actions that likely decrease student hesitation to ask for help when an issue is first perceived. Initial data also seem to indicate that students are more likely to use other college services (attending workshops, working with a writing coach, making appointments with librarians) when referred by the course assistant as they progress through the course. These initial findings are all consistent with the benefits described in traditional face-to-face supplemental instruction literature and are another way face-to-face approaches can translate into an online environment.

Skill development and transition studies are ways to support new and returning adult learners through their initial entry into higher education. The classic First-Year Experience course has been altered to fit the specific needs of adult learners in blended and online studies. Introduction to College Studies promotes academic skill evaluation and development (time management, effective writing, etc.), while promoting abilities needed for success (teamwork, understanding of active and independent learning, research techniques). Strongly promoting this course among students registering for their first term has encouraged skill preparation and development activities in the students' first term, not only after academic difficulties arise.

Drop-in hours services specifically for those students considered an online method of study is also being done. These appointments tend to focus on educating students on the differences between online learning and face-to-face or blended settings as they enroll in their first distance term. While an online option might be a more effective or efficient approach with a learner's life circumstances, the fear of the unknown may dissuade that learner from a distance-based approach. The Drop-in Hours service helps ease the transition for those students who may be hesitant or overly anxious in their first attempt at online study.

Case Study Two: Data Analytics at Rio Salado College

Rio Salado College is a community college that serves 43,000 online learners, with open enrollment terms that start 48 times per year. The institution provides access for a wide array of students with its open enrollment policy and has had particular success with improving certificate and course completion rates. The institution is able to increase course completion rates through the use of predictive data analytics with a 70% success rate of predicting student course persistence. It uses student enrollment history with student log-in history during the first 7 days of course delivery. Administrators are then able to contact students with low log-in activity, which is a predictor of dropping out, and provide personal interventions that can positively affect course completion.

In addition to effectively using predictive data analytics to improve student success, Rio Salado offers all new students services through the outreach center. Every newly enrolled student is contacted via e-mail with a variety of resources from the center that assist the student in being successful. The center also provides students with access to an online student lounge that offers social engagement and a connection to the institution, both predictors of student success and retention.

A core value at Rio Salado is relentless improvement. In keeping with this value, the institution is currently working toward adding many features to its online student services to help students with course completion as well as degree completion. While it currently offers orientation materials through the outreach center, in the future the college will offer student orientation directly built into the learning management system based on individual student characteristics, and staff will then be able to focus on each specific learner. Providing this type of personalized learning environment from a student's first contact with the institution may be effective in retaining the student throughout the length of the degree program (K. Brock, personal communication, December 19, 2011).

Implications for Online Learning Leaders

The centrality of student services to the success of online distance education has numerous implications for those who lead the enterprise. In the context of a traditional college or university, a key implication has to do with institutional culture. While student services is seen more as an administrative necessity by some mainstream academics, the online distance education leader recognizes that effective student services—and a focus on students generally—are critical to the long-term viability of distance education. As a result, the leader must be an advocate for a centralized student services function that is more active and involved in institutional practices. This may run against the culture of decentralized academic advising, but it is essential for success. It requires a consistent, long-term commitment to advocacy.

In distance education, the leader must play an active role in bringing key student services leaders to the table for strategic planning, recognizing that the information gathered by student services staff is a valuable resource for branding, marketing/recruiting, instructional design, and program planning. At the same time, student services should be represented at the policy table, so that the student's voice and needs are reflected in new policies and in the reconstruction of existing policies. In addition, student services should be at the table when quality assurance measures are developed, implemented, and evaluated.

Finally, the leader should encourage student services staff to participate in external professional development activities, such as attending national/international conferences, participating in webinars, and, where feasible, participating in external evaluation of other institutions' online learning programs. This kind of professional development will help overcome the isolation many student services staff feel in their institutions, help them discover new practices, and allow them to develop professional networks that will inform their practice in the future.

While most online distance education leaders are from outside student services, successful leaders will recognize the importance of this area, not simply as a technical specialization but as a voice for the student and as a critical contact that helps students persist and succeed. The challenge for the online distance education program leader is to ensure students' access to formal and informal support services that recognize and respond to the unique needs of adult learners who often must work in relative isolation, and that these students have a voice, through the student support function, in the ongoing development of the overall distance education program. It is a critical component of long-term sustainability.

Organizations Supporting Online Student Services Administrators

Sloan Consortium

The Sloan Consortium (www.sloanconsortium.org) organizes best practices in student services on its website. There are tracks on student services at most of its conferences, and there is a professional community of practice in student services. The consortium also publishes the *Journal of Asynchronous Learning Networks*. A special edition was devoted to student retention in online learning in 2010, and webinars are available related to promoting student success.

Center for Transforming Student Services

The Center for Transforming Student Services (CENTSS, www.centss .org), provides educational institutions with tools and training to develop and deliver high-quality student services online. Effectively implemented student services are a critical component of student retention, engagement, and satisfaction. Through CENTSS, institutions are able to blend the power of technology with the personal attention of traditional support services.

The CENTSS project was developed in cooperation with the Western Cooperative for Educational Technologies (WCET, http://wcet.wiche.edu/ wcet). WCET shares resources related to accreditation and distance learning programs and materials related to student retention, degree completion, and support for adult learners. WCET also has common interest groups related to student retention and student completion for members.

References

Abel, R. (2005). *Achieving success in Internet-supported learning in higher education: Case studies illuminate success factors, challenges, and future directions.* Lake Mary, FL: Alliance for Higher Education Competitiveness.

Allen, I. E., & Seaman, J. (2007). *Online nation: Five years of growth in online learning.* Retrieved from http://www.sloan-c.org/publications/survey/pdf/online_nation.pdf

Astin, A. (1984). Student involvement: A developmental theory for higher education. *Journal of College Student Personnel, 25*(3), 297–308.

Bates, A. W. (2000). Giving faculty ownership of technological change in the department. In A. F. Lucas (Ed.), *Leading academic change: Essential roles for department chairs* (pp. 215–245). San Francisco, CA: Jossey-Bass.

Bean, J. P., & Metzner, B. S. (1985). A conceptual model of nontraditional undergraduate student attrition. *Review of Educational Research, 55*(4), 485–540.

Betts, K., & Lanza-Gladney, M. (2010). Academic advising: Ten strategies to increase student engagement and retention by personalizing the online education experience through online human touch. *Academic Advising Today, 31*(1), 5.

Bogle, L. R. (2008). *Higher Education Cooperation Act fiscal year 2008 final project evaluation* [Evaluation on the project "Increasing Retention in Online Courses Through Peer Mentoring"]. Retrieved from http://www.ilcco.net/ILCCO/ content/resources/Reports/Increasing Online Retention Through Peer Mentoring Grant Report.pdf

Boles, E., Cass, B., Levin, C., Schroeder, R., & Smith, S. (2010). Sustaining students: Retention strategies in an online program. *EDUCAUSE Quarterly, 33*(4).

Boston, W., Diaz, S. R., Gibson, A. M., Ice, P., Richardson, J., & Swan, K. (2009). An exploration of the relationship between indicators of the Community of Inquiry framework and retention in online programs. *Journal of Asynchronous Learning Networks, 13*(3), 67–83.

Campbell, J. P., DeBlois, P. B., & Oblinger, D. (2007). Analytics: A new tool for a new era. *EDUCAUSE Quarterly, 42*(4), 41–57.

Chyung, S. Y. (2001). Systematic and systemic approaches to reducing attrition rates in online higher education. *American Journal of Distance Education, 13*(3), 36–49.

Fosse, R., Humbert, J., & Rappold, R. (2009). Rochester Institute of Technology: Analyzing student success. *Journal of Asynchronous Learning Networks, 13*(3), 63–66.

Frid, S. (2001). Supporting primary students' on-line learning in a virtual enrichment program. *Research in Education, 66*(9), 9–27.

Gopalakrishnan, S. (2011). *Best practices, leadership strategies and a change model for implementing successful online programs at universities* (Doctoral dissertation). Retrieved from http://www.fltc.wayne.edu/PDF/Sangeetha_Gopalakrishnan_Pro Quest.pdf

Green, K. (2010). *Managing online education: The campus computing project.* Retrieved from http://www.campuscomputing.net/

Hartman, J., Dziuban, C., & Moskal, P. (2007). Strategic initiatives in the online environment: Opportunities and challenges. *On the Horizon, 15*(3), 157–168.

LaPadula, M. A. (2003). Comprehensive look at online support services for distance learners. *American Journal of Distance Education, 17*(2), 119–128.

Lenrow, J. (2009). Peirce College and student success. *Journal of Asynchronous Learning Networks, 13*(3), 23–27.

Liu, S. Y., Gomez, J., & Yen, C. J. (2009). Community college online course retention and final grade: Predictability of social presence. *Journal of Interactive Online Learning, 8*(2), 165–182. Retrieved from http://ncolr.org/jiol/issues/pdf/8.2.5.pdf

Ludwig-Hardman, S., & Dunlap, J. C. (2003). Learner support services for online students: Scaffolding for success. *International Review of Research in Open and Distance Learning, 4*(1), 1–15.

Metzner, B. S., & Bean, J. (1987). The estimation of a conceptual model of nontraditional undergraduate student attrition. *Research in Higher Education, 27*(1), 15–38.

Meyer, K. A., Bruwelheide, J., & Poulin, R. (2006). Why they stayed: Near-perfect retention in an online certification program in library media. *Journal of Asynchronous Learning Networks, 10*(4), 100–115.

Moloney, J. F., & Oakley, B. (2006). Scaling online education: Increasing access to higher education. *Journal of Asynchronous Learning Networks, 10*(3), 19–34.

Otte, G., & Benke, M. (2006). Online learning: New models for leadership and organization in higher education. *Journal of Asynchronous Learning Networks, 10*(2), 23–31.

Pascarella, E. T., & Terenzini, P. T. (1980). Predicting persistence and voluntary dropout decisions from a theoretical model. *Journal of Higher Education, 51*(1) 60–75.

Phipps, R., & Merisotis, J. (2000). *Quality on the line: Benchmarks for success in Internet-based distance education.* Washington, DC: Institute for Higher Education Policy.

Pullan, M. (2011). Online support services for undergraduate millennial students. *Information Systems Education Journal, 9*(1), 67–98. Retrieved from http://isedj .org/2011-9/ ISSN: 1545-679X

Raphael, A. (2006). A needs assessment: A study of perceived need for student services by distance learners. *Online Journal of Distance Learning and Adminis- tration, 9*(2). Retrieved from http://www.westga.edu/%7Edistance/ojdla/sum mer92/raphael92.htm

Rovai, A. P. (2002). Developing an instrument to measure classroom community. *The Internet and Higher Education, 5*(3), 197–211.

Rovai, A. P. (2003). In search of higher persistence rates in distance education online programs. *The Internet and Higher Education, 6*(1), 1–16.

Sadera, W. A., Robertson, J., Song, L., & Midon, M. N. (2009). The role of com- munity in online learning success. *Merlot Journal of Online Learning and Teach- ing, 5*(2), 277–284.

Santovec, M. (2004). Virtual learning communities lead to 80 percent retention at WGI. *Distance Education Report, 8*(8), 4.

Schiffman, S. (2005). Business issues in online education. In J. Bourne & J. C. Moore (Eds.), *Elements of quality online education: Engaging communities* (Vol. 6, pp. 151–172). Needham, MA: Sloan Consortium.

Shea, P. (2006). A study of students' sense of learning community in online learning environments. *Journal of Asynchronous Learning Networks, 10*(1), 35–44.

Shea, P., & Armitage, S. (1995). *Principles of Good Practice for Electronically Offered Academic Degree and Certificate Programs.* Retrieved from http://wcet.wiche.edu/ wcet/docs/publications/PrinciplesofGoodPractice1995.pdf

Shelton, K. (2009). Does strong faculty support equal consistent course completion? It has for Dallas Baptist University. *Journal of Asynchronous Learning Networks, 13*(3), 63–66.

Sloan Consortium. (2009) *Pillar reference quick guide.* Newburyport, MA: Author. Retrieved from http://sloanconsortium.org/publications/freedownloads

Sloan Consortium. (2011). *Quality scorecard for the administration of online programs.* Newburyport, MA: Author.

Tinto, V. (1975). Dropout from higher education: A theoretical synthesis of recent research. *Review of Educational Research, 45*(1), 89–125.

Tinto, V. (1987). *Leaving college: Rethinking the causes and cures of student attrition.* Chicago, IL: University of Chicago Press.

Tinto, V. (1998). Colleges as communities: Taking research on student persistence seriously. *Review of Higher Education, 21*(2), 167–177.

Wojciechowski, A., & Palmer, L. (2005). Individual student characteristics: Can any be predictors of success in online classes? *Online Journal of Distance Learn- ing Administration, 8*(2). Retrieved from http://www.westga.edu/~distance/ojdla/ summer82/wojciechowski82.htm

8

MOVING INTO THE TECHNOLOGY MAINSTREAM

Raymond Schroeder and Gary Miller

The online environment has blurred the traditional distinctions between distance education and campus-based education, with broad implications for the distance education unit leader. Nowhere are these implications clearer than in the strategic management of online learning technology at the institutional level. This chapter explores the challenges of mainstreaming the online learning technology infrastructure, starting with a survey of some of the ways online learning is being used in campus-based education. We then explore a variety of issues surrounding the growing role of online technology as an institution-wide utility and conclude with a discussion of the implications of this trend for distance education unit leaders.

The Current Technology Environment

Shortly after the World Wide Web was formed, the need became clear for some sort of environment to be created to house online classes. In PLATO (Programmed Logic for Automatic Teaching Operations), the pre-web computer system developed in 1960, the entire system was dedicated to learning, so it was the default environment. But online, the wide range of applications made it necessary to confine a course to one domain. Variously called virtual learning environments, course management systems, or learning management systems (LMSs), with subtle differences in meanings, a wide array of online platforms have emerged over time. While many were developed in higher education institutions, most of the platforms that have survived have been commercialized and licensed to institutions. One example is WebCT, a pioneering course management system developed by Murray Goldberg at the University of British Columbia in 1996 and released as a commercial product in 1997. Defined as Web-based Course Tools, the program provided a framework for the essential academic functions of assignments, testing, and discussion. At its apex, WebCT was used by some 10 million students in 80 countries (for more on this program, see http://en.wikipedia.org/wiki/WebCT). Ultimately, WebCT was purchased by a rival, Blackboard, in 2005. Blackboard, created in 1995 shortly after WebCT was produced, was the product of Matt Pittinsky and Michael Chasen and became viable after merging with CourseInfo, a platform developed by Cornell University in 1998 (www.gilfuseducationgroup.com). Founded in 1996, eCollege was another of the early internationally marketed course management systems. It was taken over by Pearson Publishing in 2007 (Pearson, 2012). Prior to the advent of these and other major commercial systems, home-grown custom and small proprietary systems were used to support online classes.

By 2001 a number of programmers came together for the Moodle project to create an open-source system that would provide affordable access to learning management (see Dougiamis, 2001, which recorded for the first time that Moodle was up and running). According to the Moodle website, the term *moodle* is an acronym for "modular object-oriented dynamic learning environment."

> Moodle is provided freely as open source software (under the GNU public license). Basically this means Moodle is copyrighted, but that you have additional freedoms. You are allowed to copy, use and modify Moodle provided that you agree to: provide the source to others; not modify or remove the original license and copyrights, and apply this same license to any derivative work. (http://docs.moodle.org/20/en/About_Moodle)

Moodle became the most popular LMS in the world (Thibault, 2013). Joining Moodle as an open source LMS in 2005 was a collaborative project, funded by the Mellon Foundation, of four universities: Indiana University, Stanford University, University of Michigan, and Massachusetts Institute of Technology. The project was named Sakai because the University of Michigan's course support system is called CHEF, and chef Hiroyuki Sakai is one of the stars of the popular *Iron Chef* television program produced by Japan's Fuji Television. While adoption of Sakai lagged far behind Moodle, it remained important as an interinstitutional collaboration to meet the shared needs for a high-quality, affordable LMS in higher education.

The field of commercial LMSs continues to be marked by takeovers and mergers. One of the more interesting collaborations is between Pearson eCollege and Internet giant Google. Created in the Google Apps environment, this open LMS is hosted as software-as-a-service in the cloud.

As LMSs have progressed, features have been added. Early systems provided only minimal data collection for student use. Over time, more advanced data analytic features were added to enable instructors to easily access information from performance dashboards. Automated alerts are generated when students display patterns of use and performance that indicate they are having difficulty with concepts or assignments. As algorithms progress, predictive models are built that can project student performance in future assignments and even in classes.

In this environment technology is informed by research and the formulation of effective pedagogy. Teaching models are tested, most often in live credit-bearing classes, and outcome results are recorded. These results in turn help identify the features and functions that are needed to enable effective practices in online classes. As noted in Chapter 5, student engagement and interaction with the instructor have long been known to build deeper learning and greater student satisfaction. As a result, LMSs generally include discussion boards to facilitate the kind of activities the research recommends. Other technologies are developed and integrated as the research suggests. Adaptive release, for example, may provide review or additional information at the time the student exhibits a lack of understanding of a concept. It may also be used to enable automated deployment of course materials in synchronization with the course syllabus.

With the expansion of online social networks, instructors are pushing the boundaries of the LMSs, asking students to use Facebook, wikis, and virtual reality environments. The result is to shift the instructional environment into a more public, less institutionally controlled environment, thus creating additional policy and practice complications for institutions.

Online Learning in the Mainstream

As noted, the technology that underlies e-learning in distance education is inexorably working its way into the mainstream of higher education institutions. The mainstreaming process is one factor that will define the distance education leader's role as a change agent for decades to come. The mainstreaming process has several dimensions that expand the value of the technology infrastructure beyond e-learning, while moving it also closer to the mainstream. These include pedagogy, the growing role of technology as a broad-based utility for faculty and students, the use of online technology to facilitate interinstitutional and cross-sector partnerships in response to external societal needs, and the growing international movement to share online content. In the remainder of this chapter we explore these factors and the implications for policy and leadership.

Innovations in Pedagogy and Course Design

While the initial thrust of online distance education was to extend access to nontraditional learners, it quickly became clear that the online environment offered great opportunities for on-campus pedagogical innovation. In Chapter 5, Karen Swan describes the Community of Inquiry approach to learning developed by distance education theorists in Canada and the United States. It is a direct response to the opportunities presented by online technology and as the information society matures, for professionals in all disciplines who are skilled at inquiry, information analysis, teamwork, and problem solving. The online learning technology infrastructure allows institutions to incorporate the development of these skills into campus-based courses across many disciplines. As a result, we can anticipate that on-campus use of online technology will continue to become more common and more diverse.

Since 1999 the National Center for Academic Transformation (NCAT) has received funds from the Pew Charitable Trusts, the Fund for the Improvement of Postsecondary Education, and the Gates Foundation "to redesign learning environments to produce better learning outcomes for students at a reduced cost to the institution" (NCAT, 2005). NCAT has supported more than 150 large-scale course redesign projects in over 25 disciplines in mathematics, science, social sciences, humanities, and a variety of professional studies areas, such as business, nutrition, and education. Director Carol Twigg (2003) identified five different approaches to the use of online technology that have grown out of NCAT's work with institutions

> After examining the similarities and differences in how these common characteristics are arrayed in the various projects, the Program has been able to identify five distinct course-redesign models: supplemental, replacement, emporium, fully online, and buffet. A key differentiator among them is where each model lies on the continuum from fully face-to-face to fully on-line interactions with students. (p. 30)

According to Twigg (2003),

- the *supplemental* model adds out-of-class online activities to increase student engagement with content without eliminating classroom meetings;
- the *replacement* model reduces classroom meetings, replacing them with online activities;
- the *emporium* approach gives students control over the time of study; and
- the *buffet* model focuses on the student, customizing the learning environment for each individual student.

NCAT-supported projects have resulted in pedagogical innovations using the online learning infrastructure at more than 50 public and private colleges and universities. While it is certainly not the only source of innovation in the use of this technology on campus, it reflects the breadth of innovation currently under way.

As we look at the impact on the online learning technology infrastructure, it may be useful to divide these programs into three sorts: (a) web-enhanced courses that use online elements but may not require an LMS, (b) hybrid courses that replace a certain number of traditional classroom meetings, and (c) fully online courses offered as part of the campus's schedule but requiring few, if any, face-to-face sessions. The first of these categories may use the web, but may not require an LMS or other infrastructure. The latter two most likely would require an LMS and, thus, have an impact on the technology infrastructure used to provide access to off-campus students. A nuanced understanding of how the infrastructure could be used on campus is needed for the distance education leader to navigate policy, budget, and cultural issues across the institution.

Institutional Collaboration

The elimination of geography as a barrier between working adults and the academic resources they need is a significant change in the overall educational ecology. In response, institutions increasingly are forming partnerships to share resources to meet demand. This use of the online environment often begins with a distance education goal in mind. One example in the United States is the Great Plains Inter-Institutional Distance Education Alliance (www.gpidea.org/about/alliance). In this alliance, 11 institutions in the American Midwest have collaborated to develop and deliver professional graduate programs that none of the institutions could do effectively using solely its own resources.

However, institutional collaboration increasingly is attractive as a way to improve quality and scope in on-campus programs. One example of institutional collaboration to support on-campus students is CourseShare (www .cic.net/home/projects/sharedcourses/courseshare/introduction.aspx),   a collaboration among public universities in the Committee for Institutional Cooperation (the academic side of the Big Ten). CourseShare uses online technology to aggregate students from multiple institutions into on-campus sections of highly specialized or high-demand courses and in courses when specialized faculty are not widely available. The collaborative has been used to share courses in rarely taught languages (e.g., Native American languages, Tibetan, Uzbek, and Zulu) and very specialized areas such as radiation science and transnational feminism, thus allowing students at all participating institutions to benefit from the specialized faculty expertise at one university.

Internationally, the Movinter initiative among European and Latin American institutions promotes virtual mobility for Latin American students, giving them the opportunity to study at European institutions without forcing them to leave their home institutions.

Cross-Sector Collaboration

The online environment provides many opportunities for several cross-sector collaborations. These range from partnerships between higher education institutions and K–12 schools to dual enrollment courses to programs that allow recent grads working in companies to help new employees adjust to the work environment or that allow recent grads to stay in touch with faculty and other students.

Sharing Content

The Open Educational Resources movement is an international by-product of e-learning-based distance education that encourages faculty members and institutions to openly share content beyond the traditional institutional proprietary approach. The spirit of this new movement was captured in the Cape Town Open Education Declaration (n.d.) in 2007 and signed by more than 2,000 individuals representing 220 organizations worldwide:

> We call on educators, authors and institutions to release their resources openly. These open educational resources should be licensed to facilitate use, revision, translation, improvement and sharing by anyone, ideally imposing no legal constraints other than a requirement by the creator for appropriate attribution or the sharing of derivative works. Resources should be published in formats that facilitate both use and editing, and that accommodate a diversity of technical platforms. Whenever possible, they should also be available in formats that are accessible to people with disabilities and people who do not yet have access to the Internet.

Online Technology as an Empowerment Tool

Empowering Faculty

Faculty members can not only incorporate online elements into their traditional classroom courses, they can also use the environment to create informal communities among current students, alums, and students at partner institutions. They can also use it to create interinstitutional research communities.

As an example, the Worldwide Universities Network (www.wun.ac.uk/about) of 17 research universities in nine countries focuses on building research collaborations and uses online technology to bring together faculty and graduate students into global communities to share current research findings.

Empowering Students

Current students would be able to use the infrastructure outside their classes to extend the impact of student organizations, maintain linkages with international students, and improve collaboration among students in shared courses and disciplines. The environment is also increasingly used by students to create portfolios they can use with applications for employment and for graduate programs.

Empowering Student Support

Increasingly, the same technology is being used to support a variety of administrative and student support activities, including course registration, student portfolios, and advising.

Technology Infrastructure as a Utility

As e-learning technology infrastructure becomes part of the mainstream, it is enabling faculty and students to expand the context in which learning takes place. While blogs and personal websites give students and faculty members opportunities to express themselves and to participate in global discussions, the technical infrastructure supports other more specific benefits. To promote effective innovation, the infrastructure must be readily available to faculty members and students, not restricted to specific applications. Seeing the online learning infrastructure as a utility allows faculty members to innovate on a small scale and gradually expand their use of online learning. It also allows for informal applications by student groups and by student services staff to bring students together into cocurricular communities.

Decision Factors in Defining the Learning Infrastructure

The emerging learning infrastructure is a mix of hardware (e.g., servers), distribution networks, and software. Decisions regarding the infrastructure should take into account several factors:

- *Affordability:* What is the cost of maintaining the infrastructure as an institution-wide utility rather than a program-specific delivery system? If the software is licensed from a commercial firm, what are the licensing options? What percentage of the cost of acquiring and maintaining the infrastructure should be recovered from the online distance education function, and what should be considered part of the overall institutional operating expense?

- *Scalability:* Decisions about the technology infrastructure should consider two factors. First, online enrollments are growing nationally at a much faster rate than on-campus enrollments. A 2010 Sloan Consortium survey reported, "The twenty-one percent growth rate for online enrollments far exceeds the less than two percent growth of the overall higher education student population" (Allen & Seaman, 2010, p. 2). Second, while the on-campus student population is fairly stable, the use of technology by students and faculty will continue to grow in size and diversity.
- *Support:* What specific support will be needed for online distance education that is not already provided for on-campus students? For instance, will expanded help desk services be needed?
- *Training requirements:* How difficult is it to train faculty, staff, and students to use the infrastructure, considering that in the mainstreamed environment, some training will need to occur across the board, which raises the question of what additional training is needed specifically for online distance education?
- *Curricular requirements:* What special applications might be needed for specific curricula?

Mainstreaming the Technology Infrastructure: Policy Implications

For most of the past century, distance education has required that institutions invest in a set of dedicated technologies that had little if any impact on the mainstream. Correspondence study required a dedicated distribution system for books and study guides. Broadcast required that the institution either operate or collaborate with a radio or television station. Satellite required uplinks and downlinks. Today, however, online distance education relies on the technical infrastructure that has become fundamental to higher education's tripartite mission of teaching, research, and service. In this arena, it can no longer work on the periphery but must become part of a new mainstream. In the process, online distance education leaders will need to be aware of the broadening institutional impact of the technology infrastructure as they develop policies for online distance education. It will be shortsighted to limit policies to a purely distance education function, especially in areas that might affect faculty work across multiple learning settings and across the three missions of the institution: teaching, research, and service.

Online learning raises a number of institutional policy issues that take on broader implications when the technology itself is mainstreamed. In these cases, the leader cannot define policy in isolation from the rest of the institution. Several issues illustrate this need.

Copyright. The use of online technology adds a new element to the faculty member's role in the teaching process. For each course, the faculty member creates content, which is then published by the institution and made available to students. This is true whether the content is part of a fully online course being taken by students far from campus or a supplement to a traditional campus-based course. Either way, the faculty member and the institution are engaged in the development and publication of content. The need for a clear policy becomes even clearer if other faculty members want to use the content in their own courses, if the faculty member wants to sell the content to a company the faculty member consults or does research for, or if the institution wants to share the content with other institutions as open educational resources or for a fee.

The increasingly diverse potential for multiple uses of online content raises issues of ownership and responsibility. Who has the right to use this material beyond the course it was designed for? Who benefits if it is distributed beyond the institution or beyond the initial course? Who is responsible for the legality of the material, such as getting approvals for the use of third-party materials? Increasingly, these are institution-wide issues, not limited to the distance education program. The question of ownership is complicated. While it is, on the face of it, a legal issue, it also affects the academic culture itself: the relationship between a faculty member and the institution and between them and the broader community. Rodney Peterson (2003, pp. 4–5) noted that policy makers need to unbundle the idea of copyright to consider three factors: (a) Who has the creative initiative for the work? (b) Who controls the content, scope, and final expression of the work? (c) Who has invested in the creation of the work? Peterson goes on to state,

> Development of a copyright-ownership policy should involve individuals representing all interested groups, and the policy development process must be perceived as fair to all parties, including the institution. Because faculty are most affected by the policy, establishing faculty representation as the dominant force may be wise. (p. 6)

Licensing and sharing. A copyright policy will also establish a basis for the author and the institution to make decisions about using the online content beyond the institution, either on a fee basis or as open educational resources. Clear policies on distribution are critical if either the individual faculty member or the institution wants to share the content with others beyond the institution. On one hand, this can affect the ability of the institution to collaborate with other institutions on shared degree programs. Similarly, it can affect the ability of the faculty member to use the online materials in consulting work, such as noncredit training.

Faculty recognition. Increasingly, institutions will need to set policy to determine under what conditions faculty-created online materials will be considered as academic publications for promotion and tenure purposes.

Conflict of commitment. As opportunities to teach online grow, some faculty members who have full-time appointments at one institution are offered the opportunity to teach part-time as online instructors at another institution. Institutions are responding by developing conflict of commitment policies that define acceptable practice in this area.

Financing the infrastructure. In the emerging environment, the online distance education function in a traditional institution increasingly will call upon a centralized technological infrastructure rather than one devoted solely to distance education. In cases where the distance education program represents a separate revenue stream, that is, where the tuition fees for the online distance education courses go into a separate budget that supports the cost of the distance education program, two critical questions are, how does the distance education program transfer funds to support the central infrastructure, and how is the financial obligation measured? The distance education leader needs to anticipate this issue to ensure that the program has an effective voice in establishing financial policy as well as strategic planning for the infrastructure itself.

Personalization of Technology: Implications for Infrastructure Planning and Strategy

One of the challenges in the continuously evolving environment of online and mobile computing is the wide range of technical standards presented by the devices and access software used by students and faculty members. The plurality of platforms that include a variety of versions of Microsoft, Apple, and Linux operating systems using a dozen or more web browser versions and varieties can be daunting to manage. Even among "apps," there are different versions and varieties. Identifying a standard that can be supported broadly among the user base and is supported by the LMS is difficult. The decision making in this area is driven in part by user demand and in part by stability and sustainability of the platform. Decisions must be revisited several times a year to ensure that the student and faculty base is best served.

Working in the Technology Mainstream: Leadership Strategies

As these policy issues illustrate, online technology is blurring the old distinctions between distance education and campus-based education. In the emerging new mainstream, it will not be to the long-term benefit of the online program to make technology infrastructure decisions in isolation from the rest of the institution, as faculty members and students will want to easily cross these conceptual boundaries. This presents new challenges for online distance education leaders, who may be comfortable working on the periphery of the institution but are not well known or effectively positioned in the campus's mainstream administrative and academic decision-making structure.

The leader needs to develop a strategy for two basic planning situations: (a) policies that may arise first in the distance education program but have implications for the mainstream, and (b) policies that arise in the mainstream that have implications for the distance education program. In the first case, the distance education unit leader may be initiating the policy discussion. In the second, the distant education leader will need to ensure his or her place at the policy table.

Identifying and Engaging Policy Stakeholders

The first step in either situation is to identify the stakeholders—those individuals whose work will be affected by the policy being considered. In the first situation, the leader should ask an appropriate institution-wide administrator to charge the stakeholders to be a change community, with the leader as convening executive, to address the policy issue and to recommend a specific policy, business model, or infrastructure strategy. In the second situation, the leader may need to request to be added to an existing policy group.

Creating a Change Community

In a mainstreamed environment, online distance education represents one end of a continuum of how faculty members use technology in their teaching, research, and service activities. Faculty advocates can be found at many places along this continuum. The change community—the group of faculty, staff, and administrators whose experiences and ideas can provide direction to policy—can include people who are innovating at multiple places along that continuum. The change community should also include representatives of related organizations, such as the library, registration and records, advising, and so on.

Creating a Positive Business Environment

In a mainstreamed environment, online distance education should be seen as part of the core rather than as an ancillary information technology function. How the distance education unit pays its share of infrastructure costs affects how it will be seen. Working out this business relationship is key toward long-term sustainability as it sets the stage for how the distance education unit will work with the broader institution as technology needs change in the future.

Conclusion

The distance education leader will need to develop many new relationships as online learning enters the mainstream of higher education institutions. Among these relationships, creating a positive strategic and business relationship regarding technology is critical, as it affects a plethora of other relationships. These include relationships with faculty, who increasingly will want to use technology with distant and on-campus students and who will need to move easily between the two groups. It will also affect relationships with other administrative units, such as registration and student affairs, that will want similar ease of working via technology with students in both environments. And, ultimately, it will affect the students themselves who will want to move easily among technology services and platforms. Building productive, strategic relationships with the broader technology leadership and with key stakeholders will allow the leader to ensure that the technology needed for distance education is widely supported and that distance education needs are addressed in long-term strategic planning.

References

Allen, I. E., & Seaman, J. (2010). *Class differences: Online education in the United States, 2010.* Retrieved from https://docs.google.com/viewer?url=http://sloan consortium.org/sites/default/files/class_differences.pdf

Cape Town open education declaration: Unlocking the promise of open educational resources. (n.d.). Retrieved from http://www.capetowndeclaration.org/read-the -declaration

Dougiamis, M. (2001). Re: Welcome to Moodle! [Web log comment]. Retrieved from http://moodle.org/mod/forum/discuss.php?d=1

NCAT. (2005). *Who we are.* Retrieved from www.thencat.org/whoweare

Pearson. (2012). *Company history: Pearson eCollege evolves to meet the needs of education technology.* Retrieved from http://www.ecollege.com/Company.learn

Peterson, R. (2003, January 7). Ownership of online course material. *EDUCAUSE Center for Applied Research: Research Bulletin.* Retrieved from http://net.educause.edu/ir/library/pdf/erb0301.pdf

Thibault, J. (2013). *Moodle tops list of the "20 Most Popular LMS Software Solutions."* Retrieved from http://www.moodlenews.com/2013/moodle-tops-list-of-the-20-most-popular-lms-software-solutions/

Twigg, C. A. (2003). *New models for online learning.* Retrieved from https://docs.google.com/viewer?url=http://net.educause.edu/ir/library/pdf/erm0352.pdf

9

OPERATIONAL LEADERSHIP IN A STRATEGIC CONTEXT

Raymond Schroeder

It is not at all unusual for new leaders of online distance education programs to emerge from an operational role within the organization. While the emerging leader may be an expert in one area, he or she is faced with a dual challenge: how to continuously develop operational excellence that ensures continued access by distant students and how to integrate the online function into a broader strategy of sustainability over time. This chapter surveys the breadth of skills required for effective operational leadership and then explores how to create a more strategic context for leadership and how to maintain a strategic vision in times when the external context is constantly changing.

Operational Versus Strategic Leadership

The role and demands of the operational leader and the strategic leader are significantly different in duties and in perspective. An operational leader has a focus on the frontline concerns, which are many in the online initiative. The initiative has a complicated array of aspects that require intricate operations. On the other hand, a strategic leader has a focus on the broad picture of direction, placement of the institution in the increasingly competitive higher education environment, emerging trends, predicting broader social and economic factors that will affect the initiative, and a vision and the ability to communicate that vision in a way that builds loyalty and support among the various internal and external publics of the institution.

Online learning initiatives require sophisticated operational coordination at the academic and nonacademic levels as well as careful planning in a rapidly changing technological and marketplace environment. It is a complex endeavor at best. With each complexity comes the possibility of delay or failure that will have an impact on the whole initiative. Exasperating the process is the fact that many online initiatives grow either from scratch as small departmental projects or out of a significantly different model in a campus-based continuing education or correspondence study unit. In either case, the development of the online initiative requires large changes in technologies, focus, implementation, coordination, marketing and faculty/student support.

The transition from an operational leadership position to a strategic leadership position is also complex. The characteristics of the successful operational leader are not the same as those of the strategic leader. Richard Wellins (2008) succinctly describes the characteristics of the midlevel operational leader and the senior-level strategic leader. Wellins notes that operational and strategic leaders take on responsibilities that are different from the front-line manager. Thus, "the experiences, knowledge, competencies and personal attributes . . . at these levels look very different than at the frontline" (para. 1). He makes these comparisons:

Operational Leader

- Competencies: At this level, look for the ability to be innovative and think "out-of-the-box" when introducing and managing change. Additionally, operational leaders will need to develop strong internal partnerships across departments or work groups, and build strategic relationships with external clients to ensure loyalty and satisfaction.
- Knowledge: An operational leader candidate should demonstrate in-depth knowledge of the company's business model, financials, and competitive landscape. Further, they should have an understanding of the other business units' processes, products and procedures in all markets—domestic and international.
- Experience: Operational leaders should have some experience in the following areas: leading a business unit with profit/loss accountabilities, leading cross-functional teams, preparation of business plans, and managing a significant function.
- Personal Attributes: Finally, your candidate should exhibit personal attributes like receptivity to feedback, flexibility/adaptability, a strong desire for continued growth and development, and acceptable risk-taking.

Strategic Leader

- Competencies: At this level, leaders must exhibit succinct and compelling communication, the ability to inspire and lead organization-wide change, entrepreneurship, a passion for results, and tenacious drive for high performance at all levels.

- Knowledge: Strategic leaders need to make well thought-out, long-range plans and thus must intimately understand their customers' needs and the competitive landscape. They must also have the ability to understand and drive key talent management functions, such as compensation, training, and performance management and measurement.
- Experience: Leaders at the strategic level need to have experience in creating a corporate culture, cost control, and global or expat leadership assignments. This is even more crucial at this level since these senior-level leaders drive the culture and direction of the organization.
- Personal Attributes: Finally, your candidate should exhibit high levels of ambition, inquisitiveness, imagination and innovation, and a high learning orientation. (para. 3–10)

We often see great operational leaders fail when thrust into strategic leadership positions without training and development. One danger is that they tend to be comfortable with their area of operational knowledge and are hesitant to step away from operations. The common result is a micromanaging leader who is lost in the details rather than focused on the vision and broader leadership. Yet, to be a successful strategic leader, one must have an understanding of the issues and forces at play at the operational level. One of the most challenging aspects of strategic leadership can be to understand the relative importance of the elements of the operation and to carefully choose the very best operational leaders to tend to those elements.

The higher education environment is complex. The field is changing rapidly. What had once been a field dominated by nonprofit public and private institutions that held loose geographic areas of preference has now become a much different field. However, there was little strategic thought guiding the initiation of online learning in most cases in the early and mid-1990s. It was all about operations. In the early 1990s we saw a collection of entrepreneurial faculty members, often enthusiasts of the emerging World Wide Web and earlier bulletin board systems, experimenting with deploying individual unrelated courses online for their convenience and that of their students as well as simply testing the virtual waters. The early adopters were often working without full infrastructure support from the colleges and universities. They tested freeware, shareware, and openly available tools and techniques to cobble together loosely held frameworks for online classes. The online efforts at many institutions grew into a loose amalgam of faculty members and courses in a variety of curricula that were not closely tied together.

Over time, administrators of nearly all institutions recognized the need and the potential for providing a common set of tools and support for online classes.

In many cases it seemed that existing extended education or continuing education offices would be the best units to serve this nascent effort to use computer technologies to deliver a portion of the curriculum. In other cases, small units emerged within colleges to support the effort, and in a few cases, institutions with an existing mission and organizational commitment to distance education made the transition to the online environment. There is no single developmental model and, thus, no single career pathway for operational leaders.

For example, at the University of Illinois Springfield in July of 1997, I was given release time from one of my classes and one graduate assistant to create the Office of Technology-Enhanced Learning. The unit was housed in a small unused physical chemistry laboratory (complete with Bunsen burners, sinks, and an emergency drench shower). Servers to support the effort were placed on the lab tables as far distant from the emergency drench shower as practical. And, the emphasis was on encouraging faculty members to post their course syllabi online and on developing a standardized format for online class websites. In those days with very few isolated online classes, it was much more about supporting the technology and the students and far less about program development, accreditation, and institutional priorities. Thus, in the beginning of online learning, the enterprise was much more about operations—technologies, support, training for faculty members and students, student support, marketing—because the vision of where online learning might go was not fully formed, and the critical mass had not been reached to generate viable sequences, certificates, and degrees. But it was not long before these programs proliferated and strategic considerations became relevant.

The World Campus at The Pennsylvania State University evolved in a much different context. Penn State had been a pioneer in correspondence study and video-based distance education. By the mid-1990s its distance education operation was already fully developed and nationally recognized, offering courses and a limited number of degree programs from many of the university's academic colleges. At the same time, the university became an innovator with computer-based education on campus and had a well-developed technology infrastructure. Online learning was built on the shoulders of these existing operational capabilities. However, because the focus was on complete degree programs and formal undergraduate and postbaccalaureate certificate programs, in addition to individual courses, online learning also proved to be a disruptive innovation that altered the relationship between the distance education unit and other areas of the institution, moving distance education closer to the mainstream. The focus on extending undergraduate and graduate degree programs online for distant students moved the World Campus into the institutional mainstream, and in the process changed the mainstream in some ways.

Moving From Operations to Strategic Leadership

In moving beyond the day-to-day operations in support and delivery of curricula through online media, we enter the strategic realm where we begin to focus on a plan of action that takes into account a wide variety of considerations. The development and application of operations are essential elements of the overall strategic approach, but the relative emphasis, timing, and way of implementing operations are governed by strategic leadership. Long-term sustainability rather than individual program success becomes the goal here.

While many institutions involved in online distance education have now moved beyond the first generation of innovators, many of those moving into leadership positions in online programs today come from operational positions. It is not uncommon for an instructional designer, a professor of educational technology, or some other professional with a strong operational orientation to move along the promotion path into leadership. In some respects, it is the sum of the operational areas plus the university-wide vision that shapes the overall strategic vision.

The Operational Context

For the most part, operations in online learning fall into four areas that interact and intertwine to make a kind of matrix in which the online program develops and operates. Activities in these areas often carry strategic implications that have an impact on other aspects of university planning and operations. The interplay among these areas can become involved. At times, to accomplish a goal in one area, changes need to be made in another area or areas. Although three of these areas—technical services and infrastructure, student support, and faculty engagement and support—have already been discussed in preceding chapters, we discuss these briefly here. The fourth—marketing—most obviously bridges operations and strategy.

Technical services and infrastructure, the first area of operations, are at the backbone of the online system. While the goal is to make the technology transparent, there are necessary concerns regarding ensuring that the learning management system, web conferencing technologies, the reliability of a robust bandwidth, and the support desk for students and faculty members are secure and stable. Without these, the online program fails. They are the virtual classrooms, parking lots, and highways to the online campus. This operational aspect, perhaps more than any other, is subject to rapid changes, failures, opportunities and challenges.

The second area of operations is student support. Some early pioneers theorized that online learners would seek the same student services that are sought on campus, including clubs, student organizations, and activities. As the online field has grown, it has become apparent that distant students, particularly midcareer students, dominate the field. At the University of Illinois Springfield, the average online student age is 35; on campus it is in the 20s. Most of the online students have families, jobs, and careers under way. They are less interested in a chess club than they are in the career placement center. The online students do need services, but those services tend to fall in the areas of financial aid, career networking, and professional development. These are important and valued services for the online students.

Faculty engagement and support, the third area of operations, remain a critical component of most online programs. Regrettably, few doctoral programs include teaching theories, foundations, and methods in their curricula. And even among those that do, online learning is often absent. Unlike elementary and secondary schoolteachers, university faculty members are not required to take course work or obtain certifications in teaching. For hundreds of years, faculty members have taught as they were taught, creating a cycle of mediocrity in my opinion. The online program operationally needs to provide faculty development in theory, pedagogy, and best practices in teaching and learning online. Effective practices and approaches evolve over time, enlightened by empirical research. These need to be communicated and demonstrated to faculty members. In some universities, faculty development provided through the online learning program accounts for the majority of development available to the faculty.

Marketing, the fourth area of operations, is critical to the success of the online program. The marketing program tracks enrollments, identifies new groups of prospective students, and provides materials and contacts to good candidates. This operational area is important in carrying out the strategic vision of the online program. Marketing brings to bear several levels of strategy.

- Brand marketing is positioning the online program (and, by extension, the institutional image) in a marketplace that may extend well beyond the normal recruiting range of the institution.
- In each online program the marketing plan must take into account the reputation of the academic program and how faculty members are already engaged with potential students, employers that may pay for employees to take the program, and professional associations that may endorse or promote the program.
- Finally, marketing involves positioning the unit and the program to attract individual students through direct promotion, which requires an understanding of the competition and how best to reach a sometimes very narrowly defined potential student population.

- Marketing, then, involves a close working partnership between distance education staff, faculty in the programs being marketed, and those responsible for the broader institution image.

The marketing function continues to evolve with developing new media. The full range of marketing activities, from identifying and tracking prospective student characteristics for each program to identifying the most cost-effective and persuasive approach to reach and influence the identified target groups, is a fluid one. Competition, employment trends, and many other factors must be constantly monitored.

As the marketing discussion suggests, the interplay among the operational areas is dynamic. For example, marketing may identify a viable emerging market for a new degree or certificate program. But to move forward, faculty members must be engaged, best modes of delivery (e.g., mobile or fixed, online or blended) must be identified, infrastructure requirements must be identified and met (e.g., virtual laboratories or clinical placements), and needs specific to the anticipated student base must be identified. Laying all these considerations on top of the existing matrix of online learning degree and certificate programs creates yet another dimension of complexity.

Assembling a Strategic Approach

A strategic approach begins with considering the mission of the initiative. While this may seem to be a simple task, it is more complex, certainly within the university structure, than one might initially think. The interplay of internal and external factors can become complex and can ultimately distort what might have been an elegantly simple and clean statement of mission into one that is gerrymandered among several existing, although tangential, initiatives. For example, previously existing correspondence programs may carry influence in the university and suppress the emergence of newer technological and pedagogical approaches. Or other universities in the system or state may have staked a claim to delivery modes or delivering distance degrees in certain discipline areas or degree levels. Or a department or college in the university may be reluctant to cede control of planning and deployment to a more centralized unit that seeks to build university-wide synergies by gathering support for online initiatives under one umbrella. Unfortunately, because of the internal political strength of some previous initiatives, the move to a more efficient and potentially more effective centralized or coordinated approach can be thwarted. In such cases, many university initiatives can be delayed or stunted.

Mission. The first step in the process is to create a mission for the initiative. This becomes the foundation of the entire initiative and the standard for measurement of long-term success. Certainly the distance education strategy is likely to undergo modest modifications over time as the overall priorities and values of the institution change over the decades. However, the mission ideally remains essentially constant, as it is the cornerstone of the vision and operations. It is the beacon that lights the way for progress. It must be in harmony with the broader mission of the university and provide the venue for the shared goals and objectives of the institution.

As Wellins (2008) noted, one key competency of the strategic leader is not only to develop the mission but to *communicate* regularly to reinforce the core purpose of the operation.

Values. Each institution has a unique set of values that shapes its character, its orientation, its heart. These values are ideally embraced by the president down to the custodian, from the student to the dean. A famous statement of implicit values is found in the Declaration of Independence: "We hold these truths to be self-evident, that all men are created equal, that they are endowed by their Creator with certain unalienable Rights, that among these are Life, Liberty and the pursuit of Happiness." Many university mission statements include a values statement. In other cases, the values are less formally stated. A good place to begin identifying the values of the university is to carefully read the strategic plans of the university. But at times the stated values are incomplete, or they may be dated and less relevant than the values that have become clear through funding priorities, official statements, and the shifting priorities of the governing board, accrediting bodies, state legislatures, or the federal government. An assessment of all these sources should be completed.

Conflicting values. An experienced administrator may believe that he or she has a good idea of the values of the institution but may not fully understand the range of values held across the institution or how strongly held those values may be. For example one may understand the faculty values in the school of business, but may not be familiar with the fine arts faculty values or the engineering faculty. In all these cases, the student values, state and regional values, funding entity values, and accrediting agency values must all be integrated. To identify the range of values and their relative strength, an organized and coordinated process should be conducted. It is important to identify the values that are held by all stakeholders: faculty members, students, alumni, board of trustees, governing boards, and identifiable subgroups in each of those categories. Identifying these values at the start of the process can help avoid surprises later. Often, one will find conflicting values across the institution. Higher education institutions are complex social institutions with diverse cultures within individual academic units. Typically, the online learning unit is practically unique in that it works across multiple academic cultures to develop and deliver academic programs. In this environment, it is difficult to be all things to all people. The challenge is to make a selection among those differences or to find a way the online initiative can span the differing values.

Understanding the context and market. Understanding the context of the online initiative is a complex activity. The context comprises the economic, political, and social aspects of the geographic region, political region (e.g., state), and alumni base. Other components include the accrediting bodies (the regional accrediting commission and discipline area accreditors), other colleges and universities that compete with or relate to the institution, and the broadly accepted reputation of the institution. Understanding how online learning would be received in each of these areas, how it might conflict with perceptions, or where points of competition or controversy may emerge are all important to document and consider.

The marketplace can be equally complex to assess. What other universities are serving the intended market? How well are the learning needs met by existing alternatives? Where are these prospective students located? What tuition levels can they tolerate, and what financial support is available to them through the array of sources that include government agencies, private donors, corporate donors, and foundations? Some institutions may already have market research capabilities. For others, fortunately, these data can be gathered into custom reports by a contractor for a fee.

As the initiative moves into the program development phase, other strategic marketing issues arise. What is the reputation of the academic program? What are its competitors online? Does the academic unit have access to gatekeepers, such as employers or professional associations, that can open doors for the program? At this level, the distance education unit must work in tactical partnership with the academic unit. And at this level, marketing is not a technical specialty, but a key element of long-term strategy that requires multiple inputs.

Trends and Movements

Adding to the complexity of determining the programs to include in the online initiative is the monitoring of emerging trends and movement in the topical field as well as among competing institutions. For example, if there is an innovation emerging in the field, it is important to adjust the program to ensure that your institution is at the forefront of preparing for the change. And if competing institutions are offering advanced simulations, you may need to consider offering the same or better. Now that there no longer is a geographical monopoly or a preference for institutions, it is important that your program, tuition, accessibility, and features can stand up to the online comparison feature by feature.

The open educational resources movement is worthy of note. Enabled by the Internet, an incredible array of resources are available to self-directed learners, ranging from articles and monographs to simulations to learning modules to the collected materials for an entire class offering. This virtual repository of learning materials is growing at an astonishing rate. Games and simulations are freely available that promise learning outcomes that may be superior to those in the classroom. Differentiating the markets these resources appeal to from those where prospective students are willing to pay tuition and fees for directed and supported learning is critically important in this second decade of the century.

Projecting the Future

Given the already large amount of information that has been compiled, an administrator must predict the environment 3 to 5 years into the future because many programs take more than a year to secure approval from governing boards and regional accrediting agencies. It is useful to remind oneself that program development is not about today; rather it is about tomorrow. Being able to piece together the variables into projection of the context and the projected market several years before they fully emerge can put the institution ahead of the competition and on the pathway to success. This is a tricky business at best. It requires a keen understanding of the workforce direction, popularly held values, and the ability to project these into the future marketplace for higher education.

As with some other areas, the task of projecting a program development plan is best done in consultation with academic units to ensure that they are prepared to respond when the strategic opportunity presents itself. Success at the program level depends not only on the inherent quality of the academic program but on its reputation outside the traditional recruiting area, faculty depth and readiness to make a long-term commitment, and whether the potential market for the program is identifiable and reachable—often through employers and professional organizations already familiar to the academic unit.

Creating a Vision

Distilling all these considerations in the institutional context and market potential, the defining task is to create a strategic vision of the online initiative that will set the goal for the online program in 3 to 5 years. The vision should draw support across the university. The board of trustees, upper administration, deans, directors, faculty governance representatives, and others who are key to the core mission of the university should share the vision and commit the university to achieving it within the stated time frame. In some universities, this will require formal action by several committees and boards; in other cases a consensus is all that is needed. In any case, it is important to have support and clear understanding at all levels of the university. Communicating the vision, and rearticulating it as the program evolves, is a key leadership responsibility.

Creating the Strategic Path to Achieve the Vision

It is one thing to create a vision of a successful online program, and it is quite another thing to bring that vision into reality. Creating a strategic path to achieve the vision requires an understanding of the focal points and people who hold political sway in the university structure. One must take into account the historical precedents and the alliances that are informally built within the bureaucracy. For example, certain colleges and deans may hold more power than others because of the size of the student body or faculty, or the longevity or prestige of the person who is dean. Other colleges and deans may fall into line if the opinion leaders can be convinced to adopt the vision. Equally important in many institutions is the disposition of the bodies of faculty governance (e.g., faculty senate, curriculum committees) and the faculty union if collective bargaining is in place. Identifying the opinion leaders in these structures is essential. It is often productive to engage these leaders in the process of final shaping of the overall vision. They can help you formulate the vision in a way that is easily adopted and supported by others. Generating shared ownership is an important strategy in gaining acceptance and advancing the vision.

Flexibility: Adjusting and Adapting

The art and skills of a strategic leader must include those pragmatic people skills of adjusting, adapting, and compromising to the extent necessary to achieve something as close to the vision as is possible. A leader must recognize when and how to adjust to competing missions and visions for the institution. The diversity of an institution's values and emphases can be a most valuable attribute when one or another of the priorities is obfuscated or eliminated by external factors. In other cases there may be powerful interests, threats, and opportunities that demand attention, putting the online initiative in a secondary position while other initiatives take priority.

It is a measure of a successful strategic leader to put the overall mission of the institution ahead of the online initiative. To accomplish this, one must regularly revisit milestones and expectations on the path to implementation. This regular review may take place quarterly. It allows the leader to examine the progress and adapt to the unexpected. A number of minor course corrections are often preferable to a major overhaul of a master plan for development. Working for the overall good of the institution brings about synergies that enhance all aspects of the future of the university, including those of the online initiative.

Leading in a Fluid Environment

It is difficult to imagine leading in a field that is more in flux than online learning. The concept remains relatively stable: to bring learning opportunities to the learner rather than requiring the learner to come to a physical campus or classroom. But the technologies, the marketplace, the regulatory framework, and the social need for this service is changing rapidly. A leader in this field must be in constant touch with the changing context of the field. For-profit ventures are launched daily, and open ventures are launched even more frequently. The competitive landscape changes week to week and month to month.

Technology itself is changing nearly every field. Hand in hand with those technological changes comes the need for education, training, and development, which in many cases can most effectively be provided online. Opportunities abound. New opportunities emerge daily. To track these the strategic leader is best served by using technologies such as smart agents and RSS news feeds to get updates on the latest developments that may affect the field.

Thus, the ability to work in a rapidly changing environment is essential for the strategic leader in online learning today. It is not enough to merely respond to changes, but it is essential to predict changes in order to thrive in this field. Becoming part of the change itself is ideal. Balancing the risks and benefits of leading change in each instance is important. Here the art of leading meets the science of trend analysis and predictive data analytics. The very successful leaders will recognize the forces behind trends and successfully predict where they will lead the field. They will become advocates for strategic change in their institution.

Concluding Thoughts About Strategic Leadership

Leading in this field is a daunting task. It is not enough to be a good operational leader. It is not enough to be a collaborative consensus builder. It is not enough to have excellent contacts and extensive support within the university. It is not enough to be able to predict where technology and the market will take us. Rather, it is the combination of all these factors, combined with a deep understanding of all the special interests and constituencies that are affected by online learning, that enable a strategic leader in online learning to be successful. Those truly successful leaders have the ability to communicate and build loyalty in support of the initiative. Their work combines a commitment to a long-term vision, attention to shorter-term goals that contribute to the vision, and the ability to not be distracted from the vision.

Reference

Wellins, R. (2008). *Building a strong leadership pipeline^SM: Making the shift to operational and strategic leader.* Retrieved from http://www.imakenews.com/ddi/e_article001214494.cfm

PART THREE

SUSTAINING THE INNOVATION

The final section of the book focuses on the Sloan pillar of quality in online learning that involves achieving and sustaining an effective scale of operation. It deals with the ongoing leadership challenge of balancing high quality with cost-effective operations across all aspects of the distance education enterprise and its integration into the institutional mainstream. Part Three includes examples of three dimensions of the leader's role in guiding the long-term evolution of online distance education.

Bruce Chaloux's career has centered around policy issues in media-based distance education since he led the Project on Assessing Long-Distance Learning via Telecommunications, a national study of quality assurance and accreditation issues in the 1980s. In Chapter 10, "Policy Leadership in e-Learning," he takes a close look at emerging policy issues and the leadership response. He examines the roles played by national and state governments, accrediting agencies, and institutions, and the role that the distance education leader can play at all of these levels.

In Chapter 11, "Leading Beyond the Institution," Meg Benke and Gary Miller explore the importance for distance education leaders to extend their influence beyond their home institutions and to encourage others, including faculty, to do the same to better inform institutional practice and at the same time create a more welcoming external environment for the ongoing development of online learning.

Chapter 12, "Foreseeing an Actionable Future," is a roundtable discussion that gives the authors of this book an opportunity to think broadly about where online distance education is heading, the ongoing social changes that will continue to shape higher education's role, and leadership strategies for helping institutions respond to the need for continuous change.

10

POLICY LEADERSHIP IN E-LEARNING

Bruce Chaloux

> *Policy: prudence or wisdom in the management of affairs; management or procedure based primarily on material interest; a definite course or method of action selected from among alternatives and* in light of given conditions *to guide and determine present and future decisions; a high-level overall plan embracing the general goals and acceptable procedures especially of a governmental body. ("Policy," n.d.; emphasis added)*

> *Leadership: a position as a leader of a group, organization, etc.; the power or ability to lead other people; the leaders of a group, organization, or country. ("Leadership," n.d.)*

The mainstreaming of e-learning, whether still a journey under way or, as many advocates or believers suggest, a journey that is complete, has focused new attention on the myriad of policy challenges in higher education. Indeed, there seems little doubt that wherever you are on the continuum of mainstreaming, the lack of policy leadership—moving organizations and individuals forward in light of given conditions—is hampering broader efforts. Whether at the federal, state, or institutional level, the development of a coherent, reasoned policy construct in the changing dynamics of higher education that recognizes e-learning is seriously lacking. Why is this the case? What roles do the aforementioned policy organizations and others in the broader community have in changing the policy perspective? How can e-learning leaders engage in policy development? Finally, what factors are suggesting that changes happening may prove a stimulus for policy leadership? These issues are explored in this chapter.

As e-learning exploded in the late 1990s and the early part of the twenty-first century, moving inexorably to the mainstream of higher education, attention to policy concerns started to rise. In the past five years, issues of policy focusing on e-learning at the federal, state, and institution levels have increased markedly, too often to address real and many perceived inadequacies of the learning modality. With this greater focus and attention, the need for policy leadership in e-learning has emerged to help fill a void in crucial policy development. If e-learning is to become truly seated in the mainstream of higher education, policy must be developed or amended that supports and encourages this development and leadership must emerge to help facilitate these changes. It is a significant challenge for the broader higher education community.

With the growing number of institutions pursuing e-learning strategies to reach new student markets, to expand access to students across the country and around the world, or to meet the increasing demands of residential or campus-based learners, the policy disconnect has grown. Higher education policy was and too often remains focused on traditional students attending traditional campuses in traditional time frames. These policies, including the growth of the for-profit sector in e-learning, pose significant challenges for institutions focused exclusively on online delivery or for traditional institutions that are expanding their online efforts.

The national goal of universal access to higher education is moving from promise to practice with e-learning playing an increasingly significant role in providing options for learners of all ages. Institutions have moved to establishing online programming to provide greater access to student markets without regard to geographic boundaries. They have done this through flexible scheduling, competitive tuition rates, and innovative programming to overcome barriers to postsecondary education that campus-based programs often unwittingly create. Extending postsecondary education to previously underserved citizens such as working adults, those with some college credit but no degree, rural populations, and those who have found technology an effective and even better way to learn, has helped to make universal access—what the Sloan Foundation, and later the Sloan Consortium, called "anytime, anyplace" (Picciano, 2013, p. 1) learning—an achievable goal. But it cannot be achieved without changes in fundamental federal, state, and institutional policy; greater recognition of the central value and importance of e-learning to institutions and students; and an understanding that long-standing policies have been built on a traditional model that does not meet the needs of a growing number of learners.

Institutional leaders play a critical role to promote change and to serve as vocal advocates for e-learning. Leaders must recognize the emerging trends in e-learning; understand and track national, state, and institutional policy issues; and promote reasoned change in e-learning programming. Developing relationships through professional organizations and monitoring federal and state legislation that may have an impact on e-learning are essential aspects of leadership.

Setting a Policy Context for e-Learning

The historical roles of the federal and state government and statewide systems that frame and enable institutional policy provide an important dimension in understanding higher education policy development and its long-standing focus on traditional patterns of learning. The educational enterprise continues to operate in an outdated policy environment that fails to understand, and some would argue appreciate, the massive changes in students and in the delivery of higher education that have occurred over the past generation. The role of the policy developers and other influencers is instructive. These players in policy formulation help to define policy challenges or barriers for current and future leaders in e-learning. Moreover, the policy players help to define a pathway for how to move policy forward.

Federal Role

The federal role in higher education policy has expanded significantly over the past 50 years, most dramatically in the 1960s when the first wave of baby boomers drove massive increases in enrollment at colleges and universities across the United States. Institutions were ill equipped to handle the surge, and federal efforts to help address these challenges during this period altered federal influence on higher education policy since that time. Before that growth spurt, federal involvement and policy tended to focus on promoting broader national goals and targeted efforts to assist and extend educational opportunity. Several landmark efforts helped to establish the federal interest. Three highlight the early impact of the federal government and policy prior to the 1960s.

- The Morrill Act of 1862, often referred to as the Land-Grant College Act, established a set of institutions designed to "promote the liberal and practical education of the industrial classes in the several pursuits and professions of life" (Morrill Act, 1862, § 4). The second land-grant act, the Morrill Act of 1890, focused on the former Confederate states and the establishment of institutions to serve "colored students" (§ 1). This act led to the development of the current network of historically Black colleges and universities.
- The Serviceman's Readjustment Act of 1944, often referred to as the GI Bill, provided educational opportunities that nearly eight million military veterans took advantage of upon their return from World War II. While the act had several financial aspects for veterans (e.g., low or no interest home loans, weekly support for those looking for work), it is hailed, appropriately so, as the most successful incursion of the federal government into higher education, supporting the

educational pursuits of veterans, many of whom would otherwise not have had the opportunity to start or restart college studies. The act dramatically altered the higher education landscape, well beyond the postwar period of the 1940s and 1950s, helping to instill within the American culture the importance, value, and expectation of a higher education for millions two decades later ("GI Bill's History," 2012).

- The National Defense Education Act of 1958 promoted efforts, particularly at the graduate level, to provide expanded programs in math, science, and engineering. It was primarily a response to the Russian launch of Sputnik in 1957 out of concern that the United States was falling behind the Soviet Union. The act was designed to provide for a greater military defense, but had as its focus upgrading educational efforts to help build a larger cadre of highly educated scientists and engineers in disciplines essential to the country's future development (Flattau et al., 2007).

These three major legislative acts, and several other smaller ones leading up to the 1960s, all took a longer-term view of national needs while addressing, at least in the latter cases, a particular challenge (how to help the millions of returning GIs and national defense). Federal legislation from the 1960s and through the first decade of the twenty-first century has moved more to immediate crises and to providing financial assistance to millions of students and their families.

This latest change in the federal role first emerged in response to the explosion of demand and subsequent enrollments of the baby boom population in the 1960s. Many refer to this period as the golden age of higher education, when a succession of major legislation actions and growing interest and support for higher education emerged. Highlighting the series of major legislative actions were the Higher Education Act (HEA) of 1965 and the Higher Education Facilities Act of 1965, which changed the role, scope, and influence of the federal government in educational policy. The 1965 HEA was designed "to strengthen the educational resources of our colleges and universities and to provide financial assistance for students in postsecondary and higher education" (HEA, 1965, p. 1). This started the federal government's role in student financial aid support, a construct that continues to this day and that has grown significantly to become an essential part of college and university support. While it has provided needed assistance for millions of students, it has fueled dramatic increases in tuition and fees and made federal grants and loans a near necessity. The Higher Education Facilities Act recognized the emerging issue that colleges and universities were not prepared to handle the massive growth of the 1960s and sought (and achieved) success in helping institutions build, quickly, campus infrastructure to support enrollment growth. It also recognized for the first time community colleges as important and central entities in higher education (Cervantes et al., 2005).

So how does this increasing federal role over the last 50 plus years affect e-learning? This is addressed in more detail later in this chapter, but in short, the clear emphasis of federal action has focused and continues to focus on traditional bricks-and-mortar campuses that provide traditional classes in person to full-time students. There has been little support, or more important, recognition, of any activity that wanders from this mind-set. While there are some signs that a greater awareness of e-learning is emerging, much of the policy continues to focus on what was a realistic picture of students in the 1950s through the 1990s, which does not fit with the contemporary picture of students in the new century nor the emerging model of students in the future.

Moreover, federal involvement (some suggest intervention), with dollars flowing from the federal level to states, institutions, and students, essentially has resulted in actions at the state and institutional levels that ensure that federal guidelines are met. Guidelines have become de facto policies that states and institutions are unable or unwilling to adjust.

State Role

The role of states and state government in postsecondary education is generally held as a constitutional privilege, with constitutional authority for education left to states. Amendments to the original Higher Education Act of 1965, in particular those in the 1972 Amendments that articulated needs for states to undertake greater planning efforts, reflected the astonishing growth in higher education over a period of two decades. During this period of great expansion, including the earliest forms of technology-based programming that crossed state lines, a new era of state involvement and policy emerged. The role of states and state policy has not waned in the past five decades.

Numerous people at the state level leverage and affect policy development. Governors and legislators exercise broad authority. They define many factors for public institutions in their states, including the level of funding, operational considerations, and direction. State higher education agencies, either governing or coordinating in nature, have a range of authority and power (impact) on policy, ranging from those in governing structures, with significant legal powers, to coordinating agencies, with limited or no control but with a focus on coordinating statewide educational efforts, data collection, and compliance with state requirements.

The role of states in developing e-learning policy has varied dramatically. Most have not defined or articulated a clear plan for a broad e-learning strategy, despite several efforts to establish virtual campuses or collaboratives. Early efforts were mostly online catalogs of courses and programs, although refinement in many states is under way as the demand for e-learning increases and states seek ways to expand access and reduce costs. Still, few of the states that are developing such plans have articulated policy changes that reflect the changing nature of teaching and learning that technology has affected. It is typically the case that existing policies (on teaching workload, calculation of full-time equivalents, support for infrastructure, etc.) remain based on traditional policy models.

The growth and impact of statewide agencies, many of which were established to manage growth in the 1960s and 1970s, occurred in reaction to the increased federal push for stronger coordination and planning promulgated by the 1972 Amendments to HEA. An emerging issue from the 1970s—state authorization of institutions to operate within their borders—surfaced during that period of expansion as institutions wandered far afield from their home campuses to establish beachheads through branch campuses, off-campus centers, and rented office and hotel space to hold classes. Many of these efforts crossed home state boundaries. In response, states acted to ensure that their residents could be assured of postsecondary education of acceptable quality from a legitimate provider. Efforts to license, approve, or authorize (all of these terms are used by states) these out-of-state providers typically focused on those that had established a physical presence in that state. Those efforts, while often difficult and at times expensive to institutional providers, were generally viewed as a legitimate responsibility of states. As electronic distance education emerged, initially through the use of video, satellite, and later more contemporary online delivery modes, new challenges emerged for states and institutions. E-learning poses the latest and more problem-causing challenge to states, with states unsure about what entity might be operating in their states without some evidence of institutional activity (e.g., advertising, student complaints). Efforts by the federal government designed to regulate such activities provide a real case study of policy challenges and conflict and is discussed in more detail later in this chapter.

Institutional Role

At the bottom of this policy funnel rest institutions, which craft local policy in response to federal and state (and state system, as appropriate) dictates while seeking to balance those demands with the often competing interests and demands of faculty, staff, students, and alumni. At the institutional level broader governmental/system policy is refined to an operational level to ensure quality and continuous efforts to ensure the best teaching and learning experiences for the educational community.

It is also at the institutional level where e-learning has emerged and where a succession of studies suggest a gap or disconnect between the strategic value and importance of e-learning as noted by chief academic officers and its broader acceptance by faculty, too many of whom still embrace the qualities of traditional learning at all costs. Further driving this challenge is an unabated demand by students on traditional campuses and nontraditional students of all ages and locations, many who cannot gain easy access to campuses because of work, family, geography, and increasingly, because of their interest in the flexibility and convenience of e-learning.

The increasing demand, grudging acceptance on the part of some institutions to embrace e-learning (although that is changing), and some much publicized failures to develop virtual campuses that operate as shadow campuses to institutions have fostered several new players on the higher education stage. A growing number of for-profit institutions with national footprints have emerged, building programs and services fully online with resultant dramatic increases in enrollment. These programs are high cost, highly promoted, and designed to provide services for busy adults wanting to balance work, family, and study obligations. Until recent studies, increasing federal interest in the use of Title IV financial aid support, and growing default rates in the for-profit sector stalled growth, a large percentage of the overall increases in online enrollments could be attributed to for-profit institutions. They are sleek and streamlined, not burdened by a large full-time faculty or workload considerations (many rely heavily on adjunct faculty), offer courses in shorter terms or ones that are self-paced, and turn on the proverbial dime when markets or demand dictates. These institutions have also tapped federal student financial aid programs and now are at the top of many of the lists of the largest recipients of federal student aid support. This has brought about greater scrutiny by the federal government, scrutiny that now touches all postsecondary institutions that engage in online learning.

With the changing nature of the student market, growing acceptance of e-learning as an option preferred by many learners, limited resources, and increasing competition from for-profit institutions and from others in the nonprofit sector, e-learning leaders face a myriad of challenges. At the same time, they have a significant opportunity to continue to move e-learning into the mainstream.

Policy Influencers

Beyond these major policy developers are several policy influencers, organizations, agencies, and entities that play a role in policy formulation. These range from accrediting bodies, national educational organizations, and discipline-based learning societies to business and industry, a growing educational vendor community, and professional e-learning organizations. Each brings its own perspective and influences policy formulation, often with the goal of retaining the status quo and not adjusting to the changing landscape of higher education. Most prominent among these are

- Accrediting bodies, which include regional, national, and specialized (discipline-based) nongovernmental agencies that seek to ensure institutional quality. While the accreditation process is considered voluntary, eligibility for Title IV financial aid, recognition of credit, and having a stamp of legitimacy in the higher education community makes accreditation a basic requirement for any academic institution. With the expansion of e-learning and multistate and multiregional programming, accrediting agencies have moved, some quickly, some not so fast, to accommodate e-learning efforts. These organizations do have a significant impact on institutional activities and in recent years on e-learning efforts.
- National education associations, which are historically the major voice of higher education. These and several large institutional membership organizations have addressed e-learning policy issues that have an impact on their membership. Some have embraced e-learning and have it as a major agenda item, while others have engaged in national discussions in a more limited way. Their impact can be, and has at times been, important; but most have broader agendas.
- Professional associations, which are sometimes referred to as *learned societies*. These are faculty-based membership organizations that work to sustain and promote excellence in disciplinary areas. While some have embraced e-learning, many have not and continue to promote traditional faculty arrangements.
- E-learning organizations, membership organizations that have emerged with a specific focus on e-learning and the growing e-learning community. Organizations such as the Sloan Consortium, the Western Cooperative for Educational Technology, the American Distance Education Consortium, and the U.S. Distance Learning Association have emerged over the past two decades and have provided a professional home for many in the e-learning community. These organizations have begun to find their voice for having an impact on policy, but they will likely become more vocal and influential in the years ahead.
- Business and industry, a major beneficiary of the U.S. higher education system, which influences the broader acceptance and recognition of e-learning. While more and more employers accept and recognize e-learning and the quality of graduates, this is not universal.

- Educational vendors, which are the providers of technology, instructional tools, textbooks, and a host of services for faculty and learners that have increasing influence on e-learning development and strategies. While most are responsive to institutional needs, some influence direction through their products and services.
- E-learning students—prospective students may be the most significant influencer of all as they vote through participation/enrollment in online programs and help redirect policies and planning efforts at the state and institutional levels. The increasing enrollment in for-profit institutions using e-learning has forced more systems and institutions to reconsider program strategies to remain competitive and viable.

In summary, those who make policy and those who influence policy makers have helped to move e-learning efforts forward. But higher education policy, at all levels, fails to take into account and address the changing landscape of educational delivery and student demand. Policy remains a barrier, albeit an inconspicuous one. The need for leadership in e-learning has never been greater. The environment at the federal, state, and institutional levels to effect policy change has never been more accommodating. Framing a fair policy construct for e-learning is achievable. Can leadership emerge from the e-learning community to seize the opportunity?

Institutional Policy: The Inconspicuous Barrier to e-Learning Remains

The notion that policy was an inconspicuous barrier to e-learning was outlined by Chaloux (2004). A national survey conducted by the Babson Survey Research Group for the Sloan Consortium (Allen & Seaman, 2003), the first in what was to become part of a series of such reports, suggested all but a small percentage of institutions had e-learning programs as part of their mission. The report noted, however, that real barriers existed to the continuing development and expansion of e-learning. The tenth annual report in that series (Allen & Seaman, 2012a) highlighted the continuing growth in enrollments in online learning and the strategic importance of e-learning in institutional missions but also paints a picture of the continuing challenge of faculty acceptance and support for e-learning and the perception that the quality of programming is not at the level of more traditional classroom instruction. The finding that "less than one-third of chief academic officers believe their faculty accept the value and legitimacy of online learning" (p. 5) is troublesome. The fact that this percentage "has changed little over the last eight years" (p. 5) is damning. After so many years of continual growth in enrollments, far outstripping growth in traditional delivery and hailed by a growing number of students as the preferred way to study, how can there be such a disconnect between sellers and buyers? Moreover, with online learning expected to continue to grow, how can this disconnect be addressed? While there are many plausible answers, the existing policy construct at the federal, state, and institutional levels remains one of the major factors in this gap. And the lack of policy leadership at each of these levels is a contributing factor.

The policy challenges may be less conspicuous than a decade ago, but they remain a barrier to the broader understanding and acceptance of online learning. The barriers are real but unobtrusive threats to e-learning. Most are long-standing policies, defined and instituted many years ago, that have helped students, in some cases generations of students, pursue a higher education. These policies were written in a different time for different students and certainly for different delivery modes, often with no consideration for application to a new generation of students who are no longer on the periphery but are now in the mainstream, although exactly where is much debated. In many ways, the traditional policies of the past that helped so many now become barriers for the new breed of e-learners.

Five policy areas that have emerged as barriers to the new e-learner are outlined in this section. The policy issues emerge from work over the past decade by the Southern Regional Education Board (SREB). One of four regional compacts in the United States, SREB works with political and educational leaders in its 16 member states (Alabama, Arkansas, Delaware, Florida, Georgia, Kentucky, Louisiana, Maryland, Mississippi, North Carolina, Oklahoma, South Carolina, Tennessee, Texas, Virginia, and West Virginia) to promote improvement in the South through educational attainment. SREB has embraced technology as a strategy for increased access and success in postsecondary education, including the establishment of its Educational Technology Cooperative, and with the creation of the Electronic Campus in 1998, it established a southern marketplace of online courses, programs, and a variety of services to support online learners. Soon after the launch of the Electronic Campus, it became clear that policy lagged well behind delivery and that barriers to learners and institutions were emerging. Accordingly, SREB established the Distance Learning Policy Laboratory (DLPL) to focus attention on several key policy issues or barriers. Among the barriers addressed in a series of DLPL (2002a, 2002b, 2002c) reports several years ago, the following remain ostensibly unchanged and remain barriers to e-learning expansion: tuition, transfer credit, state and campus budgeting and allocation, federal and state financial aid, and student support services.

Tuition policies. Tuition increases, dramatic in some instances over the past few years as state budgets have suffered, are reaching levels that place higher learning out of reach for many needy students. While there may be little that can be done to stem the tide of tuition increases, the pricing of courses and programs in e-learning can be effectively addressed through a more market-oriented pricing structure and by eliminating pricing based on residency.

Traditional methods of charging based on residency or "seat time" are inappropriate or even unworkable in e-learning. Out-of-state tuition, for example, may be a barrier to competitive marketing and to achieving economies of scale in enrollment. It is a real and growing problem for e-learners who have newfound access to programs from colleges hundreds or thousands of miles away, yet are faced with an anachronistic policy based upon geographic boundaries that are irrelevant in e-learning.

One favored approach is an electronic tuition rate policy (Mingle & Chaloux, 2002) that encourages institutions to establish an appropriate market tuition rate for courses and programs delivered electronically, a rate independent of the student's state, regional, or even national residency. Many students taking an e-learning course from an institution in their home state are farther away from the campus than other students in a neighboring state. In addition, whether in state or out of state, students use campus resources in the same way and access instructional support in the same way, neither of which has much if anything to do with their residency. Adopting an electronic tuition rate policy allows institutions to set a single rate for all learners. This policy creates additional access, uses unused capacity, and increases tuition revenue for colleges. Furthermore, the policy permits market pricing, an approach that would permit different course offerings to be priced differently based on market interest and demand.

The potential benefits of an electronic tuition rates policy are significant for students and institutions. Students would have increased access to educational opportunities, greater choices, and greater affordability of e-learning with less need for financial aid. Institutions would have expanded markets for courses and programs, increased revenues, and operating efficiency; better use of unused capacity, which also can increase revenues and efficiency; and reduced expenses from unnecessary duplication of courses.

Several institutions participating in SREB's Electronic Campus now offer courses and programs at a single rate, but the number that embrace or have adopted this policy remains well below half. Students hundreds of miles and a dozen states away from the campus of the providing institution have the same access as students a few miles from the campus who opt to study online. Their residence is immaterial and limits access unnecessarily.

Although online learning was long thought to be a more inexpensive way to deliver instruction, most institutions have discovered that high-quality e-learning can be expensive and requires an investment that when scaled can be less expensive over time than traditional campus-based costs. But in this era of dramatic increases in tuition and fees, some institutions are now charging higher fees, using market-rate pricing for charging a convenience fee (the convenience for the e-learner). The cost of securing a higher education, even with growth in e-learning, remains a significant barrier to many.

Transfer credit policies. E-learning is increasing access to higher education by making it possible for students to fit education into work and family schedules and by providing greater programmatic choices. As a consequence, a new breed of student is emerging who is characterized less by connection to a single institution than by selection of courses designed to meet particular learning needs. The advent of multiple-institution students (sometimes labeled as *swirling students*) who simultaneously enroll in more than one institution to achieve their particular learning goals is increasing as e-learning provides greater access and a greater selection of offerings for students to choose. While historically these students were forced to bridge general education, prerequisites, academic majors, and other institutional requirements, outcomes-based learning and new institutions dubbed *aggregators* that are emerging reduce the need for a home institution in the traditional sense (DLPL, 2002c).

The growth of e-learning changes the very nature of education: how it is administered, delivered, supported, and monitored. As larger numbers of students take advantage of the benefits of anytime/anywhere learning, more students will encounter difficulty with credit transfer. While transfer disagreements between institutions have existed for many years, the distance learning environment aggravates preexisting transfer problems because of the greater number of institutions that can be involved in the education of a single student. Disagreements over credit transfer and degree requirements mean higher costs and more time required for students to reach their education goals. The promise of learning via technology is undermined when students are required to repeat certain courses or enroll in a single institution to meet degree requirements.

Policies easing transfer should be adopted first on the state system level. However, state systems of higher education can no longer work in isolation if the full potential of e-learning is to be realized. Because e-learning is independent of physical place and is not contained by state boundaries, transfer principles should be adopted regionally and eventually, nationally. Just as state systems have adopted statewide policies on articulation and transfer, it is time for regional or national transfer policies, including major field and residency requirements. The needs and interests of the learner, not of the institution, should be paramount.

In an increasingly mobile society, it is in the best interest of the student and the institution to accommodate movement across states and institutions. Students should have the option to change programs and take courses that meet their educational needs, whether the courses are offered by one or several institutions. Given a changing environment, one strategy proposed by SREB is the establishment of degree completer entities, at least one in every state. A degree completer entity might be a virtual campus, an institution, or group of institutions that would use mutually agreed upon criteria to integrate various course credits into a meaningful, coherent degree. States would identify one or more highly visible institutions or consortia to act as degree completers.

Complicating existing transfer credit policies is the emergence of competency-based learning programs and institutions (e.g., Western Governors University, now with branch campuses in several states) and a reawakening of prior learning assessment, in particular a new effort called Learning Counts by the Council for Adult and Experiential Learning, an online portfolio development program. Many of these efforts have focused on a renewed emphasis on degree completion, particularly for the more than 40 million working-age adults with some college credit and no credential. It offers learners the opportunity to demonstrate or document knowledge of required competencies, which can often shorten time to degree and keep students out of courses in which they already have requisite knowledge. In the end, the challenge remains the broader acceptance of these credits toward meeting program requirements by colleges and universities.

State and campus budgeting and allocation policies. In the early years of the growth in e-learning, states and many institutions treated the delivery mode as a special budget category and funded it through one-time appropriations. This was particularly true of first-generation technical infrastructure and the early reliance on course or learning management systems. More recently, most institutions adopted these powerful tools and have such systems in place for use by faculty, not only for e-learning students but also for students in traditional campus-based learning situations. Over time, states and institutions have grown to appreciate that technology infrastructure is a core budget item. Still, most states and institutions fail to embrace business models that use e-learning to reduce costs and increase instructional productivity in the same way that for-profit institutions have with great success.

Current funding policy approaches, while appropriate for the traditional campus-based programs, fail to provide sufficient support or flexibility at the institution level to provide the necessary fiscal elbow room to expand e-learning programs and services. Areas of concern include

- Funding methods. Life-cycle funding for e-learning technology is critical if it is to become a core resource. While this is becoming the norm, technology funding often is not clearly correlated with important objectives, and accountability reporting may not be established. Funding methods should incorporate incentives to support the change process necessary for effective technology usage.
- Education as e-commerce. Increasingly, fundamental business processes of education are handled electronically. Education is moving in the direction of e-commerce for core functionalities, and yet many administrative practices and business policies are not designed to enable this move (Katz & Oblinger, 2000).
- Revenue sharing. Some institutions have sought to develop new revenue sharing approaches that share revenue generated by e-learning enrollments. This model has proven effective in many institutions, particularly those that have embraced the e-commerce model that puts e-learning programming in a more traditional business model, where state or institutional support through traditional funding mechanisms such as full-time-equivalent students are not used for e-learners.

It is still not the norm that e-learning, and technology to support e-learning, is treated as a core resource and funded as such. This leaves e-learning out of regular funding cycles and subject to funding inconsistencies and variations. Thus while e-learning has become a central part of the mission of most colleges and universities, fiscal policies have not followed suit. This problem is further exacerbated by the lack of support for the preparation and continued development of human capital or personnel infrastructure.

Clearly the primary cost factors of technology initiatives are people costs, not hardware or software. Most human resource, or personnel infrastructure, costs are associated with educational personnel, primarily faculty and related instructional support personnel. Thus finance policy must address this central and significant part of the cost equation. This can be done by encouraging greater institutional support for faculty to improve their productivity and effectiveness as teachers; supporting cooperative activities that will achieve economies of scale and qualitative improvements; implementing team approaches to curriculum development and any required changes in contracts, workload, and compensation policies; and finally by creating hiring, promotion, and review process policies that encourage and support teaching, the creation of digital learning materials, and the effective use of those materials.

The alternative that more institutions are moving toward is to rely more heavily on adjunct faculty, often using faculty from other institutions and from an increasing pool of faculty with online teaching experience who teach at multiple institutions online.

The increasing reliance on an adjunct faculty model, while holding great promise in the short term, portends a longer-term challenge for e-learning leaders. First, the impact on traditional faculty is troublesome for those in the academy and for the future of the traditional role of faculty in higher education. Second, the reticence of traditional faculty to embrace e-learning may, in some instances, be attributed to this concern. E-learning leaders must find ways to continue to develop traditional faculty, to make them aware of the benefits of e-learning to create better teaching and learning environments, and to ensure that full-time faculty remain a central and important part of emerging instructional models.

Federal and state financial aid policies. As more adult students seek to take advantage of the convenience of e-learning and pursue study in alternative modes, particularly as part-time learners, more are facing real financial challenges. Financially, these learners are often the neediest as they try to balance work, family, and education. While billions of dollars of financial aid is made available by federal and state governments annually, little is available to the distance learner. Financial aid mechanisms at the federal and state levels that were established over the past 50 years and designed to expand access, often limit aid for students who are not traditional age, full-time, or on campus. These are barriers that must be removed to get financial aid to the fastest growing population of higher education students (DLPL, 2002c).

The broader and fundamental goal of financial aid systems at all levels should be to make higher education available to all who can benefit and to remove or lessen financial hurdles to access. Financial aid systems must be fair and reasonable to all learners, and policies should encompass a broader definition of *student learner* than the current traditional classification. It is clear that learning is no longer confined to a campus setting in face-to-face classrooms or in defined blocks of time, as students are increasingly learning in part-time, extended, or contracted time formats. These learning arrangements should not preclude participating learners from access to financial aid.

In short, financial aid systems must become more student-centric and responsive to how, where, and when students learn. A variety of steps can be taken to accomplish this. Policy makers should consider devising strategies to provide greater flexibility in financial aid for the e-learner and financial aid providers, including assessing the practicality, efficiency, and effectiveness of shifting financial aid disbursement from an institution-based process to a student-based process. Another avenue could be to promote changes in existing federal financial aid statutes and regulations that are tied to time and place. For example, new policies and regulations could redefine academic learning periods (standard term, nonstandard term, and nonterm), allowing institutions and students to use overlapping terms, self-paced learning, short and sequential course enrollment, and multiple or rolling start dates. Another change that would respond to e-learner needs is the development of procedures that permit specific e-learning expenses to be included in the cost of attendance and need calculations. One specific idea is to develop a regional financial aid clearinghouse for e-learners that would facilitate financial aid efforts that are multistate and multi-institutional, particularly important for the e-learner enrolled in multiple institutions at the same time.

Student support services. Student support services play a direct, central, and critical role in students' academic performance, personal growth, and retention to completion. While colleges and universities have moved rapidly in the past decade to develop online courses and complete degree programs that are independent of time and place, only recently have equal effort and financial commitment been provided to develop important support services that must be provided to all learners. Services should be available at the same times that academic courses are, yet few institutions provide a full array of academic and administrative services that can be accessed at any time from any place (DLPL, 2002c).

Findings from most surveys show that students typically report a higher satisfaction with the active, self-directed learning required by e-learning courses. However, many returning adults may lack requisite basic skills or be unprepared for the self-discipline needed to be successful. Many have unrealistic expectations regarding the time, effort, and skills necessary to succeed. The emergence of so-called concierge services, an academic suite of assistance akin to what might be enjoyed at a hotel, have proven successful in the last few years. With e-learning placing a greater responsibility for learning on the individual student, specialized services may be required to support the learning process.

Evidence is mounting that services designed to serve e-learners also better serve on-campus students. As institutions move toward a model in which services are designed around the needs of the student and not the institution, policies to ensure the adequacy of such services will be required. Policies are needed that extend a variety of traditional campus-based services to e-learners, such as business office functions, bookstore purchases, financial aid, admission, registration, library, advising, career counseling, and testing. Some services may need significant modification for learners whose work schedules or physical distance impede them from traveling to campus. The growing use of instructional technology in on-campus and off-campus education demands new student services as well as new delivery formats.

It is clear that e-learning has become the most significant strategy to ensuring greater access to learning. But higher education is hamstrung by a myriad of policies and practices that are ineffective or a barrier to access for the e-learner population. Achieving universal access through the development of an accessible and affordable ubiquitous technical infrastructure will take many years. Meanwhile, policies on pricing, access to financial aid for part-time e-learners, and more equitable credit transfer and articulation arrangements should be developed to approximate success over time.

These specific challenges and policy development or change surrounding each is borne out by other studies including the latest annual Sloan survey (Allen & Seaman, 2012a).

e-Learning Policy Comes to the Fore?

The impetus for major policy change often is an event, or chain of events, that most would not consider to have great impact. What many perceived as an innocuous set of regulations promulgated by the U.S. Department of Education in October 2010 may have been the event that thrust e-learning into the middle of the higher education policy debate. Part of a package of regulations under the heading "Program Integrity Rules" (2010; regulations 34 C.F.R. § 600.9, commonly referred to as 600.9), has mobilized the e-learning community and may be the genesis of much-needed policy leadership. It is a case study that is still evolving, and while it remains unresolved in 2013, the issuance of a report by the Commission on the Regulation of Distance Education (2013) has created a potential pathway for dealing with the state authorization issue. In many respects, this one issue has already had a far-reaching impact and may push e-learning into the policy mainstream.

The impetus for the new rules, indeed the concerns of the Department of Education, was the growth in the use of federal financial aid dollars by for-profit institutions, more specifically those for-profit organizations that have high student default rates. Moreover, the department sought to ensure that e-learning institutions that delivered online instruction to students in states outside their home states were properly licensed, or approved, by the nonhome state. Specifically, the regulations in § 600.9 stated,

- Institutions must be authorized to conduct business in a state and may not be exempt from this requirement on the basis of accreditation or years in operation.

- Institutions that offer education through distance education to students in a state in which they are not physically located, must meet that state's requirements.
- Failure to have appropriate authorization could lead to the loss of Title IV federal financial aid dollars used for e-learners.

These requirements for state approval, while not new and historically a requirement in most states, forced hundreds of institutions, the majority of which were not-for-profit public and private institutions, to undertake a review of their status in states. Many found they could not easily determine where students were located, and the majority of institutions, excluding several with a national footprint, knew nothing about state authorization requirements (and for those that did, many simply opted not to pursue authorization).

The issuance of the regulations created a firestorm of protest, activity, and energy at the institutional and state levels. The broader e-learning community, indeed many of the major educational associations, responded by voicing opposition and seeking to either overturn or at least delay implementation of the new regulations. The Association of Private Sector Colleges and Universities ultimately filed suit against the Department of Education (*Career College Association v. Duncan*, 2011). They were successful to some extent in delaying implementation before a July 2011 Court of Appeals ruling that set aside one key element of the regulations on procedural grounds. The U.S. Department of Education appealed that decision, and in June, 2012, the Court of Appeals issued a ruling upholding the lower court's decision and vacating the federal requirement that institutions must demonstrate state approval. Other regulations in 600.9 were left untouched and in effect (*Association of Private Sector Colleges and Universities v. Duncan*, 2012). In July of that year the Department of Education issued a Dear Colleague Letter indicating it would abide by the court's ruling and would not appeal the decision (Department of Education, July 2012). While ending the federal requirement, the impact on e-learning efforts was significant as it heightened awareness of the level of activity by colleges and universities outside their home state boundaries. While leaving existing state authorization requirements intact, it exposed the variety and differences among states and still posed a threat that could thwart expansion by institutions outside their home states, rolling back the significant enrollment increases enjoyed by many institutions over the past decade.

To address this concern, a new national reciprocal model for state authorization of e-learning has emerged. Suggested as early as the 1980s in the Project for Assessing Long-Distance Learning via Telecommunications (Project ALLTEL), and implemented on a regional basis for SREB's 16-state Electronic Campus, albeit with several limitations, the approach would shift responsibility for authorization to the institution's home state rather than the current model of institutions needing to be authorized in each individual state where they enroll students (Chaloux, 1985). In the proposed approach, an institution offering programs in all 50 states would not have to seek authorization or a waiver from every state that requires such authorization but rather could meet requirements through the compact arrangement. The proposed agreement, the State Authorization Reciprocity Agreement (known as SARA), would allow institutions to operate freely since they would have been certified by their home state. It would operate in a fashion similar to drivers' licenses, which are issued by states and recognized by other states. This model was developed with support from a Lumina Foundation for Education grant to the President's Forum, a national organization focusing on e-learning and related policy issues, and the Council of State Governments.

This effort led to the establishment of a national commission to address several key issues regarding state authorization. With a start-up grant from the Sloan Consortium, the Association of Public and Land-grant Universities and the State Higher Education Executive Officers Association established the Commission on Regulation of Postsecondary Distance Education with an initial charge/focus "to develop and provide recommendations that will address the costs and inefficiencies faced by postsecondary institutions that must comply with multiple (often inconsistent) state laws and regulations," and further, "the Commission will be called upon to address key issues associated with appropriate government oversight, consumer protection, and educational quality related to distance education" (EducationCounsel, 2012, p. 1). The commission membership "reflect . . . major thought leaders and . . . an array of perspectives important in shaping the commission guidance and recommendations," and include representation from major national presidential organizations and several key e-learning groups (P. McPherson and P. Lingenfelter, personal communication, May 22, 2012).

The final report issued by the Commission on the Regulation of Distance Education in April 2013, offered support for the SARA model report and outlined a national plan, working through the four regional education compacts in the United States (New England Board of Higher Education, Midwest Higher Education Compact, Southern Regional Education Board, and the Western Interstate Commission on Higher Education) to establish this national reciprocal approach. It is being heavily scrutinized and debated since it was presented to the broader higher education community. States' approval of SARA will require legislative action in most states, and adoption and implementation of the model by a majority of states is not likely before 2014.

But a significant and potentially game-changing offshoot of the 600.9 matter is the new focus on policy that has galvanized the e-learning community like no other issue. In addition to the SARA and Commission efforts noted earlier, other new initiatives have emerged that focus on affecting e-learning policy with an eye toward longer-term issues and policy considerations, not just the immediate state authorization issue. These efforts include:

- The National E-Learning Alliance (NELA). This interorganizational group is currently an informal initiative led by the University Professional and Continuing Education Association and with participation of the Sloan Consortium, American Distance Education Consortium, Cooperative for Educational Technology, EDUCAUSE, and the Association for Continuing Higher Education. Designed to advance the interests of online learning and adult learners with federal and state policy makers and campus leadership, NELA outlined its charge as follows:
    1. Develop a set of issues-oriented recommendations for the advancement of quality and scale in online learning.
    2. Develop recommendations that will help inform and be useful to the accreditation process.
    3. Develop an interorganizational mechanism for (a) rapid and longer-term *responses* to federal policy developments and media coverage of online learning; and (b) a *proactive* agenda to help shape public policy and public opinion" (R. Hansen, personal communication, June 25, 2012).

- The Congressional E-Learning Caucus. Through the initial efforts and leadership of the Government Strategies Group at Dow Lohnes, PLLC, and in collaboration with a number of e-learning organizations noted previously in this chapter, this caucus was established under the leadership of representatives Kristi Noem (R–SD) and Jared Polis (D–CO). The caucus has a K–12 and a postsecondary emphasis and is being established to "help ensure the continued growth of eLearning in the United States . . . [as] an advocate in Congress for the use of information technology to enable all learners—from pre-school to high school, from college to the workplace—to have access to the highest quality of instructional materials and best-in-class instructors regardless of location or income level. . . . [and] to support, encourage and to ensure innovative educational delivery to all Americans" (K. Noem & J. Polis, letter to fellow members of U.S. House of Representatives, October 5, 2011).

Exerting Leadership in Policy

So how does the e-learning leader engage in policy development? What avenues at the federal, state, system, and institutional levels might be available to be at the policy table? Four approaches are suggested.

1. *Get educated.* A prerequisite for policy leadership is knowing what the current policy issues in higher education are and what the implications might be for e-learning. Several sources of information are readily available, including national associations and membership organizations that monitor and track federal policy, state governing or coordinating agencies that typically focus on state policy, and national and regional policy think tanks that publish updates on policy. Check with your local government affairs or relations office for what they are monitoring and tracking. In all these examples, organizational websites offer easy and free access to materials.

2. *Get involved.* There is no better way to engage in policy leadership than to get directly involved in the process. Make known your interest in the policy arena, participate in policy forums, and attend national and regional meetings of e-learning organizations—most will have sessions focusing on key policy issues. Volunteer to serve on accrediting teams, institutional evaluations/self assessments, and state reviews that can provide great insight into policy issues. Many organizations need the help, and overtures to become involved often will be warmly received.

3. *Get moving.* Those who work in policy often say the real work and development of policy at all levels occurs well before any public pronouncements are made. Effective policy leadership demands proactive, not reactive, efforts. This has not been the norm in e-learning, where the broader community is often caught trying to respond to policy change after the fact (as was the case in SARA [2012]). Getting educated about policy issues and getting involved in the process can get you moving in a more proactive way.

4. *Educate the policy makers.* Despite the rapid growth, acceptance, and increasing quality of e-learning, too many policy makers and their staffs don't understand what e-learning is, how effective it has become, and how it can address access, workforce, economic competitiveness/development, and other national and state priorities. As noted earlier, policy remains focused on traditional campuses, and delivery and the lack of understanding and awareness of the virtues of e-learning remain. E-learning leaders need to be cognizant of this and continue to seek ways to educate those who make policy.

A Closing Thought

Despite the dramatic and well-documented growth of e-learning in the United States, there is ample evidence that a coherent and supportive policy at the federal, state, and institutional levels has failed to emerge thus far. There has been a vacuum in leadership in the e-learning community, which has been reactive and not proactive in policy considerations. If a more supportive and appropriate policy construct is be achieved, more engagement with policy makers, more communications to educate those at all levels, including boards at the institutional level, is required. There are signs that the community is mobilizing, and mechanisms to help affect policy development are or will soon be available. The e-learning community must take advantage of this opportunity, must be ready to articulate its needs and the areas of policy that must be addressed to ensure the continuous growth in development of learning.

For institutional e-learning leaders, the opportunity is at hand. It is time for leadership to step up, be heard, and articulate a reasoned, sound, and supportive policy construct for higher education now and into the future. E-learning leaders must become vocal advocates for e-learning, within the institution and in state and national policy matters. They must engage policy makers at all levels and work more closely with e-learning organizations in crafting and articulating e-learning needs. They must articulate the meaning and potential impact of policy for faculty, administration, staff, and learners to secure their support. In summary, they must address the earlier definitions of *policy* and *leadership*: to demonstrate the power to lead a group in light of given conditions. The leadership challenge, and opportunity, is at hand.

References

Allen, I. E., & Seaman, J. (2003). *Sizing the opportunity: The quality and extent of online education in the United States, 2002 and 2003*. Wellesley, MA: Sloan Center for Online Education.

Allen, I. E., & Seaman, J. (2012a). *Changing course: Ten years of tracking online learning in the United States, 2012*. Wellesley, MA: Babson Survey Research Group.

Allen, I. E., & Seaman, J. (2012b). *Going the distance: Online education in the United States, 2011*. Wellesley, MA: Babson Survey Research Group.

Association of Private Sector Colleges and Universities v. Duncan, 681 F. 3d 427 (2012).

Career College Association v. Duncan, 796 F. Supp. 2d 108 (2011).

Cervantes, A., Creusere, M., McMillion, R., McQueen, C., Short, M., Steiner, M., & J. Webster, (2005). *Opening the doors to higher education: Perspectives on the Higher Education Act 40 years later*. Round Rock, TX: TG Research and Analytical Services.

Chaloux, B. N. (1985). *The project on assessing long distance learning via telecommunications. Project ALLTEL: A summary report*. Washington, DC: Council on Postsecondary Accreditation.

Chaloux, B. N. (2004). Policy: The inconspicuous barrier to expanding e-learning in community colleges. In B. L. Bower & K P. Hardy (Eds.), *From distance education to e-learning: Lessons along the way* (pp. 79–84). San Francisco, CA: Jossey-Bass.

Commission on the Regulation of Distance Education. (2013). *Advancing access through regulatory reform: Findings, principles, and recommendations for the State Authorization Reciprocity Agreement (SARA).* Washington, DC: Association of Public and Land-grant Universities.

Department of Education "Dear Colleague Letter" issued July 27, 2012.

Distance Learning Policy Laboratory. (2002a). *Distance learning and the transfer of academic credit: A report of the SREB Distance Learning Policy Laboratory Credit Issues Subcommittee.* Atlanta, GA: Southern Regional Education Board.

Distance Learning Policy Laboratory. (2002b). *Using finance policy to advance distance learning: A report of the SREB Distance Learning Policy Laboratory Finance Subcommittee.* Atlanta, GA: Southern Regional Education Board.

Distance Learning Policy Laboratory. (2002c). *Creating financial aid programs that work for distance learners: A report of the SREB Distance Learning Policy Laboratory Financial Aid Subcommittee.* Atlanta, GA: Southern Regional Education Board.

Education Amendments, 20. U.S.C. 1681 et seq.; Public Law 92–318 (1972).

EducationCounsel. (2012). *A call to action in light of federal and state legal and policy issues and trends: A working white paper to inform commission deliberations and recommendations.* Retrieved from http://ide.sreb.org/fedregs/Commission%20 White%20Paper%20Final-Updated%20post%20June%20meeting%20Final%20 II%20.pdf.

Flattau, P. E., Bracken, J., Van Atta, R., Bandeh-Ahmadi, A., de la Cruz, R., & Sullivan, K. (2006). *The National Defense Education Act of 1958: Selected outcomes.* Washington, DC: Institute for Defense Analyses.

GI Bill's history. (2012). Retrieved from U.S. Department of Veterans Affairs website: http://www.gibill.va.gov/benefits/history_timeline/index.html

Higher Education Act of 1965. Pub. L. No. 89-329, 79 Stat. 1219 (1965). Available from ftp://ftp.resource.org/gao.gov/89-329/00004C57.pdf

Higher Education Facilities Act, 20 U.S.C. (1965). §1132a et seq.

Katz, R. N., & Oblinger, A. G. (2000). (Eds.). *The "e" is for everything: E-commerce, e-business and e-learning in the future of higher education.* San Francisco, CA, Jossey-Bass.

Leadership. (n.d.). In *Merriam-Webster's learner's dictionary.* Retrieved from www .learnersdictionary.com/search/leadership

Mingle, J. R., & Chaloux, B. N. (2002). *Technology can extend access to postsecondary education: An action agenda for the South.* Atlanta, GA: Southern Regional Education Board.

Morrill Act, 7 U.S.C. § 301 et seq. (1862).

Morrill Act, 26 Stat. 417, 7 U.S.C. 321 et seq. (1890).

Picciano, A. (2013). *Pioneering higher education's digital future: An evaluation of the Alfred P. Sloan Foundation's Anytime, Anyplace Learning Program (1992–2012).*

Policy. (n.d.). In *Merriam-Webster's collegiate dictionary* (10th ed.).

Program Integrity Rules, 34 C.F.R. § 600.9 66832-66975. (2010).

11

LEADING BEYOND THE INSTITUTION

Meg Benke and Gary Miller

Any leadership in distance education also carries elements of leading beyond the institution. Perhaps because distance education originated on the edges of higher education, leadership is necessary to raise visibility, translate trends, justify resources, and affect accreditation and policy. There is also a role for administrative leaders to promote and support faculty leadership and engagement in the research, discipline, or other professional association areas.

This chapter highlights leadership in several sectors, including engagement in professional associations, leadership in accreditation, and advocacy in government or other policy areas.

Engaging in Professional Associations

Participation in national and international professional associations can provide significant benefits for the online distance education leader.

Professional networking. Leading the online enterprise can be a lonely journey at many institutions. Often, the online leader is one of a very small number of leaders in the institution who work across all academic units to develop and deliver degree programs to off-campus audiences. And often the leader is leading what is perceived by many as a disruptive change that threatens the institutional culture. For these leaders, participation in professional associations is a way to meet peers at other institutions and to establish professional networks that can be helpful in finding solutions to problems at home. Professional associations can become a safe harbor where leaders can discuss ideas with peers from other institutions who understand the issues and who are having similar experiences at their own institutions. For example, for many years prior to the advent of online learning, the National University Extension

Association (now the University Continuing and Professional Education Association) maintained a Division of Correspondence Study that not only scheduled its own sessions during the association national conferences but also organized a national catalog of correspondence study courses and programs.

Developing leadership skills. Participation in professional associations provides opportunities for professionals to develop leadership skills. Opportunities range from committees to communities of practice to the governing board of the association itself. Leading in a volunteer environment is excellent training for leading in the highly decentralized environment of many higher education institutions. In addition, this kind of experience can add to the leader's credibility at the home institution, provided that the external work does not interfere with institutional responsibilities.

Identifying an expert community. Participation in professional associations gives the online distance education program leader access to a national, and potentially international, expert community whose members can be called upon to visit the institution and offer advice and expertise. Being the source of this kind of expertise can be a strategic advantage at one's home institution. At the same time, the leader may become an external expert for other institutions, helping to enhance one's reputation at home.

Leadership Opportunities in Accreditation

The distance educator in a leadership capacity should develop particular expertise in accreditation, regional accreditation, and professional program accreditation. Expertise can be developed by having an understanding of the leading quality indicators in the field and becoming familiar with accreditation standards. Opportunities usually start with being a lead member of one's own accreditation self-study team. As expertise is developed, volunteering to serve on a collegial, state, or regional team is a good opportunity to contribute to the field and to expand knowledge and expertise. Many regional associations now require that at least one team member have expertise in distance education.

Academic professional accreditation groups also generally have requirements related to distance and online education. Developing an understanding of the requirements and participating in peer reviews is a way to lead beyond the institution. Many associations also have subgroups dedicated to better understanding distance education, another opportunity for leadership.

Leadership Opportunities Regionally or in the State

Many states also have distance learning consortia where administrators and faculty can promote leadership and exchange. The State University of New York (SUNY) Learning Network (SLN) is a partnership with SUNY campuses to provide support in the areas of pedagogy, technology, student and faculty support, and marketing services. SLN sponsors research, conferences, and webinars. The Illinois Council of Continuing Higher Education (ICCHE) is a collaboration of private and public colleges and universities in the state. The council promotes development and research in online and continuing education. ICCHE brings practitioners together at forums around the state to share best practices and develop collaborations and partnerships (www.icche.org). With workshops, newsletters, and conferences, the council builds ties that bridge the public and private university sectors. The Illinois Faculty Summer Institute is an annual three-day conference sponsored by the Illinois Online Network (www.conferences.uiuc .edu/facultysummerinstitute). It provides faculty development in the form of workshops, presentations, and plenary sessions. The conference is for higher education instructors and other professionals. Participants come from Illinois state universities, community colleges, private institutions, and out-of-state universities.

Encouraging Faculty Leadership

In addition to becoming personally involved in external leadership, leaders of online programs are in a rare position, as administrators who work across academic units, to encourage faculty to lead in their own ways beyond the institution. Encouraging faculty leadership opens new strategic opportunities for the distance education unit and for the institution generally. These faculty leaders, who are informed through their external activity about issues affecting the field, can in turn help lead in the institution by representing the faculty perspective in policy development, serving as peer leaders in the professional development of other faculty, and representing the field with their colleagues.

Participate in online learning and distance education professional associations. While many professional associations in the field are targeted to professional staff and administrators, there are opportunities for faculty members to become involved through presenting papers at national and international conferences and joining association-sponsored interest groups related to teaching and course or program design. This could include discipline-based associations and also the major national organizations focused on online learning and distance education, such as EDUCAUSE, the Sloan Consortium, the Western Cooperative for Educational Technology, and the International Council for Open and Distance Education as well as a wide range of other education and service-related organizations that have an interest in online learning as it relates to their specific mission (e.g., UNESCO).

While some faculty members may be a bit uncomfortable initially to work outside their normal disciplinary community, the experience will give them insights into how the field is unfolding nationally and internationally, give them the opportunity to compare experiences with others who are teaching or designing courses in other institutional environments, and better understand the broader strategic and policy context in which their own online teaching is done. As a result, these faculty members may well become peer leaders, helping other faculty in their own program and even across disciplines. The online distance education administrator can enhance the benefit even further by reserving some revenue each year for a faculty leadership fund that could be awarded competitively to faculty members who teach online and who have papers accepted at conferences, with previous awardees helping to judge applications.

Support related research. The University of Central Florida is an example of an institution that set aside funds specifically to create research support teams for faculty who are involved in online course development. Such support encourages faculty to conduct research that contributes to teaching in the faculty member's specialty and to informing the practice of online learning generally.

Develop collaborative instructional models. Online leaders can also support faculty involvement beyond the institution by encouraging program and course design models that allow faculty to coteach with peers at other institutions. One example of this is the master of distance education developed by the University of Maryland University College. The instructional approach encourages teaching faculty to bring into courses theorists, researchers, and policy leaders from other institutions internationally. The result is a very rich graduate experience for the students and the opportunity for teaching faculty to become part of a global peer community of academic and policy leaders.

Encourage interinstitutional course sharing. Similarly, leaders can facilitate faculty sharing and collaboration with peers at other institutions by creating the institutional policies and distribution mechanisms and procedures to allow them to share online courses and course materials with other institutions. One example is the CourseShare initiative of the Committee for Institutional Cooperation (the academic counterpart of the Big Ten athletic cooperative) in which universities agree to share online versions of courses with students at their institutions. This allows the institutions to reduce costs and improve access to courses that are rarely taught or when there is a shortage of qualified faculty or not enough students at any one campus to support a local course section. Encouraging faculty to offer such shared courses expands their reach and creates the possibility of new relationships with peers at other participating institutions. Similarly, the Open Educational Resources movement encourages faculty members to share online course materials with colleagues at other institutions, especially in developing economies. The movement has become an increasingly widespread mechanism for faculty members to create global communities to share resources and to enhance the value of each other's online publications.

The New Century Learning Consortium, led by the University of Illinois Springfield, assists with the implementation of high-quality large-scale online and blended learning programs (www.uis.edu/colrs/service/outreach/nclc). This organization shares best practices to expand the student base and stabilize enrollments for institutions. The consortium includes institutions with deep experience in distance education but also works with Hispanic-serving institutions and others that are newcomers to distance education. This organization encourages collaboration between faculty and professionals. This kind of collaboration can add significant value to a faculty member's teaching role. However, it also requires that the institution have in place policies (on copyrights, for instance) and procedures to support the work. The online learning leader can facilitate faculty leadership by advocating for the necessary policies and procedures at the institutional level.

Encourage consulting. Many faculty members consult with outside organizations in their area of academic expertise. Leaders can encourage faculty who have solid experience in online learning to add this as an element of their consulting work. This will bring them into contact with new dimensions of online learning for training, social development, and other applications.

Academic specialization in distance education. A number of institutions have developed graduate programs in distance education and, correspondingly, developed leadership in research through faculty leadership, collaborative student research, and research institutes that network faculty and students and faculty from the institution and beyond. Athabasca University in Canada developed a research institute called the Canadian Institute for Distance Education (http://cider.athabascau.ca). Spain's Open University of Catalonia has an Internet Interdisciplinary Institute at http://in3.uoc.edu/opencms_porta lin3/opencms/en. The University of Wisconsin and the University of Maryland have developed master's degrees and certificates in distance education. Some adult learning graduate programs also allow for specialized learning in distance education (such as SUNY Empire State College and The Pennsylvania State University). For instance, The Pennsylvania State University, which founded the American Center for the Study of Distance Education in the 1980s, offered a pioneering synchronous online program of graduate courses as early as 1987; the master of adult education was the first graduate program offered by the Penn State World Campus. The SLN collaborates with faculty at SUNY Albany in areas such as working with community college faculty and administrators interested in research and applied research. Karen Swan is the Stukel

Distinguished Professor of Educational Leadership and a faculty associate in the Center for Online Learning, Research, and Service at the University of Illinois Springfield. Creating a chair in distance education, or a research center, enhances the visibility of these institutions and contributes to leadership in research and innovation.

Trends and Future Leadership

Some leaders, particularly faculty and instructional designers, also become involved in cutting-edge issues and future trends. Those in distance education, an emerging field, always have an eye to futures perspectives. Leaders emerge as translators and national speakers or experts on emerging trends in technology and education. A particular type of leader is more capable at scanning and connecting ideas, tools, and perspectives. Communities develop, and clear voices emerge as leaders.

Chapter 12 gives a number of perspectives related to how the authors of this book became involved as leaders and what motivated each to pursue a higher level of engagement in the field. Emerging leaders have a great number of opportunities, starting with the Institute for Online Learning delivered by The Pennsylvania State University and the Sloan Consortium.

The major professional associations all have communities of practice and boards of directors, and there are opportunities to be part of conference planning committees or to present seminars or workshops.

Examples of Professional Associations

The following list of professional associations is a representative sample of what is available to professionals who are interested in working with like-minded colleagues, learning about professional development opportunities, and better understanding the national and international scope of their work. There are also opportunities for people to connect through LinkedIn groups, which most of the associations offer, as do groups targeting a specified population such as technology-using professors.

Sector-Based Associations

The University Professional and Continuing Education Association (UPCEA): According to its website, UPCEA "attaches high priority to meeting the professional development needs of its members. Through its programs, publications, conferences, institutes, seminars, and public advocacy, the Association seeks to advance university professional and continuing education." (www.upcea.edu)

American Association of Community Colleges (AACC): AACC "supports and promotes its member colleges through policy initiatives, innovative programs, research and information and strategic outreach to business and industry and the national news media. Its efforts are focused in five strategic actions areas: Recognition and Advocacy for Community Colleges; Student Access, Learning and Success; Community College Leadership Development; Economic and Workforce Development; and Global and Intercultural Education." (www.aacc.nche.edu)

American Distance Education Consortium (ADEC): ADEC is a nonprofit distance education consortium composed of 61 state universities and land-grant colleges. The consortium was conceived and developed to promote the creation and provision of high-quality, economical distance education programs and services to diverse audiences by the land-grant community of colleges and universities through the most appropriate information technologies available. (www.adec.edu)

Online Learning Organizations

The Sloan Consortium (Sloan-C): Sloan-C is "an institutional and professional leadership organization dedicated to integrating online education into the mainstream of higher education, helping institutions and individual educators improve the quality, scale, and breadth of online education. Membership in the Sloan Consortium provides knowledge, practice, community, and direction for educators." (http://sloanconsortium.org)

EDUCAUSE: A nonprofit association whose mission is to advance higher education by promoting the intelligent use of information technology, EDUCAUSE helps those who lead, manage, and use information resources to shape strategic decisions at every level. A comprehensive range of resources and activities is available to all interested employees at EDUCAUSE member organizations, with special opportunities open to designated member representatives. (www.educause.edu)

The Western Interstate Commission for Higher Education (WICHE) maintains the WICHE Cooperative for Educational Technologies (WCET): WCET "accelerates the adoption of effective practices and policies, advancing excellence in technology-enhanced teaching and learning in higher education." Focus area for the cooperative include: student authentication, mobility, adult learners, accountability, student retention, and student completion. (http://wcet.wiche.edu)

Distance Education Organizations

National University Technology Network (NUTN): NUTN "is a consortium of higher education institutions and provides a networking and professional development arena for the advancement of teaching and learning." (www .nutn.org)

United States Distance Learning Association (USDLA): USDLA, through its mission, "serves the distance learning community by providing advocacy, information, networking and opportunity." (www.usdla.org)

Adult Education Organizations

Council for Adult and Experiential Education (CAEL): Under its vision to support meaningful learning, credentials, and work for all adults, CAEL "pursues work at all levels within the public and private sectors to enhance learning opportunities for adults around the world." It offers members professional development opportunities including conferences and journal discounts. (www.cael.org/About-Us)

American Society for Training and Development (ASTD): According to its website, ASTD is the world's largest association dedicated to workforce training and development. Through conferences, networking opportunities, and resources, it offers members multiple opportunities to expand their knowledge in the field. (www.astd.org)

American Association for Adult and Continuing Education (AAACE): "The mission of AAACE is to provide leadership for the field of adult and continuing education by expanding opportunities for adult growth and development; unifying adult educators; fostering the development and dissemination of theory, research, information, and best practices; promoting identity and standards for the profession; and advocating relevant public policy and social change initiatives." (www.aaace.org)

International Organizations

International Council for Open and Distance Education (ICDE): The ICDE is the leading global membership organization for the open and distance education community and is open to institutions, educational authorities, commercial actors, and individuals. It offers a biennial World Conference as well as networking opportunities for members to work on projects together. ICDE maintains an excellent directory of open and distance education associations on the website. (www.icde.org)

Inter-American Distance Education Consortium (CREAD): Located on Nova Southeastern University's campus, CREAD is committed to creating strong partnerships that use local potential for the development of each country, improving the standard of living and quality of life through educational opportunities, fostering a better understanding of different cultures and identities, and enhancing cooperation between countries through shared action. (www.cread.org)

The European Distance and E-Learning Network (EDEN) exists to share knowledge and improve understanding among professionals in distance and e-learning and to promote policy and practice across the whole of Europe and beyond (www.eden-online.org). Multiple European networks are devoted to e-learning and distance learning. The Open University of Catalonia is an excellent resource for such networks (www.uoc.edu/portal/en).

Faculty Research Organizations

Adult Education Research Conference (AERC): The purpose of AERC is to promote the improvement of research and evaluation in adult education, to foster professional collaboration among people who promote research, and to conduct research or use research findings in the field of adult education. (www.adulterc.org)

Society for the Study of Emerging Adulthood (SSEA): SSEA is an international, multidisciplinary organization focused on theoretical, empirical, and policy research issues related to emerging adults, ages 18 to 29. It hosts a biannual international conference and offers members access to a database of publications on the topic as well as a venue for networking. (www.ssea.org)

Product User Groups

Blackboard: Blackboard users come together to form connections that help them become more successful by learning from their peers or like institutions that have tackled similar problems. (www.blackboard.com/Platforms/Learn/Resources/Community-Programs/User-Groups.aspx)

Moodle: With a common interest in Moodle, users can sponsor conferences or community groups and post them at MoodleMoots (http://docs.moodle.org/19/en/MoodleMoot) or at the Moodle Conference Center (http://moodle.org/course/view.php?id=33).

Open Education Associations

Creative Commons: Its vision is to realize the full potential of the Internet—universal access to research and education, full participation in culture—to drive a new era of development, growth, and productivity. (http://creativecommons.org)

WikiEducator: WikiEducator is a community project working collaboratively with the Free Culture Movement to create a free version of the education curriculum by 2015. Its focus is on building capacity, free content, community networks, and new technologies. (http://wikieducator.org)

Open Educational Resources (OER) university: The OER university is a virtual collaboration of like-minded institutions committed to creating flexible pathways for OER learners to gain formal academic credit. The OER university aims to provide free learning to all students worldwide using OER learning materials with pathways to gain credible qualifications from recognized education institutions. It is rooted in the community service and outreach mission to develop a parallel learning universe to augment and add value to traditional delivery systems in postsecondary education. Through the community service mission of participating institutions pathways are available for OER learners to earn formal academic credit and pay reduced fees for assessment and credit. (www.wikieducator.org/OER_university)

OpenCourseWare Consortium: The OCW Consortium is a collaboration of higher education institutions and associated organizations from around the world creating a broad and deep body of open educational content using a shared model. (http://ocwconsortium.org)

12

FORESEEING AN ACTIONABLE FUTURE

Gary Miller, Meg Benke, Bruce Chaloux, Lawrence C. Ragan,
Raymond Schroeder, Wayne Smutz, and Karen Swan

A s we conclude this look at the role of the emerging generation of distance education professionals in leading change in higher education, the authors offer their opinions about the future and anticipate what kinds of changes are yet to come and what the implications might be for the distance education leader. This chapter is organized as a virtual roundtable, with each author commenting in turn on questions about the future of our field.

Part 1: Currents of Change

This group of first-generation online leaders comes from a variety of professional backgrounds, from public media to nontraditional adult learning, public school teaching, and educational technology. In what ways is online distance education like or unlike previous generations of distance education you have been involved with?

Gary Miller: Distance education has had a long history in the United States, starting in 1892. When online learning came along, I was surprised to find myself part of a new and quite different community of people who had come to distance education either from an academic unit or from the computer technology. Distance education has attracted many new institutions, and as a result many new colleagues from a wide diversity of backgrounds into our field. It is as diverse as higher education itself. It is also increasingly international, one of the implications of overcoming geographic barriers. Perhaps more important is the vastly increased range of programs being offered through online education, from high school courses to doctoral level graduate programs, in a very diverse array of academic and professional subjects. At the same time, the online environment has blurred the distinctions between distance education and traditional education. These differences highlight the fact that online learning is an example of the transformation under way in society and a tool for higher education to adapt to that transformation. Its impact is much more powerful than what we experienced with educational broadcasting and satellite, for instance.

Meg Benke: In more historical forms of distance education, institutions developed expertise at providing services at a distance, but most of these were individualized. My own institution became expert at highly personalized relationships with students that promoted success, but online brought this to a significantly higher capacity. The online environment allowed for learners to interact and use services directly and collaboratively and many times to receive services without the need for staff involvement. This released staff time to invest in a higher standard of relationships with students and programmatic improvements.

Ray Schroeder: Online distance education is interactive. That is the essential difference and the essential advantage over the video-, audio-, radio-sideband-, and satellite-delivered learning with which I had previously been engaged. The dual asynchronous and synchronous aspects also give enormous value to this form of learning delivery. Engagement, that is, interaction between the students and the instructor, in the prior modes was either not personal or nonexistent using interactive television or satellite systems.

Larry Ragan: Although there are many similarities between online learning and previous versions of distance education models such as print-based correspondence study, I believe the primary difference is the immediacy of connection between all participants of the learning community. In the theory of transactional distance, Michael G. Moore speaks of the "a psychological and communication space to be crossed, a space of potential misunderstanding between the inputs of instructor and those of the learner" (Moore, 1997, p. 22). Online learning bridges that distance by connecting learners, instructor, and learning systems in synchronous and asynchronous methods. The power to connect these elements of the learning system significantly affects the dynamics of the online classroom. Online learning, through the use of technology and pedagogy, has the potential to increase rather than decrease that connectivity.

Bruce Chaloux: Historically, distance learning was focused on reaching nontraditional learners, those who could not be served through traditional campuses, are older students, or who do not fit the traditional student model. I think that has changed with the explosion of online delivery, which is being used for students sitting in a dormitory across the campus green from a classroom or to a student halfway around the world. Distance, as measured in feet or miles, is simply no longer a major factor. Online learning is transforming how, when, and where we learn (and teach) and has become far more individualized, or personalized, to meet the needs of the student (consumer) rather than the needs or interests of the institution or provider. This is broadly true in almost every other social institution, so why wouldn't this be the case for higher education? I still love the campus but believe that the best education will combine online strategies with more traditional in-person settings—blended or hybrid learning models if you will.

Online learning has been described as a vehicle for the radical transformation of higher education. What do you see as some of the main elements of the transformation that is under way?

Bruce Chaloux: Given the traditions of higher education, almost any new approach or strategy that evolves is considered a radical transformation. I recall in the 1970s the evolution of applied doctoral programs, some which brought students together on weekends in hotels or church basements hundreds of miles from the main campus. The response by the higher education community was not surprising—you can't deliver quality graduate education in that format, and a doctoral degree can't be applied but must be theoretical and contribute new knowledge. Certainly this was a radical transformation that 30 years later is now commonly accepted in terms of the applied nature of graduate education as well as the different construction of academic terms. It certainly is not radical today. Similarly, online learning won't be considered radical in another decade or so, just a commonly accepted strategy for teaching and learning.

Are elements emerging to suggest this is the case? Certainly. More students are engaged in online learning than ever before, and the annual increases are multiple times greater than traditional learning. The explosive growth of for-profit providers, most using online strategies, is telling; these institutions don't go into markets that are not attractive or profitable, and the increases in their enrollments suggest learners are looking for more personalized learning.

But the most significant elements relate directly to the growing acceptance, somewhat grudgingly, by traditional faculty who are slowly but surely embracing online learning, even for their traditional campus-based programming. Faculty are now understanding that creating the best learning environment is enhanced dramatically by online strategies. It takes many out of their comfort zone, but doesn't any radical transformation do that? We successfully moved from horse and buggy to automobiles, trains to jet aircraft, and departments stores to online shopping, so why not higher education? The revolution is over, the evolution is continuing unabated.

Ray Schroeder: Online learning truly is transformative. It is changing education at the very foundation of its centuries-old delivery principles. Previously, the students traveled to the scholar, to the campus, to the institution to engage in learning. To be sure, there were a few exceptions in correspondence and tutorial experiences even with audio or video technologies, but none of these took off because they lacked the interactive elements that seemed essential to the process. The vast majority of learning was expected to take place at a central physical location. Online learning shifts that model. The learning takes place at home, in the workplace, in a bus, on a train, on a plane, or on the beach. As a result, online learning opens opportunities to the vast range of students who otherwise would not be able to come to the campus: the full-time worker with family obligations, the disabled who cannot easily make the trip to campus, those who are caring for others day and night, and many more.

Gary Miller: The transformation now under way, and that has been under way for some time now, is to adapt higher education to better meet the needs of people and society as a whole as the information age matures. It has become obvious that today access to information has grown exponentially. The challenge for education is not simply to transfer knowledge but to help people turn information into reliable knowledge and to develop their skill in using that knowledge to solve problems. This applies to their professional lives and their lives as members of a community. It is also clear that higher education has become essential for most people to be able to make a good living in today's world and that education is not a one-time event but a continuing need throughout one's career. Higher education is being transformed to meet these new needs.

Ray Schroeder: I often think of online learning as the virtual third Morrill Act in the United States. The first Morrill Act (1862), a vision of Abraham Lincoln, provided land grants so that education was more accessible to those in rural parts of the country. The second Morrill Act (1890) provided access for the slaves who had been freed. And online learning now brings learning opportunities, not just to the neighborhood, but right into the hands of the learners wherever they may be.

Wayne Smutz: I see a number of key elements in this transformation. One is movement away from a faculty paradigm to a student paradigm in the learning process. Given much access to content, faculty's role is more about how they facilitate learning and less about how they share content. Since many faculty in Research 1 institutions focus their lives on content, this is a major change. Second is the issue of personalizing learning. With advances in technology, we are rapidly approaching the time when the learning process can be customized to the personal preference of individuals. This will not only facilitate learning for all, it will also speed it up in many important ways. Third is the issue of the technology itself. From my perspective, it is really technology and not just online learning that is revolutionizing education. Mobile technology, for example, will soon make it possible for formal learning to occur almost anywhere. Finally, online and technology-based education have the potential to reduce the cost of higher education, putting it within reach of more people. We have to figure out better how to achieve scale in both enrollments and number of programs/courses, but I do believe that is the path we are headed down.

Karen Swan: Henry Jenkins (2008) writes that media are characterized not only by the technologies they employ but by the cultural practices that surround their use. Similarly, what distinguishes online learning from traditional higher education, and indeed from the distance education of a previous era, is not just the digital technologies it is named for, but, more important, the pedagogical approaches they enable. Where the latter is teacher centered, online learning is student centered; where traditional higher education is focused on instruction, online learning is focused on learning; and where traditional higher education is grounded in behaviorist and cognitive psychology, online learning is grounded in constructivist learning theory. I am not at all sure that online learning could be seen as the cause for such fundamental reconceptualization of the learning process, but I do believe it is extremely well suited to a radically changing larger culture.

Larry Ragan: There are many forces of change enabling online learning to serve as a vehicle for radical transformation in higher education. The two I have recognized over the past 25 years have to do with a deeper understanding in the cognitive sciences of how people learn coupled with the impact of new and emerging technologies. This confluence has created a tidal wave of energy and focus on the construction of new learning spaces where students are actively engaged, and the instructor directs the learning process. This trend is also substantiated by the current language in higher education that refers to student learning rather than instructors teaching. The rapid emergence of teaching and learning technologies has served as a catalyst to hasten this pedagogical shift. The role of online technology as a catalyst is also evident in the changing dynamics of the face-to-face classrooms. The boundaries and borders of online and face-to-face learning spaces continues to blur as faculty embrace the power and capabilities of these technologies to extend the learning space, and the students demand increased access to and control of their learning environment. This radical transformation may appear subtle at first, but the undercurrent of change in the dynamics of the teaching and learning enterprise are increasingly evident in our classrooms, physical and virtual.

If online education is a "disruptive innovation," what aspects of the academy need to change to accommodate it? What are the characteristics of online learning that cause it to be a disruptive innovation?

Karen Swan: From what I understand of Christensen's (Christensen, Horn, & Johnson, 2008) work, a disruptive innovation is one that creates a new market that eventually disrupts an existing market and displaces an earlier technology. If online education is a disruptive innovation, then one might assume that the technology it would replace is the bricks-and-mortar, lecture-and-text technology of teaching and learning that developed after the invention of printing, and hence that the academy can't change to accommodate it and remain the academy as we know it. It also seems to me that the really disruptive aspects of online learning are those practiced by for-profit institutions and some community colleges (such as Rio Salado), such as employing very few tenured faculty, which allows them to respond to demand and greatly expand course offerings very quickly and keep costs down. These characteristics, together with issues of access common to all online learning, are what I think make it a disruptive innovation.

Gary Miller: Two characteristics of online learning are the most disruptive. First, online learning eliminates time and geography as defining factors in the relationship between an institution and its students and faculty. This means that an institution's online programs are available to any student, anywhere. In essence, students can choose to study at many different institutions, regardless of where they live. They can also decide to study at times and locations that are most convenient to them. At the same time, institutions can attract teaching faculty from anywhere in the world, ensuring that their students have access to the best possible instruction. Second, online learning allows institutions to deliver at scale the kind of active, collaborative, inquiry-based learning environment that previously was limited to graduate study. This dramatically improves the quality of undergraduate education for distant students and for nearby and even on-campus students.

Ray Schroeder: Online learning is disruptive to the entire field of education. As with so many other disruptive technologies or approaches, it becomes viable only in the greater context of society. The personal computer, for example, would have been far less important in the industrial age. It was the move to the information age that created the fertile ground for the personal computer to make such an important contribution to society, so much so that we cannot easily separate the two.

Online learning is similarly tied to the economy. While online learning is certainly viable in a robust economy because of the access and quality aspects it provides to selected segments, it will accelerate as the economy continues to languish. Affordable, accessible online learning will become the norm, supplemented by face-to-face sessions where needed.

Meg Benke: I believe that online learning and open education communities will start to converge, and these communities have different foundations and strengths. Open institutions from around the world have developed methods to reach huge numbers of learners through more independently used materials. More elite educational institutions in the United States have developed open education resources. Much of online education in the United States has focused most on working with smaller groups of learners with faculty in a somewhat closed classroom space. As these communities converge, a next wave of radical transformation could be the opening of online classroom space for more easily used exchanges of open resources, for learners in other programs and other countries, and even greater exchanges. Online and open learning will be disruptive if they can help learners to reach their goals more quickly, or in a less costly manner, or with greater attention to the learning outcomes.

Wayne Smutz: What makes online or technology-based education disruptive has to do with a several things. First, it has unlocked the gates to content. Faculty are no longer the key holders of content anymore. It can be obtained in other ways. Second, it has the potential to scale education in a way never possible before. Third, again, it can personalize the learning process. And finally, technology has made it possible to disconnect or de-couple elements of what colleges and universities do. Whether in the administrative processes or in the educational ones, entrepreneurs are developing new solutions for colleges and universities in marketing, recruiting, teaching, grading, advising, and more. These entrepreneurs are able to develop highly effective solutions because that is all that they do. Not only is it no longer practical for colleges and universities to do everything, it's probably not even the way to be successful because they can't keep up with the better solutions created by external entities. The result is likely to be higher education institutions that are connected to lots of other companies that provide them with services. In terms of the educational process, I believe this is the most significant change that will occur. But all of these are disruptive to the existing structure of higher education and will bring about change.

Larry Ragan: A foundation of the academy that needs to change is the explicit or implicit agreement between the learner and the institution with regard to the roles and responsibilities as well as the dynamics of the educational transaction. For the disruptive innovation to truly create a groundswell of change, learner and teacher need to recognize and embrace a new set of classroom dynamics. In the past, industrialized model of education, content is the commodity, and the education system represents the transfer of content from one vessel to another. This system resulted in the desire to design the most efficient and effective method to support the transfer of content. Online learning offers the opportunity to redefine the educational model from content transfer to content generation and deeper levels of internalizing and understanding. For this to occur, however, learner and teacher will be required to embrace radically different roles and take greater responsibility in the educational interchange.

Wayne Smutz: The biggest change has to come from the faculty. Higher education essentially is a craft industry now. Individual faculty produce individual courses one by one. While there is no doubt of significant added value in this approach at the graduate level, I'm not sure it can be demonstrated at the undergraduate level or at the lower division level. (Indeed, I've never seen any effort to demonstrate the value of this approach.) There is nothing inherently wrong with this approach. But when it drives the cost of higher education up and up, thereby limiting accessibility, it's a problem. But since the whole structure of a university is built on a faculty paradigm, then the whole structure, system, and administration is also built on this paradigm. All of that will have to change as the way is made to a learning-focused paradigm. That change will not come easily or in many cases willingly.

Gary Miller: Institutions will need to do several things to fully embrace the potential for transformation that online learning presents. First, and most immediately, institutions that offer online courses and programs need to develop new ways to engage students in noninstructional aspects of being a student. They need to eliminate geography and time as defining factors in these support services. Students need to be able to conduct all their interactions with the institution at a distance: advising and counseling, registration, access to the online infrastructure, library services, delivery of books and other physical resources, testing, and so on. They also need to ensure that faculty members have available to them the instructional design and media development resources that are needed to optimize the online learning environment. And they need to develop policies for engaging faculty at a distance in the life of the academic department. Most fundamentally, institutions will need to develop business models—costing and revenue distribution models—that allow online learning to have a broader impact as a change agent across the institution.

Just as online learning blurs the geographic boundaries between institutions and students, it is blurring boundaries between institutions themselves. One impact of online learning will be to encourage new relationships between higher education and K–12 schools—dual enrollment courses, accelerated degree programs, and such. This could be a significant change that is enabled by online learning. Similarly, we are already seeing interinstitutional collaborations; institutions will need to develop standards, and cultural mores, to support long-term collaborations across state and national boundaries.

Online learning has stimulated new kinds of degree-granting organizations, including for-profit corporations and multistate collaborations, that are stimulating new state and federal policies. What do you see as the major public policy issues leaders will need to confront in the coming years?

Ray Schroeder: The phenomenon of the higher education bubble more than anything else has stimulated these changes, and the resulting oversight movements among regulators. We are shifting to a new economy that in many ways no longer needs the institutions and learning models of the industrial age. I see the advent of more just-in-time and continuing professional education supplanting formal degree programs at the postsecondary level. This will ease the regulatory pressure because it will fracture the learning into so many microcertificates and programs that will thrive or die based on the perceived value in the marketplace of employers and industries.

Karen Swan: There seem to be quite a few public policy issues on the horizon that are being driven by online education; state credentialing of online programs, interinstitutional acceptance of credits, and performance measures of learning are all ones I think will need to be addressed soon.

Larry Ragan: The emergence of new and unique educational delivery systems will tax the current policy of accountability for and equality of what constitutes a unit of measurement from these systems. Coupled with this shift to more diverse learning systems is the need for agreement on how the unit of measurement will be valued, transferred, and accounted for over time. The current policy of regional accreditation may not be sustainable or practical in a more global and distributed educational model.

In addition, whereas traditional educational delivery systems were largely confined by boundaries of time and geography, online learning presents challenges of these dimensions as irrelevant and useless. Existing policies defining educational domains by geographic region or time zones are no longer adequate in a global educational framework. Policies established to enforce standards of quality, costs, or customer service will need reconstituting to serve local and global constituents.

Bruce Chaloux: Great, and challenging, question. It seems clear that the major public policy issues, indeed the greatest challenge to the higher education establishment is the growing perception that a higher education is not a great investment, or that the return on the investment is insufficient given the escalating and unabated increases in the costs of securing a higher education. Online learning has contributed to this quandary by demonstrating that quality learning can be delivered anywhere and anytime and can be structured to meet the needs of the learner and not institutions, particularly traditional colleges and universities. So the greatest public policy issues will center on the value proposition of a higher education. This plays out in several ways, ranging from quality control (e.g., the current debate about state authorization), federal financial aid support, teaching loads, class sizes, and a litany of other dimensions in higher education. While we recognize the social value of what a college and university experience provides, there seems to be a refocusing on learning and learning outcomes, and this will challenge many conventional ideas.

Clearly, for-profit providers are emerging in response to the need for innovation. How does the traditional academy respond?

Larry Ragan: The impact of for-profit educational providers on the traditional academy has been threatening, challenging, constructive, and presents a tremendous opportunity for dramatic change to the status quo. Operating from a fundamentally different set of values and parameters, the for-profits have stimulated new conversations in the academy of their core value and business proposition. In many cases, this reflection and examination has led to a renewed examination of why these institutions exist and how they respond in times of dramatic innovation and change. The most fundamental belief the for-profits have threatened is that the traditional institutions are the sole source, and perhaps the preferred source, of higher educational programming for all. The rapid growth of the for-profit educational providers suggests this is clearly not the case. The wake-up call for mainstream higher education is that although there is a continual need for and recognition of the value of a traditional degree, alternative products also hold value in the educational marketplace. My belief is that there is ample room in the online learning marketplace for for-profits and nonprofits alike to operate and, indeed, to learn from each other to improve learning for all.

Karen Swan: There are things the traditional academy does that for-profit providers do not and cannot do. The most important of these is probably the creation of knowledge (and the concomitant evaluation and synthesis of ideas). In addition, for-profit providers are not grounded in either the notion of the importance of a liberal education or of educating citizens, both of which I think are especially critical today. These are things I believe the academy must foreground to distinguish what it does from what for-profit education does, or what training at any institution or institutional level does for that matter, so that neither society in general nor the academy itself loses sight of the distinction. Beyond that, I believe we have a lot to learn from for-profit providers, and it is about time the academy was shaken up.

Wayne Smutz: The for-profit providers have brought good and bad with them to higher education. The pressure to generate profit has at least in part contributed to making getting students a priority over what's best for the student. There have been questions of quality from their own students as well as others. But the for-profit sector has also made positive contributions. For-profits serve the adult learner population that was primarily being ignored by higher education. They developed a customer service orientation that was long overdue in higher education, especially as the cost of higher education has risen. And they are attacking the learning outcomes issue aggressively and are likely to make progress. All of this was happening while all of

American higher education was becoming a market-based industry over the last 40 years. The traditional academy has been responding, some institutions faster than others. The student service orientation is much more prevalent. Adult learners are a major part of much of higher education. Attention to serious learning outcomes is emerging. And there is at least some initial movement toward trying to create efficiencies in higher education, something that has long been needed. These kinds of changes will continue.

Ray Schroeder: The traditional academy has no choice other than change. With very rare exceptions, we will no longer have state-supported institutions. All universities will become private institutions either for-profit or nonprofit. One good place to look to the future is among the for-profit and nonprofit health care institutions. Higher education will do well to study the models of hospitals that have existed in this environment for decades.

Bruce Chaloux: The traditional academy response to date has been to discount the value, quality, and legitimacy of the for-profit sector. It would appear that the finger pointing is not working, as for-profit enrollments continue to climb (although some in the sector are seeing decreased enrollment because of financial aid practices). Indeed, there appears to be a growing interest on the part of some segments of the academy to pursue markets that were left to the for-profits, a great example being the 40 million or so adult learners 25 and over who have some college credit but no credential or degree. I think more institutions recognize that the best way to address the for-profit sector is to become more competitive, more responsive to student interests and needs, and to use their name recognition, brand, and generally lower costs to attract more students.

Gary Miller: Traditional institutions should respond primarily through the peer-review process, ensuring generally accepted standards for how for-profit providers operate in the broader higher education community. This will allow them to reach some general accords related to several issues.

What are the implications for peer-review-based regional accreditation?

Karen Swan: I would guess there will be a need for better communication between regions or some sort of national accreditation, and these will all need to be much more focused on assessments of learning and performance beyond the institution.

Larry Ragan: One implication is the value of locally or regionally created standards for accreditation in a global environment with an increasing number of for-profit providers. Many of the measurement criteria may need to be reconsidered in light of the crowded educational marketplace. National or even global standards may need to be established as well as agreement on the quality and value of the learning outcome.

Wayne Smutz: I think that there are a couple of implications. One is that the movement toward greater use of technology has exposed peer review as a system for maintaining the status quo. It doesn't necessarily have to be like this. And there are some signs that accrediting bodies are trying to show they can act independently (e.g., the push for learning outcomes). But that is a reaction and not leadership. The second and more threatening potential implication is that accreditation may no longer be the right kind of vehicle to ensure quality. I would hate to see quality assurance centralized. That's likely to push quality to the lowest common denominator. Those in higher education need to think carefully and deeply about this. The quality of much of higher education has been based on the quality of the students (e.g., what comes in) and not on the quality of the teaching and learning that occurs. That has to change because all humankind deserves access to quality education.

Gary Miller: The primary challenge for regional accreditation is to ensure that for-profit degree-granting companies meet the definition of a higher education institution. For instance, the Middle States Commission for Higher Education uses this definition: "An institution of higher education is a community dedicated to the pursuit and dissemination of knowledge, to the study and clarification of values, and to the advancement of the society it serves" (Middle States Commission on Higher Education, 2008, p. iv). The question for peer review and regional accreditation is whether the company meets all three facets that define an institution of higher education. In addition, regional agencies need to develop clearer accreditation rules for member organizations that break federal or state laws related to admissions, financial aid, and so forth. Similarly, regional accrediting groups should be concerned that interinstitutional collaborations, especially when they cross regional or national boundaries, operate according to generally accepted academic and administrative standards. Just as the regional accrediting associations developed standards for distance education as technology-based distance education was emerging, they need to do the same now to ensure quality in a range of collaborations, from open educational resources to fully integrated collaborative degree programs.

Ray Schroeder: The future of regional accreditation is not at all certain. There currently is a struggle between a micromanaging Congress and the Department of Education carrying out the perceived wishes of Congress and the regional accrediting bodies. This bifurcated system is further broken down into state regulatory bodies. Meantime, content is changing at the speed of technology. At some point in the near future it will become clear that regulation beyond the cornerstone of primary and secondary education is no longer needed. We will see deregulation of postsecondary education.

Some fields may continue to offer accreditation by discipline (e.g., American Association of Colleges and Schools of Business), but employers and others will assess learning. Postsecondary education will become granular, that is, short courses, sequences of courses, and certificates will predominate without the overriding regulation that was needed previously.

Bruce Chaloux: Regional accreditation, long a distinct feature of the American higher education landscape, is under attack. The apparent unevenness across the regional bodies in standards and, more important, the assessment against those standards, has created new challenges for the peer review system. Online learning has been a central and continual challenge to the accrediting bodies, which still tend to focus on traditional campuses and delivery approaches. The role of regional accreditation, dictated in part by the federal government's insistence that these bodies take on new responsibilities, and the relationship to state charter and authorization or licensure, has weakened and muddied the roles of the members of the triad of states, accrediting bodies, and federal oversight. The greater concern is, what are the alternatives? Most in the higher education community would not like to move toward an international model of a central federal entity that oversees/authorizes/certifies quality, yet there appears to be some evidence of this creeping into the American model. The leadership in regional accrediting associations and institutional leadership (which establishes the standards and accreditation processes for each of the regions) will be challenged in the coming years.

As online learning becomes more prevalent in our institutions, will it result in a permanent centralized structure, or will it be decentralized over time? What factors should institutions consider?

Bruce Chaloux: Decentralized, and this is already occurring at institutions that have embraced online learning as simply part of their teaching and learning environment. Places like the University of Central Florida, Virginia Tech, and the University of Illinois Springfield are three examples. While some levels of centralization remain, particularly for specialized services or needs, these institutions have fully integrated online learning into their learning environment. I suspect more institutions will follow this path and create a singular model of learning with a variety of dimensions. What should institutions consider in doing this? Cost is typically the greatest factor, but I would argue that a broad acceptance of online learning as part of the institutional makeup, how it operates and distributes learning, are the most relevant factors.

Gary Miller: Most institutions had to create centralized services to launch something as innovative as online learning. However, over time some of the centralized services should become decentralized but with oversight from central administration to ensure that the distant student is equitably served. For instance, our experience has been that as academic departments become more involved in online delivery, they want to integrate instructional design professionals into their department rather than call upon a central service. Over time, other services might also be decentralized as the need and processes become better defined.

Some things that are likely to remain centralized are marketing, managing client relations, registration and records, and so on. These are also functions that tend to be centralized in the traditional campus environment.

Ray Schroeder: Those institutions that choose to offer online learning will absorb the delivery mode into the content areas. This is the growing trend at the time of writing this book. A movement is taking place across the country to consider online learning as simply learning. Just as some classes have had lectures, others have had labs, some have had case studies and group projects, we now are absorbing online learning into the mainstream. Support for the online classrooms is akin to janitorial support for the physical classrooms. It all becomes one.

Karen Swan: I anticipate a time when there will be no separation between online, blended, or enhanced classes, but I could be wrong.

Meg Benke: A recent trend in institutions has been the merger or connections between faculty development centers, teaching research centers, and the expertise developed in instructional design units of online learning programs. Creating an effective learning design and evaluating the success of it, no matter the delivery approach, is what is important.

Wayne Smutz: The push and pull of centralization and decentralization will continue. The pendulum will continue to swing. There will just be different forces at play to make the pendulum move. The force for centralization will come from the efficiencies (and the effectiveness) that can be acquired because of technology. It will also come from the brand effectiveness for institutions as opposed to colleges or schools. The push to be more socially relevant in terms of programs (focused on problems rather than disciplines) will also push for centralization to bring different players together.

There will continue to be advantages to decentralization. The speed at which change can occur is one of them. Smaller units can adopt new types of technology more easily than large ones. Smaller units are also more likely to experiment with new approaches and new technologies. These are not unimportant considerations. The key, in my opinion, will be in determining the best balance.

Larry Ragan: The methods of and organizational structures and services an institution uses to organize the online learning initiative are largely an outgrowth of the desired mission of the institution. The institution is powerless to confine the use of online learning in a single delivery system. One of the most rewarding aspects of online learning is the blurring of the boundaries of delivery formats. No longer constricted to dimensions of time and location, online learning continues to have an impact on the quality of instruction by extending the learning event and including all participants. This evolution cannot and will not be reversed. Whether the online learning efforts are centralized or decentralized is dependent upon the vision and mission for the outreach of the learning programs. Online learning constructed to serve localized (including regional geographically defined populations) may flourish best in a decentralized administrative model. Online learning initiatives that seek to expand the reach of the institution beyond a region tend to benefit from centralized coordination of presence and delivery, especially in service areas such as technical and advising support as well as business functions such as marketing and finances.

Bruce Chaloux: As several of my colleagues and fellow contributors have suggested, the blurring is well under way, and the environment for faculty is and will continue to change. The changing nature and role of faculty has already begun. In the online environment, those who are most successful use teams to help in the development and design of courses, support services, and a variety of activities that were once the sole domain of faculty. There is a movement toward more part-time and adjunct faculty, often based on cost considerations. And the advent of third-party providers who employ and deploy faculty for institutions all point to the changing nature of faculty in the academy.

Are structural changes needed? Do we need to disaggregate research and the creation of new knowledge from who teaches the new knowledge? Some sectors of higher education (community colleges and 4-year teaching institutions) already emphasize teaching and teaching loads, and expectations are different at those institutions than at research and comprehensive institutions. These are questions and difficult challenges for the next generation of academic leaders.

How will mainstreaming—blurring the distinctions between online distance education and online-assisted resident instruction, for instance—change faculties' work environment? What are the implications for online learning leaders?

Karen Swan: I think mainstreaming isn't the issue, the issue is the changing nature of faculties (from tenure track to adjunct and clinical faculty).

Ray Schroeder: As I mentioned in response to the prior question, the distinction between online and on-campus learning will evaporate as will the entire spectrum of blending modes of delivery. For the future, I see that a core group of faculty members will remain campus based, but the rest of the faculty, full-time and part-time, will be geographically dispersed. Those on campus will serve face-to-face needs, but the dispersed faculty members will do the same only through virtual face-to-face individual web conferences.

Larry Ragan: In many ways, blurring the distinctions between online distance education and online-assisted resident instruction provides faculty with the best of both instructional formats. I see it as an enriched palette to select instructional strategies, techniques, and methods to craft their learning space. Many faculty recognize the potential of these two learning systems and already easily move between the two, blurring and blending and melding the two formats. This blending of delivery formats also enables faculty to adjust what and how they use each medium to increase learning efficiency and effectiveness. For example, if faculty can now offload the delivery of their course content to the online format, allowing multiple avenues of access as necessary for student comprehension, they find they can use the face-to-face meetings for deeper exploration of topics and dynamic discussion of the course content.

This richer teaching palette will require an increased awareness and skill set on the part of the faculty to understand and use the delivery formats appropriately. This may also require the institution to provide professional development programming to assist faculty in adjusting to the blended learning and enhanced face-to-face format.

Wayne Smutz: The biggest change for faculty members brought about by online learning (and technology) is a change of their role from dispensers of content to facilitators of individual student learning. There are multiple implications if this is in fact what happens:

- It has to be acknowledged that we actually know something about teaching and learning from research. The myth that PhDs with no background in education can produce effective learning has to end. Significant training in education for college teachers must begin.
- The idea that success or failure at learning is entirely the student's responsibility has to end. What are faculty accountable for? Who's at fault if 50% of the students in a class fail? Why shouldn't it be the responsibility of faculty to help *all* students succeed?
- Questions will need to be raised about what makes a really good teacher at the postsecondary level. Many will say one has to be an expert in the content. That's probably true. But having a research background necessary to do that is a separate issue. A pipeline for faculty has been created over the past 60 years that emphasizes research skills. While not necessarily individualistic, research often is. So we have recruited into the faculty many individuals who are narrowly focused on content and heavily individualistic as well. Are those the traits necessary for excellent teachers who help students learn? Teaching and

learning are primarily social activities. Is there a mismatch between who faculty are and what's needed in faculty in the years ahead?

- With the changes occurring in higher education (fewer state funds, people reaching limits of their ability to pay tuition, problems with the U.S. economy), who will pay for research? To date, the federal government, foundations, some state money, and tuition have paid for it, but all those sources are being squeezed. There are likely to be much fewer research dollars to go around.

With all these changes, the big challenge for online leaders is helping the academy understand what's happening and helping online education to be seen as a source of help in this environment. It could easily be seen as a villain in the coming years unless leaders assert that what's happening is positive.

Gary Miller: As the current distinctions blur, online courses and traditional courses will have the same weight in determining a faculty member's full-time workload and in promotion and tenure. Ultimately, one could argue the materials a faculty member creates for an online course should be available for peer review and used in the promotion/tenure process, especially if those materials are shared with other faculty or other institutions.

The implication for online learning leaders is that they should be prepared to be advocates on behalf of the faculty across academic units. Online leaders need to be willing to become involved in the faculty senate and other academic governance organizations to argue the case on behalf of faculty. Few leaders in our institutions work with faculty on academic programs across multiple academic departments and at the undergraduate and graduate levels. This is an almost unique position in academia—one that online learning leaders need to use to the advantage of the whole institution.

Some faculty now have full-time appointments at one institution but teach online for another. How do you see online learning as it matures affecting the role of faculty members in an institution and the relationship between faculty members and their institutions?

Karen Swan: It isn't just teaching online for another institution, it is teaching in general. Ratios of tenured and tenure-track faculty to all faculty have shrunk from 70% to 30% in the past 25 years. What this results in is a large class of itinerant teachers with doctorates. We need to find a better use for these folks. A mind is a terrible thing to waste.

Ray Schroeder: The professoriate as we have known is gone forever. The economy of part-time contract hires of specialized faculty members to teach just-in-time and specialized courses are significant. As certainly as water seeks its own level, we will see an end to the tenured, mostly-residential faculty base.

Larry Ragan: I believe that much of the response of faculty to extended opportunities, such as teaching at multiple institutions, may be determined in large part by the existing relationship between the instructor and his or her institution. In research-based higher education settings only a portion of the faculty may be interested in extending their teaching to institutions external to their primary employer. It is quite possible that online instructors who have fixed-term, adjunct, or part-time relationships may be more predisposed to seek arrangements with multiple institutions. Certainly the potential for multiple teaching assignments across institutions will appeal to some online instructors because of the relative ease of access and convenience.

Gary Miller: Each institution should establish its own standards to guide faculty members in interinstitutional collaborative programs and to avoid conflict of commitment when faculty members with full-time commitments at one institution teach independently at another institution.

Bruce Chaloux: For years institutions have been concerned about conflict of interest. The greater challenge may actually have been, and likely is today, a conflict of commitment. Online learning has likely contributed to this growing challenge, allowing faculty to supplement their full-time activities by teaching online for an institution hundreds of miles away. A growing online adjunct faculty community has emerged and threatens to alter the long-standing relationship of faculty to an institution. The professoriate as we know it, as my colleague Ray Schroeder noted earlier, is gone forever.

Part 2: Leading Continuous Change

As a member of the first generation of online distance education leaders, what new skills will the emerging generation of leaders need to develop during their careers?

Gary Miller: Distance education has operated for decades at the periphery of our institutions. For the most part it has been a self-contained function. Leaders owned the delivery infrastructure and worked largely with part-time faculty. Online learning has brought distance education into the mainstream. This requires new skills for a generation of leaders who will be innovating in the mainstream. This generation will need to be able to work with other administrative and academic leaders who see online distance education as a threat rather than as an opportunity or who reject the transformation that is fundamental to the mainstreaming of online learning. This requires great diplomacy and tact. It also requires online learning leaders to be scholars in their own right, so they can operate credibly in the academic mainstream.

Larry Ragan: One of the critical leadership skills for the emerging leader in online learning is the ability to grasp basic knowledge and concepts across multiple dimensions. Online learning requires literacy in educational technology, pedagogy, and the business of the global marketplace. Having a basic working knowledge in each of these areas is necessary because of the convergence of these fields in e-learning. In addition, leadership in online learning must be able not only to aggregate this information but also be able to identify the trends and directions in a rapidly evolving field. As online learning is assimilated into higher education as an integral component of the face-to-face and blended classroom as well as a viable stand-alone delivery system, leadership in online learning will require vision, direction, and focus to guide the process.

Ray Schroeder: The skills of the successful leader in this field are many. Certainly, one needs to be able to carefully track the trends and opportunities of the field on a daily basis. A successful leader needs to be able to predict where the trends will lead. Key skills include understanding what is relevant and what are irrelevant data, as well as a good understanding of analytics and predictive algorithms. Interpersonal communication skills have been and will always remain important.

Bruce Chaloux: I think strong leadership, either in a traditional campus setting, an online institution, or a hybrid of the two, actually requires similar skills. One of the great leaders in the past 50 years was the highly successful basketball coach at University of California, Los Angeles, John Wooden. Beyond having a brilliant mind for basketball, he did not subscribe to a single style of play, rather he let his leadership approach be dictated by the talent on hand. So he won by assessing the talent he had and adjusting his coaching style to fit the abilities of his players. I think leaders in higher education should follow the example of Coach Wooden, indeed, I would argue that great leaders do this. The leadership qualities of integrity, creativity, dedication, an openness to the ideas of others, and decisiveness, to name a few, are essential. When coupled with an understanding of and appreciation for online learning, what it is, how it works, and that it is moving into the mainstream of institutions, the next generation of leaders will be ready to move higher education forward. Unfortunately, at the moment there is no knowledge, understanding, or appreciation for online learning in institutional leadership, including at the board and executive levels of our institutions.

The first generation of online learning was focused primarily on the question of access and, related to that, scale—the scope of courses, programs, and enrollments generated by an online initiative. What do you think will be the focus of the second generation? What are the leadership implications?

Meg Benke: Access and scale are still important, but growing importance is placed on the measurement of the success of what we do with our investments in education. Growing attention is placed on our capability to segment groups of learners and to devise services and programs appropriate to their goals and approaches to learning.

Karen Swan: I believe that scale and access will continue to be very important issues, but I also believe they will be within a context that focuses on learning and the assessment of learning. The obvious leadership implication is that e-learning leaders will need to become knowledgeable in the use of data and learning analytics and get themselves good statisticians and learning management systems people who can get data out of the courses.

Ray Schroeder: Certainly quality, access, and scale will not go away as priorities in the delivery of education. But the just-in-time aspect of nimble response to new technologies, trends, and needs will be the focus of the near term. To be able to respond within two or three weeks to something new, to provide deep guidance and detailed instruction on the continuous stream of innovations will define the winners in this field.

Larry Ragan: Seamlessness and immediacy of learning is evolving as the next challenge for online learning. As the field continues to develop and evidence is gathered that this model can lead to effective learning, the demand for a continual stream of ready access and portability will need to be met. This demand will put increased pressure on administrators of traditional learning systems to reconsider their value proposition to meet the educational needs. As alternative learning systems develop, such as open learning, for profits, and self-directed learning, institutions of higher education will need to respond regarding the advantages of investing in a college education. Leadership in online learning will also require the ability to meet the demands of today's learner in a radically different educational landscape.

Gary Miller: The second generation is going to be focused more on the subject areas and skills that are needed in society than on simply reaching new audiences with existing programs. We can envision new partnerships among institutions and between institutions and employers and other agencies (including high schools) as we work to meet changing social workforce and citizenship needs. In the process, our next generation of leaders will need to be translators and ambassadors, bringing information about the changes in society to the institutions.

Bruce Chaloux: The second generation of online learning, while continuing to focus on access and scale, will shift significantly to success. We are already seeing that change occur, with states in particular demanding greater levels of success for the investments they have made in higher education. When graduate rates nationally are less than 33%, and we have dropped to the middle of the pack in the 30 industrialized nations, we must refocus attention on completion (or success). This focus will not include significant increases in support or great expansion of physical facilities on traditional campuses, but rather will be on greater online efforts. Our leadership will need to be more creative, less focused on the traditions of the past, and more on being efficient and effective in targeting success. Business as usual will not be the norm or an acceptable standard, and our success will be measured in degree completion and not simply on creating greater access. We have won the latter, now it's time to focus on the former.

How do you see the technology of online learning changing in the next decade?

Gary Miller: Technology will become increasingly personalized. It will be more and more difficult to contain the online environment within a learning management system.

Ray Schroeder: Ubiquitous mobile broadband access will be the hallmark of this new decade. Three-dimension displays will make a significant difference in the sciences and many other fields. Gaming and simulation will make advances into realistic 3-D environments. This will be an exciting decade of rapid change.

Larry Ragan: It would have been hard to imagine just 15 years ago that in such a short period we would be experiencing the power and strength of connectivity as we see today in online learning. Technology has served as the catalyst for tremendous change for the design and development of globally distributed learning environments that serve an even more diverse set of learning needs in a rapidly evolving marketplace. Increased technology capabilities of communications, connectivity, and new ways to interact will continue to challenge educators to innovate and develop learning systems that meet an increasingly diverse set of learner needs.

Bruce Chaloux: This question is asked often, and typically my response comes with a caveat, being that if asked this question even 5 years ago, my ability to predict the kinds of technology we have today would have been well off the mark. Few of us could have predicted the increasing power of smaller and smaller devices, lower costs of technology, the advent of social media, and the broader acceptance of these devices as components of our everyday living. That said, there are four broader notions of technology that we need to keep in mind:

- We will witness near ubiquitous broadband access.
- Devices will be more personalized, more powerful, and increasingly inexpensive.
- These devices will become the learning tools of the current generation and will have an impact on instructional strategies at colleges and universities (and elementary and secondary schools for that matter).
- Technology breakthroughs will alter our thinking.

Whatever the next great technology fad is, leaders must embrace the technology and not commit to any specific approach or model. The dustbin of leadership includes many institutions that committed to a particular technology, failed to adjust to changes, and got left in the wake of change. Leadership in this area demands nimbleness.

Globally, online learning has stimulated a new level of collaboration and resource sharing among academic communities and institutions, such as the open educational resources movement. How will these movements affect online learning and higher education in the future?

Meg Benke: As a founding U.S. partner in Open Educational Resources university (OERu), SUNY Empire State College administrators see a connection to historical methods of assessing learning through prior learning assessment and the use of open educational resources. Learners will work informally, with a volunteer mentor and then when considering a degree or credential, get that learning validated through assessment by an accredited institution.

Ray Schroeder: The Open Educational Resources university movement has the potential to remake higher education. This movement cuts to the essence of the delivery and certification of higher education. For many years we have had advanced placement credit, College Level Examination Program, credit for prior learning, and other models of granting credit for learning outside the classroom. The OERu model takes this much further. We are today entering the field of granting credit at 10% of the cost of taking classes. Entire degrees will be offered to students who learn via the robust resources online. Mentors will be engaged on a voluntary or low-cost basis to assist those students in mastery of the course material. The OERu model then has the students stand for assessment at a university such as Empire State College. Only the cost of actually administering the final assessment is charged. If successful, the student receives full credit for the course.

Larry Ragan: The open education movement will put increased pressure on administrators of traditional higher education delivery systems to reevaluate their methods, business models, and accreditation processes. The movement also provides new opportunities for traditional higher education to work in new and creative ways with other education providers to create new learning models and products.

Gary Miller: Much depends on how seriously higher education institution administrators take the opportunity to collaborate, which tends to run against the historical geographically centered culture of higher education. The best future will be one in which institutions routinely work together to ensure that all students everywhere have access to the best thinkers in the field, as this will enrich education at all participating institutions. This has incredible potential to create new global scholarly communities as well as learning communities. It will, however, require a self-conscious effort among institutions to change long-standing habits.

Bruce Chaloux: Collaboration is easy to promote and difficult to achieve. Too much of higher education is still tied to the concept of we build it here. Online learning strategies are breaking this down to some extent, with more faculty beginning to share resources, to collaborate in greater ways, and to place the emphasis more on the learner and his or her needs. The open educational resources movement has helped to spur this, but that model is also changing and likely will continue to change. Stanford University's free online courses in computer science attracted some 120,000 enrollments, portending a look at the future.

A key question will be what mechanisms will be in place and will be needed to recognize learning in this open environment. Few, if any of these mechanisms, are currently in place as we move to a more outcomes-oriented model.

Part 3: Imagining the Future

Taking a look a bit farther toward the horizon, how do you imagine higher education will look at midcentury?

Karen Swan: I am old enough to remember if not the introduction of television, at least my parents' first TV (*Howdy Doody* and the McCarthy hearings). There is no way I would have guessed either the extent or the quality of the media changes that have transformed our culture. Indeed, sometimes I feel quite overwhelmed by it. Thus, I am quite sure I have no idea what the media culture will look like at midcentury. I am reasonably certain, however, that education at all levels will have morphed from a print-based to a digital culture or will be well on its way to becoming irrelevant.

Larry Ragan: I am not certain the term *higher education* will be relevant by midcentury. Education as a system may become less segmented and more integrated as a seamless mix of resources, credentials, and learning experiences designed to meet the needs of learners from cradle to grave. The institutions that survive the impact of the globalization of education and the development of more diverse methods of learning may constitute a web of learning opportunities in which the learner navigates based on his or her employment needs. I can imagine institutions forming complex learning ecosystems that offer multiple points of entry as well as multiple outcomes of varying market value. The challenge for any one institution—and maybe a critical success factor—may be more about developing an astute business plan that fits into this global educational economy.

Gary Miller: At midcentury, I imagine higher education will be more of a network of institutions with linkages with K–12 education, employers and industries, other sectors of higher education, and other peer institutions globally. I also imagine the curriculum will be more focused on developing information skills—inquiry, analysis, problem solving, collaboration—around a body of knowledge rather than the transfer of knowledge itself. Students will be affiliated with an institution and return to it (or to a partner institution) often to continue their education; practicums and credit for experience will become more integrated as part of an ongoing educational certification system.

Ray Schroeder: I imagine higher education in the traditional baccalaureate sense for the masses will be offered through open educational resources. Students will retain mentors online and will form their own local study groups to complete their degrees. Advanced education and specialized learning will take place online through just-in-time offerings tailored to the needs of individuals and small groups spread around the world. The professoriate as we know it will be gone. In its place we will have an active group of engaged professionals who will teach online.

Bruce Chaloux: A great question to end our roundtable discussion. My vision of higher education in midcentury is one of openness, with learners having options to pursue instruction when they want it and from whomever they wish to get it from. It will likely provide options for fully online traditional classroom instruction or hybrid forms, with the user determining the format. Traditional terms will be a remnant of a bygone era with learners beginning instruction when they wish. Credit will be recognized based upon outcomes, with third-party entities serving as credit banks for students. Credentials will no longer be the sole domain of colleges and universities but rather credentialing bodies awarding degrees.

Traditional campuses will still be in vogue, but how instruction is delivered on those campuses, and to whom, will be markedly different. Those institutions will embrace technology and online learning principles. Sadly, I predict these traditional campuses will serve students as they did a century earlier (1950s), a model that was elitist and not the egalitarian model of the latter half of the twentieth century. This will force more and more students to online programming as mentioned earlier, with for-profit institutions and a dramatically larger number of international providers from all corners of the globe serving U.S. students.

The implications for leadership will obviously be dramatic. The emergence of diverse pathways of innovation, should these emerge, will make it difficult for any specific leadership training to be offered to meet all of the new challenges. That said, an adherence to fundamental leadership principles, and as noted earlier a need to remain nimble, will prove to be the features of success.

I hope to be around, with some semblance of a reasonable mind, to see if any of my or my colleague's projections 35 years out prove to be correct.

References

Christensen, C. M., Horn, M. B., & Johnson, C. W. (2008). *Disrupting class: How disruptive innovation will change the way the world learns.* New York, NY: McGraw-Hill.

Jenkins, H. (2008). *Convergence culture: Where old and new media collide.* New York, NY: New York University Press.

Middle States Commission on Higher Education. (2008). *Characteristics of excellence in higher education* (12th ed.). Philadelphia, PA: Author.

Moore, M. G. (1997). Theory of transactional distance. In Keegan, D. (Ed.), *Theoretical principles of distance education* (pp. 22–38). New York, NY: Routledge.

Morrill Act, 7 U.S.C. § 301 et seq. (1862).

Morrill Act, 26 Stat. 417, 7 U.S.C. 321 et seq. (1890).

*L*eading the e-Learning Transformation of Higher Education offers the rising generation of leaders the perspectives and benefit of the experiences of seven leaders who have pioneered online distance education at their institutions. All have had leadership roles in national and international distance education organizations. Five were recognized as members of the inaugural class of Sloan Consortium (Sloan-C) Fellows in 2010. The authors collaborated in 2009 to establish the Institute for Emerging Leaders in Online Learning, an annual professional development program offered through a partnership between Sloan-C and The Pennsylvania State University World Campus. They have led the first generation of the e-learning transformation at their institutions. In this book, they share their personal experiences and perspectives on the new leadership challenges facing the field.

Meg Benke is professor, School of Graduate Studies, and previously provost and acting president at Empire State College, State University of New York. Benke has worked professionally in distance learning for 25 years, most recently serving as vice provost for Online and Global Programs at Empire State College and administered the Center for Distance Learning, which is the largest provider of online education in New York state and one of the largest programs in the country. She served as president of Sloan from 2010 to 2013. Benke was recognized for the Most Outstanding Achievement in Online Learning by an Individual in 2007 by Sloan-C. Benke has worked with Empire State College to build partnerships with unions, corporations, and the military to encourage employees to pursue college degrees. She has been instrumental in providing programs for the military and organizations such as the American Association of Retired Persons employee program, and several other programs, to increase access to college educations for technical employees. Benke serves on the board of directors for Sloan-C and serves as president for 2010. She chaired the consortium's national conference for 2007 and 2008 and directed the best practices area in student satisfaction for Sloan-C. Benke also serves on the board of directors for the Girl Scouts of Northeastern New York. Benke holds a doctorate in student personnel from Ohio University and a bachelor of science in business from Youngstown State University. She teaches in the areas of human systems and behavior, performance measurement, learning organizations, organizational change, and training and development in the graduate and undergraduate programs of Empire State College.

"My grounding in higher education is with nontraditional and adult education," Benke notes, "but I have always been interested in the intersections between employment, communities, and degree access for adults. Working in online learning was a solid foundation for my administrative work as provost and acting president. Networking and seeing opportunities for engagement and development are key to all leadership roles."

Bruce Chaloux was executive director and chief executive officer of the Sloan Consortium, until his passing during the production of this volume, and had served as a member of the board of directors of Sloan-C and as president from 2008 to 2010. Chaloux previously directed the 16-state Electronic Campus initiative of the Southern Region Education Board, which includes more than 50,000 credit courses and more than 2,500 degree programs from 300 colleges and universities in the southern United States. For 13 years he served in the Graduate School of Virginia Tech, including 4 years as associate dean for Extended Campus Programs and 9 years as associate dean and director of the university's Graduate Campus in suburban Washington, DC. In the 1980s Chaloux led a national study of the use of technology in U.S. higher education for the Council of Graduate Schools and on quality assurance and accreditation issues in the Project on Assessing Long-Distance Learning via Telecommunications.

"I was involved with the precedents to online learning, often described as distance learning," Chaloux reported at the time of writing. "Indeed, my initial involvement in what were alternative delivery methods dates to the 1970s and the emergence of television, video, and satellite transmission, which we called telecommunicated learning. Much of my focus was on quality assurance including state licensing and authorization and the role of the federal government and accrediting bodies. Leadership has always been a focus of my work and, in particular, efforts to move traditional higher education thinking beyond the confines of the campus. I have long believed that we have not served a huge number of learners whose personal situation or circumstances (family, work, geography, time constraints) simply did not permit them to enjoy the benefits of postsecondary education. Telecommunicated learning helped some, but the emergence of online learning has allowed the educational community to reach new markets of students who previously could not access traditional campus programs."

Gary Miller is executive director emeritus of the Pennsylvania State World Campus, the e-learning campus of The Pennsylvania State University. As the founding executive director of the World Campus, Miller led the development of what has become recognized as one of the leading e-learning institutions in the United States. From 1987 to 1993 he served as associate vice president for Program Development and executive director of the International University Consortium at the University of Maryland University College. In 2004 he was inducted into the International Adult and Continuing Education Hall of Fame and served as chair of the board for 2010. He received the 2004 Wedemeyer Award from the University of Wisconsin and the *American Journal of Distance Education* and the 2007 Irving Award from the American Distance Education Consortium for his contributions to distance education. Miller was recognized for lifetime contributions to the field by Sloan-C and the National University Telecommunications Network in 2008 and by the International Council for Open and Distance Education in 2009. He was named a Sloan Fellow in 2010. He is the author of *The Meaning of General Education* (New York, NY: Teachers College Press, 1988) and numerous articles and book chapters on distance education, the latest being "Organization and Technology of Distance Education" in *An Introduction to Distance Education* (M. F. Cleveland-Innes & D. R. Garrison, Eds., New York, NY: Routledge, 2010).

Miller notes that his entire career was in the broad area of university outreach or continuing education. "We often were perceived by academics as being on the business side of the university, more interested in making money than education itself," he reports. "When online learning came along, our role changed. Suddenly, we were working with academic units on complete undergraduate and graduate degree programs. It required that I broaden my vision and my understanding of the academic culture. I could no longer afford to sit on the periphery but needed not only to learn how to operate at a higher administrative level but to be an advocate for our academic partners in that process."

Lawrence C. Ragan is codirector for the Center for Online Innovation in Learning at The Pennsylvania State University, where he helps direct the center's mission of research, scholarship, technology innovation, and leadership development programming. He has been a part of the creation and management of the Penn State World Campus since its inception in 1998. Until 2008 Ragan served as director for instructional design, providing leadership in the design, development, and delivery of World Campus courses. Before taking on his current role, he led the World Campus faculty development initiative, which offers a range of professional development opportunities to ensure success for Penn State faculty involved in online and continuing education. Since 2009, Ragan has served as codirector of the Institute for Emerging Leadership in Online Learning (IELOL). He also has served in leadership roles as codirector and faculty of the EDUCAUSE Learning Technology Leadership program (2005 to 2007). He is also active in the design and delivery of international leadership development institutes.

Ragan has taught online from 2001 through 2007 as an affiliate faculty in the College of Agriculture, and as part of the IELOL program. Ragan maintains research and publication activities focusing on a range of topics including the definition of competencies necessary for online teaching success, quality of instruction in online learning, and a framework for quality assurance in faculty development programming.

Ragan began his career as a public school teacher, teaching agriculture in a rural Pennsylvania school. "In the agricultural education classroom," he recalls, "student leadership is taught as a part of the curriculum. This early exposure to a high school classroom not only allowed me a personal formation opportunity but also allowed me the time to work with the adult leaders in the community. Upon returning to Penn State to complete my master's I immediately began teaching educational computing to the faculty and staff. This began my career as an adult educator. The leadership opportunities I recognized and embraced during these years, although modest in scope, provided me with the opportunity to practice and develop my own leadership style. I discovered a passion for adult education and was presented many opportunities over the years to learn from talented and equally passionate leaders. A most critical leadership skill I developed throughout this experience has been the ability to listen to and appreciate insights from multiple perspectives."

Raymond Schroeder is professor emeritus and associate vice chancellor for online learning at the University of Illinois Springfield. Schroeder has numerous national presentations and publications in online and technology-enhanced learning. He has published the popular "Online Learning Update" and "Educational Technology" blogs for the past decade. He was a Sloan Consortium Distinguished Scholar in Online Learning 2002–2003, recipient of the 2002 Sloan-C award for the Most Outstanding Achievement in Online Teaching and Learning by an Individual, a University of Southern Maine Visiting Scholar in Online Learning 2006–2009, and cofounder of the New Century Learning Consortium. Schroeder was named the inaugural 2010 recipient of Sloan-C's highest individual award, the A. Frank Mayadas Leadership Award. Schroeder is an inaugural Sloan Fellow.

With a background in public radio and television under his belt, along with a stint as president of the faculty union, Schroeder had several opportunities for leadership but chose to focus on online learning. "The skills of leading a larger institute on the campus along with the technology understanding I had built over the years served me well," he reports, adding, "I needed to refine skills in the area of academic leadership. The confidence and trust I had built over the years of leadership in the nonacademic areas of the campus served me well in leading the online initiatives."

Wayne Smutz is associate vice president for academic outreach and executive director of the World Campus at The Pennsylvania State University. In these roles he oversees the delivery of credit-based programs for adult learners online through the World Campus and through Continuing Education. Smutz has been at Penn State and in continuing education for nearly 30 years, serving in roles related to credit and noncredit program development, needs assessment, conferencing, marketing, and e-learning. He is the recipient of numerous awards including the 2011 Sloan-C Award for Outstanding Achievement by an Individual, national and regional programming awards from the University Professional and Continuing Education Association (UPCEA), and numerous leadership awards. Smutz currently serves on the boards of Sloan-C and the American Distance Education Consortium. He recently stepped down from the UPCEA board, concluding a two-year term as treasurer. Smutz speaks frequently on issues related to e-learning, continuing education, organizational culture, and adult learners. His latest article is "Economic Development in Challenging Times: The Penn State Outreach Response" (*Continuing Higher Education Review*, *72*[2008], 44–56). Smutz holds a doctorate in higher education and a master's degree in political science from Penn State. He received a bachelor's degree in history from the University of California, Berkeley.

"I have proudly spent my entire career working at the margins of higher education as part of continuing and distance education units," Smutz reports. "It's been an exhilarating ride. I have found the opportunities for creativity and innovation unending. Most important for me has been the opportunity to provide leadership in support of expanding access to higher education and in working to create institutional support structures for learners that maximize their chances for transformation through education. Way too much human potential is wasted locally, nationally, and globally. The world of online education is an important tool for channeling that potential into productive pathways for the benefit of individuals and society. I've been fortunate enough to make a contribution."

Karen Swan is the James J. Stukel Distinguished Professor of Educational Leadership at the University of Illinois Springfield. Swan's research is in the area of media, technology, and learning on which she has published and presented extensively. She has written over 100 publications on educational technology topics as well as several hypermedia programs and two books, and led several grants for organizations such as the National Science Foundation, the U.S. Department of Education, the New York City Board of Education, AT&T, and the Cleveland Foundation. Her current research interests center on online learning, ubiquitous computing, and data literacy. Swan received the 2006 Sloan-C award for Outstanding Achievement in Online Learning by an Individual, and in 2010 was inducted into the first class of Sloan-C Fellows. She also received a Distinguished Alumnus award from Teachers College, Columbia University, her alma mater, in that same year.

"Like many of us, my first interest was in video," Swan remembers, "but early on I was drawn to Logo programming not only because of its emphasis on the child teaching the computer but also because I found myself understanding basic mathematical concepts through programming that had eluded me most of my life. Because my area is learning technologies I have of course experimented with many different technologies throughout my career. I experimented with video conferencing as a distance technology, for example, but found it unsatisfying. So when I was asked to teach online for the State University of New York Learning Network in 1997, I felt I had to try it, but I wasn't overly enthusiastic. Who knew? I was immediately taken with the medium, especially asynchronous discussion, and I have been deeply and passionately involved with online learning ever since."

Foreword Author

Michael Grahame Moore, Distinguished Professor Emeritus of Education, The Pennsylvania State University, is known in academic circles for pioneering the scholarly study of distance education, nowadays commonly referred to as e-learning and online learning. Since he published the first theory about "transactional distance" in 1972, he has achieved many other notable "firsts" in laying the foundations of this field. While teaching the first course on distance education theory at University of Wisconsin–Madison in the mid-1970s he helped found the first national conference there. Coming to Penn State in 1986, he established the first sequence of taught graduate courses, as well as one of the first online professional networks (Distance Education Online Symposium), and founded the first American research journal in the field, *The American Journal of Distance Education.*

In recognition of this scholarship, he was inducted into the United States Distance Learning Association's Hall of Fame in 2002, and into The International Adult and Continuing Education Hall of Fame in 2013. Other recognitions include a Visiting Fellowship at the University of Cambridge, UK, and Visiting Professorships at The Open University, UK, the Shanghai Open University and the Universidad del Salvador, Argentina. An Honorary Doctorate of University of Guadalajara was awarded in recognition of contributions to establishing distance education in Mexican universities. At The Pennsylvania State University he was awarded a Lifetime Achievement award and appointed a Distinguished Professor in recognition of his "exceptional record of teaching, research and service."

Retiring from teaching in 2013, Moore now consults internationally and focuses on his editorial work, especially *The American Journal of Distance Education* and the Stylus Publishing series Online Learning and Distance Education.

AAACE. *See* American Association for Adult and Continuing Education
AACC. *See* American Association of Community Colleges
academic affairs, 15, 136
academic culture, 59
access, 8, 21, 105, 193
   challenges, 117–18
   to higher education, 50, 68, 178
   to programs, 23
   to student support, 9, 134
accountability, 20, 71, 112, 190
   academic, 84, 91
   choice for, 48, 66
   learning and, 77
   self-, 44
   teaching and, 77
accreditation, 200, 201
   bodies, 50, 183–84
   Chaloux on, 222
   Miller on, 221
   Ragan on, 220
   regional, 13, 19, 20, 134, 171, 184
   Schroeder on, 221–22
   Smutz on, 221
   Swan on, 220
achievement, 77, 87, 92–93
ADEC. *See* American Distance Education Consortium
administration, 15, 17, 18–19, 24, 59, 61
Adult Education Research Conference (AERC), 208
Adult Learners: Stories of Transformation, 57
advising, 9, 69

AERC. *See* Adult Education Research Conference
agonism, 60–61, 62
Agricultural Satellite (Ag*SAT), 7
agriculture, 5
Ag*SAT. *See* Agricultural Satellite
Alcoholics Anonymous, 43
Alfred P. Sloan Foundation, 132, 178. *See also* Five Pillars of Quality Online Education; Sloan Consortium
   funding by, 13–14, 53, 126–27
   initiatives of, 8–9
Allen, I. Elaine, 12, 21, 29–30
ALS-6. *See* Applications Technology Satellite-6
Amendments to HEA (1972), 182
American Association for Adult and Continuing Education (AAACE), 207
American Association of Community Colleges (AACC), 206
American Center for the Study of Distance Education, 204
American Distance Education Consortium (ADEC), 184, 195, 206
American Federation of Teachers, 127
American Military University. *See* American Public University System
American Public University System (APUS), 27, 36, 91
   business model for, 28
   institutional culture at, 33–35
   services at, 31, 139

American Society for Training and Development (ASTD), 207
andragogy, 119
Annenberg Foundation, 7
APLU. *See* Association of Public Land-grant Universities
Appalachian Educational Satellite Program, 6
Appalachian Regional Commission, 6
Apple, 158
Applications Technology Satellite-6 (ALS-6), 6
APUS. *See* American Public University System
Arbaugh, J. Ben, 89
Arizona, 27
Armitage, S., 134
The Art of the Long View (Schwartz), 43, 46
assessment, 89–90, 104, 113, 123–24
Association for Continuing Higher Education, 195
Association of Private Sector Colleges and Universities, 194
Association of Public Land-grant Universities (APLU), 15–19, 78, 196
Association of Public Land-grant Universities-Sloan National Commission on Online Learning, 29–30
ASTD. *See* American Society for Training and Development
Athabasca University, 204
AT&T, 52
attendance, 192
audio, 91
Authentic Conversations (Showkeir & Showkeir), 66–67, 72
authenticity, 66–67, 72–73
automobile industry, 6
Aviv, R., 89

Babson Survey Research Group, 12, 185
BBC. *See* British Broadcasting Company

Bean, J. P., 140
behavior, 64
beliefs, 55, 67–68
benchmarks, 134–35
Benke, Meg, 76
  on disruptive innovations, 215–16
  on distance education, 211
  on focus of online learning, 228–29
  on online learning structure, 223
  on open educational resources movement, 231
Blackboard, 150, 208
Blackley, J. A., 94
Black Panthers, 60
Boston, Wally, 31, 34, 91
Boyer, Ernest, 26
Bransford, J. D., 82
British Broadcasting Company (BBC), 6
British Open University. *See* Open University of the United Kingdom
Brock, Kishia, 132n1
Brown, A. L., 82
Brown, M. B., 77
Bruno, L. F. C., 64
Buban, Jill, 132n1
budgeting, 189–91
Burge, Elizabeth, 44
Bush, Vannevar, 84
business, 89
  model for APUS, 28
  model for Empire State College, 28
  model for Pennsylvania State University World Campus, 28
  model for Rio Salado College, 28
  model for UIS, 28
  models and leadership, 27–28
  models for online distance education, 27–28
  organizations, 183, 184
  sectors, 39
Bustamante, Chris, 31, 34

CAEL. *See* Council for Adult and Experiential Learning
California State University, Chico, 87, 89

campus, 18–19, 21–22, 26, 189–91
Canada, 90, 152, 204
Canadian Institute for Distance
    Education, 204
Cape Town Open Education
    Declaration, 154
Caterpillar, 126
Center for Technology in Learning,
    78–79
Center for Transforming Student
    Services (CENTSS), 146
Chaloux, Bruce, 1, 185
    on accreditation, 222
    on distance education, 211–12
    on faculty, 227
    on focus of online learning, 229–30
    on higher education, 233–34
    on online learning, 212–13
    on online learning structure,
        222, 224
    on open educational resources
        movement, 232
    on public policy issues, 218
    on skills, 228
    on technology, 230–31
change, 19, 50, 60, 159–60
    currents of, 210–27
    environmental, 68
character, 48
Chasen, Michael, 150
CHEF, 150
Christensen, C. M., 214
Chronicle of Higher Education, 20
Class Differences (Allen & Seaman), 12
classroom, 12, 115, 126
Cocking, R. R., 82
cognitive presence, 82–83, 107
CoI. *See* Community of Inquiry
collaboration, 19, 70, 73, 203
    cross-sector, 154
    between faculty, 13–14, 24
    focus on, 80
    institutional, 153–54
    opportunities for, 13–14
    teamwork and, 11–12

colleges, 53. *See also* community
    colleges
    Black, 5
    land grant, 4–5, 12, 26, 179
    microcontext of, 59–61, 112
Collins, Jim, 2, 39, 45
Columbia University's Fathom
    and AllLearn, 8
Commission on the Regulation
    of Distance Education, 193, 195
commitment, 9–10
    conflict of, 158
    to goals, 68, 72–73
    importance of, 60, 64, 66
Committee for Institutional
    Cooperation, 153, 203
communication, 5, 16, 169
    high-tech, 79–80
    standards, 117
    systems, 113–14
communities, 11, 33, 201
    change, 159–60
    e-learning, 8–10, 141
    of faculty practitioners, 124–25
    of practice, 124
    promotion of, 139–40, 141
community colleges, 6–7, 12,
    27, 206
Community of Inquiry (CoI), 78,
    91, 152
    framework, 82–83, 90
    learning and, 82–83
    survey, 106–7
computer languages, 8, 149
Congressional E-Learning Caucus, 196
consensus, true, 62
conservatism, 59
constructivism, 80–81, 89, 90, 94
consulting, 204
control, illusion of, 50, 62–63
Cooperative for Educational
    Technology, 195
copyrights, 118–19, 126, 157
Cornell University, 150
Corporation for Public Broadcasting, 7

correspondence programs, 5–6, 25, 168
costs, 9
  recovery, 18, 28
  technology, 10, 190–91
  tuition, 134
Council for Adult and Experiential
  Learning (CAEL), 189, 207
Council of State Governments, 195
course, 141, 149–50, 203–4
  construction and delivery team
    processes, 119
  content of, 126
  design, 110
  development, 53, 109
  grades, 92, 113
  hybrid, 153
  interactivity and utility of, 86
  introduction and overview, 103
  online, 12, 87, 91
  participants, 115
  technology, 80, 105
  tele, 6–7
CourseInfo, 150
CourseShare, 153, 203
Court of Appeals, U.S., 194
CREAD. *See* Inter-American Distance
  Education Consortium
Creative Commons, 208
curriculum, 9

Danarajan, Rai, 45
data
  analysis and collection of, 77–78
  analytics, 144
  -based decision making, 78,
    83–86
  faculty respondent, 17
  growth of, 84
  outcome, 92
  support, 63
decision making, 42, 59, 68
  data-based, 78, 83–86
  process, 129
degree, 134, 139
  completer entities, 189

completion rates, 12, 14, 20, 51, 77
  programs, 7–8, 23
Department of Education, U.S.
  goals of, 12, 14, 20, 51
  meta-analysis by, 78–79, 94
  "Program Integrity Rules" of,
    193, 195
  regulations, 193–94
DePree, Max, 62
disability services, 9
distance education
  academic specialization in, 204–5
  Benke on, 211
  Chaloux on, 211–12
  development of, 5–7
  evolution of, 3–4, 8–10, 47
  historical perspective of, 1, 3–12
  Industrial Revolution and, 4–5
  international, 6
  Miller on, 210–11
  professional associations, 206–7
  Ragan on, 211
  regulation of, 19–21
  roots of, 5
  Schroeder on, 211
distance education, online. *See also*
  e-learning; online learning
  business models for, 27–28
  challenges of, 110
  courses, 12, 87, 91
  criterias for, 39–40
  degrees obtained through, 7–8, 23
  diversity of, 111, 116
  endurance of, 40
  enrollment, 8, 28
  ethical realism and, 41–44, 45–46
  evolution of, 1, 8–10, 109
  excellence of, 40–41
  functions of, 23–24
  greatness in, 39–40
  impact of, 12–13, 40
  implications for, 144–45
  initiatives, 8–10
  institutional models for, 24–27
  leadership of, 23–25, 120–26

legalities of, 118–19
long-term strategies for, 29–30
as mainstream, 151
persistence in, 140
policies for, 24
purpose of, 1, 40
quality assurance of, 117, 145
regulation of, 19–21
resource engine of, 41
role of, 24, 40–41
service function outsourcing
    for, 136–37
vision for, 24, 29–30, 32
Distance Educational and Training
    Council, 19
Distance Learning Policy Laboratory
    (DLPL), 186
Drexel University, 141
Dweck, Carol, 54
Dziuban, Chuck D., 87

eCollege, 150
EDEN. *See* European Distance
    and E-Learning Network
To Educate the People Consortium, 6
Educating the Net Generation
    (Oblinger & Oblinger), 14
education, 12–15, 35, 196–97
    adult, 207
    associations and organizations,
        183–85, 206–9
    business, 89
    continuing or extended, 165
    distance, 206–7
    as e-commerce, 190
    leadership and, 58
    nontraditional, 70
    open, 208–9
    public policy on, 19–21
    as transformative, 68–69, 73
education, postsecondary, 65, 182
    goals of, 12, 14, 20, 51, 77
Educational Technology
    Cooperative, 186
EDUCAUSE, 195, 202, 206

Learning Initiative, 84
    policy review, 20
e-learning
    communities, 8–10, 141
    development and expansion of,
        185–93
    effectiveness of, 77–78
    environments, 89–91, 140
    federal role in, 179–81
    higher education and, 3, 6
    innovations, 3, 7
    inputs to, 86–88
    institutional role in, 182–83
    organizations, 184
    outcomes, 91–94
    policy context for, 179–85
    policy influencers of, 183–85,
        197–98
    policy leadership in, 177–78,
        196–98
    process, 85–86
    programs, 15–19
    quality of, 188
    roots of, 3, 7
    state role in, 181–82, 201–2
    student, 185
    traditional instruction against,
        78–79, 80–81
    transfer credit policies for, 188–89
Electronic Peer Network, 139
Empire State College, 76, 132n1, 135
    academic support services at,
        142–43
    business model for, 28
    Center for Distance Learning at, 26,
        31, 33
    Center for Graduate Studies at, 26
    institutional culture at, 33–35
    as model, 26, 36
    program development at, 31
    services at, 32, 141–42
employers, 21
"enduring understandings," 92–93
Energy Providers Consortium
    for Education, 21

enrollment
  online distance education, 8, 28
  at Pennsylvania State University
    World Campus, 54, 56, 72
  semester to semester, 92
environments, 68, 160, 173
  e-learning, 89–91, 140
  image-rich, 14
  learning, 14, 45–46, 141–42
  policy, 125–26
  student-centered, 76, 80–81, 134
  teacher-centered, 80–81
  technology supports and, 86
*Ethical Realism: A Vision for
  America's Role in the World*
  (Lieven & Hulsman), 41
ethics, 44
Europe, 7, 19, 154
European Commission, 19
European Distance and E-Learning
  Network (EDEN), 208
exams, 93
Excelsior College, 139
exercise, 55

Facebook, 151
faculty, 27, 93, 202–5
  adjunct, 191
  blended programs and, 13
  burnout, 125
  capacity issues, 111–13
  Chaloux on, 227
  collaboration between, 13–14, 24
  compensation and incentives for, 10,
    121–22, 126
  development and preparation of, 86,
    108–9, 113–19, 121–26, 128–29
  development programs at
    SUNY, 110
  diverse profiles of, 111–13
  empowerment of, 154–55
  engagement of, 68–69, 95,
    126–28, 167
  Miller on, 227
  organizations, 121

  perceptions of, 18–19
  practitioners, communities of,
    124–25
  Ragan on, 227
  recognition of, 158
  research professional
    associations, 208
  resources for, 16
  respondent data, 17
  role of, 51, 109
  satisfaction, 10, 39
  Schroeder on, 226
  services, 108
  structures, 31
  success, 108, 112
  support of, 120, 167
  surveys, 15–19, 30
  Swan on, 226
  training, 18
  workload, 10, 125
financial aid, 15
  federal, 20–21, 50, 191–92, 193–94
  for-profit providers and federal,
    20–21, 50, 193–94
  state, 20, 50, 191–92
  Title IV, 184, 194
financial exigency, 125
First International Conference on
  Learning Analytics and
  Knowledge, 84
Five Pillars of Quality Online
  Education, 9, 75, 132
*Flexible Higher Education: Reflections
  From Expert Experience* (Burge), 44
for-profit providers, 3. *See also*
  American Public University
  System
  emergence and growth of, 13,
    20–21, 51
  federal financial aid and, 20–21,
    50, 193–94
  Miller on, 220
  Ragan on, 219
  Schroeder on, 220
  service approach at, 65

Smutz on, 219–20
Swan on, 219
Free Culture Movement, 208
Friedman, T. L., 11
Fund for the Improvement of
    Postsecondary Education,
    87, 152
funding, 158
    by Alfred P. Sloan Foundation,
        13–14, 53, 126–27
    campus and state, 189–91
    life-cycle, 190
    methods, 190
    by Sloan Consortium, 126–27,
        128, 135
    sustainable, 17–18
*The Future of Learning: Preparing for
    Change* (Redecker), 19

Gates Foundation, 84
GI Bill. *See* Serviceman's Readjustment
    Act of 1944
Gibson, Chere, 45
globalization, 11
Globalization 3.0, 11
goals, 23, 53
    commitment to, 68, 72–73
    of Department of Education, U.S.,
        12, 14, 20
    of postsecondary education, 12, 14,
        20, 51, 77
    strategies and, 50, 57–59
Goldberg, Murray, 149
Goleman, D., 63, 68
*Good to Great in the Social Sectors:
    A Monograph to Accompany Good
    to Great* (Collins), 2, 39
goodwill, 63
Google, 150
governance, 24, 59, 61, 62, 129
Government Accountability
    Office, 20
Government Strategies Group at Dow
    Lohnes, 196
graduates, high school, 12, 14, 20

Granger, Dan, 45
Great Plains Interactive Distance
    Education Alliance, 14, 153

HEA. *See* Higher Education Act of
    1965
hedgehog concept, 40–41, 45–46
higher education
    as academic innovators, 39, 43, 57
    access to, 50, 68, 178
    Chaloux on, 233–34
    context and, 50–57, 112
    e-learning and, 3, 6
    institutions, 5, 46–47, 90
    as mainstream, 8, 21, 38–39,
        41–44, 127
    Miller on, 233
    organizational structure within, 17
    Ragan on, 232
    Schroeder on, 233
    as social organization, 2, 39, 40–41
    of student, 12, 14, 20
    Swan on, 232
    transformation of, 8–10
Higher Education Act of 1965 (HEA),
    180–81
Higher Education Facilities Act of
    1965, 180–81
Hillman, D. C., 89
Holocaust, 70
Horizon Report, 84
*How People Learn: Brain, Mind,
    Experience, and School* (Bransford,
    Brown & Cocking), 82
Hulsman, John, 41–44
human needs, 39
humility, 43, 44

ICCHE. *See* Illinois Council of
    Continuing Higher Education
ICDE. *See* International Council for
    Open and Distance Education
Illinois Council of Continuing Higher
    Education (ICCHE), 202
Illinois Faculty Summer Institute, 202

Illinois Federation of Teachers, 127
immigration, 4
Indiana University, 150
inductive discovery, 14
industrialization, 3, 4–5
Industrial Revolution, 3, 4–5
informalization, 19
information, 5–7, 9, 11–12, 17, 43, 47
Information Revolution, 47. *See also*
    World Wide Web
  emergence of, 5–7, 11–12
  knowledge and, 12
Information Technology, 17
innovations
  in academia, 39, 43, 57
  Benke on disruptive, 215–16
  e-learning, 3, 7
  Miller on disruptive, 215, 217
  Ragan on disruptive, 216
  Schroeder on disruptive, 215
  skills and, 11
  Smutz on disruptive, 216, 217
  sustainment of, 175
  Swan on disruptive, 214–15
Institute for Higher Education Policy,
    133–34
institutional culture
  at APUS, 33–35
  at Empire State College, 33–35
  at Pennsylvania State University
    World Campus, 33–35
  at Rio Salado College, 33–36
  at UIS, 33–35
institutions, 9–10
  collaboration between, 153–54
  goals of, 23
  higher education, 5, 46–47, 90
  mission and purpose of, 1, 8, 35,
    39–41, 128
  online learning, 15–19, 119
  resources of, 17–18
  role of, 109
  task forces or advisory councils
    within, 16–17

instructional design
  Chico's Rubric for Online
    Instruction for, 87, 89
  principles of, 87–88
  QM Rubric Standards for, 87–88,
    103–5, 117
instructional designers, 10, 18, 119
  hiring of, 67
  review process by, 88
instructional materials, 104
instructor, online
  development and preparation of,
    108–9, 113–19
  role and responsibilities of,
    109–11
  time and workload management of,
    115–16
integrity, 49, 60, 118, 193, 195
intention, 63
Inter-American Distance Education
    Consortium (CREAD), 207
International Consortium for
    Telecommunications in
    Teaching, 6
International Council for Open and
    Distance Education (ICDE),
    202, 207
Internet, 7–8, 12, 14, 79, 134
Iron Chef, 150

Jenkins, Henry, 80
Jiang, M., 90
John Deere, 126
*Journal of Asynchronous Learning
    Network,* 145

Kennan, George, 42
knowledge, 12, 45, 81, 84, 163–64
Kouzes, J. M., 69

Lamb, Craig, 132n1
Land-Grant College Act. *See* Morrill
    Land Grant Act of 1862
LaPadula, M. A., 138

Latin America, 154
leadership, 1, 35–36, 178, 205
    arenas, 24–25
    business models and, 27–28
    campus, 18–19, 21–22
    challenges and issues, 14–19,
        21–22, 50
    confidence and, 54, 73
    context and, 50–57, 112, 120–22
    development program at
        Pennsylvania State University, 24
    education and, 58
    e-learning and policy, 177–78,
        196–98
    elements of, 120–26
    excellence and, 55
    factors, 15, 120–22
    goals, 50, 57–59
    online distance education, 23–25,
        120–26
    opportunities, 201–2
    organizational culture and, 64–67
    organizational success and, 66,
        69–72
    partnerships, relationships and,
        62–64, 70, 73
    as personal, 2, 48–50, 51, 54, 55, 58,
        60, 62, 68–73
    policy, 186, 197–98
    principles and values of, 42–44,
        67–68
    program development and, 30–31
    prudent, 42
    skills, 201
    Smutz on, 48–50, 51, 54, 55, 58, 60,
        62, 68–73
    social justice and, 60
    strategies, 2, 16–17, 57–59,
        159–60
    student services, 133
    student success and, 68–69
    vision and, 29, 50, 54–57, 109
    vocation and, 49
leadership, operational, 174
    approaches to, 168–70
    attributes of, 163
    competency in, 163
    context of, 166–73
    experience of, 163
    flexibility within, 172–73
    in fluid environment, 173
    future projection and, 171
    knowledge within, 163
    mission of, 169
    movements and trends for,
        170–71
    strategic compared to, 162–65
    values of, 169–70
    vision of, 171–72
leadership, strategic, 174
    approaches to, 168–70
    attributes of, 164
    competency in, 163
    context of, 166–73
    experience of, 164
    flexibility within, 172–73
    in fluid environment, 173
    future projection and, 171
    knowledge within, 164
    mission of, 169
    movements and trends for,
        170–71
    operational compared to, 162–65
    values of, 169–70
    vision of, 171–72
Leading Without Power (DePree), 62
learned societies, 184
learner, 105
    centric, 56, 64
    characteristics, 86, 113, 116
    engagement and interaction, 104,
        140–41
    programs, competency-based, 189
    retention, 92
    satisfaction, 92
learner, adult, 7, 26, 40, 57
    markets for, 65–67, 68
    programs for, 71

learning
  accountability and, 77
  analytics, 69, 78, 83–86, 139
  assessment of, 89–90, 104, 113,
    123–24
  blended, 78–79
  CoI and, 82–83
  effectiveness of, 10, 77–78
  environments, 14, 45–46, 141–42
  face-to-face, 78–79, 112
  infrastructure, 155–56
  institutions and online, 15–19, 119
  lifetime, 57
  management platforms and
    systems, 136
  objectives, 103
  organized, 19
  preferences, 14
Learning Counts, 189
learning management systems (LMSs),
    79, 89, 149–51, 158–59
learning outcomes, 50
  measurement of, 91–94, 104
  review process and, 88
learning process, 53
  effects on, 91
  measurement of, 90–91, 104
Legon, R., 88
Leslie, Larry, 54
Let Your Life Speak (Palmer), 49
library, 9
Lieven, Anatol, 41–44
Linux, 158
LMSs. See learning management
    systems
loyalty, 43
Ludwig-Hardman, S., 138
Lumina Foundation for Education, 195

Mackey, Thomas, 31, 33
mail, 5
mainstream
  higher education on, 8, 21, 38–39,
    41–44, 127
  Miller on, 226

online distance education as, 151
  Ragan on, 225
  Schroeder on, 224–25
  Smutz on, 225–26
  Swan on, 224
  technology as, 156–57, 159–60
Manning, Sylvia, 126, 127
Maricopa Community College System,
    27
marketing, 9, 170
  brand, 167
  through direct promotion, 167–68
  plan, 167
markets, 65
  for adult learner, 65–67, 68
  for student, 4, 12, 21, 178
MarylandOnline, 87
Massachusetts Institute of Technology
    (MIT), 150
Mayadas, Frank, 8
Means, Barbara, 78–79
Mellon Foundation, 150
mentoring, 140
Mexico, 7
Michigan, 6
Microsoft, 158
Milgram, Stanley, 69
Miller, Gary E., 1, 2, 23, 52–54, 67, 76
  on accreditation, 221
  on disruptive innovations, 215, 217
  on distance education, 210–11
  on faculty, 227
  on focus of online learning, 229
  on for-profit providers, 220
  on higher education, 233
  on mainstream, 226
  on online learning, 213
  on online learning structure, 222–23
  on open educational resources move-
    ment, 231–32
  on skills, 227
  on technology, 230
Mindset (Dweck), 54
mission
  core, 8, 39–41

institution's purpose and, 1, 8, 35, 39–41, 128
of operational leadership, 169
of strategic leadership, 169
vision and, 45
MIT. *See* Massachusetts Institute of Technology
Modular Object-Oriented Dynamic Learning Environment (MOO-DLE), 150, 208
MOODLE. *See* Modular Object-Oriented Dynamic Learning Environment
Moore, Michael G., 89
Morgenthau, Hans, 42, 43
Morrill Land-Grant Act of 1862, 4–5, 179
Motorola, 126
Movinter initiative, 154

National Aeronautics and Space Administration (NASA), 6
National Center for Academic Transformation (NCAT), 152–53
National Commission on Online Learning, 196
National Defense Education Act of 1958, 180
National e-Learning Alliance (NELA), 195–96
National Survey of Student Engagement (NSSE), 79–80
National Technological Degree Consortium, 7
National Technological University, 7
National University Extension Association, 200–201
National University Technology Network (NUTN), 206–7
National University Teleconference Network, 7
NCAT. *See* National Center for Academic Transformation
NELA. *See* National e-Learning Alliance

Nesler, M. S., 94
Net Generation, 14, 21
New Century Learning Consortium, 204
New York Institute of Technology, 137–38
Next Generation Learning Challenges, 84
Niebuhr, Reinhold, 42, 43
Noem, Kristi, 196
Nova Southeastern University, 207
NSSE. *See* National Survey of Student Engagement
Nuremberg laws (1935), 70
NUTN. *See* National University Technology Network

Oakley, Burks, 126
obedience, 69
objectivism, 89
Oblinger, Diana, 14
Oblinger, J., 14
OCW Consortium. *See* OpenCourse Ware Consortium
OERU. *See* Open Educational Resources University
Online Human Touch, 141
online learning
    Benke on focus of, 228–29
    Benke on structure of, 223
    Chaloux on, 212–13
    Chaloux on focus of, 229–30
    Chaloux on structure of, 222, 224
    institutions and, 15–19, 119
    Miller on, 213
    Miller on focus of, 229
    Miller on structure of, 222–23
    professional associations, 206
    Ragan on, 214
    Ragan on focus of, 229
    Ragan on structure of, 223–24
    Schroeder on, 213
    Schroeder on focus of, 229
    Schroeder on structure of, 223
    Smutz on, 213–14

Smutz on structure of, 223
Swan on, 214
Swan on focus of, 229
Swan on structure of, 223
OpenCourse Ware Consortium
    (OCW Consortium), 209
open educational resources movement,
    13, 33, 154, 157–58, 203–4
    associations, 208–9
    Benke on, 231
    Chaloux on, 232
    Miller on, 231–32
    Ragan on, 231
    Schroeder on, 231
Open Educational Resources University
    (OERU), 203–4, 209, 231
Open University of the United
    Kingdom (OU), 6, 26, 137, 139
organizational culture, 50
    leadership and, 64–67
    values and, 65
OU. *See* Open University of the United
    Kingdom
Oxford University, 8

Palmer, Parker, 49
Parker, D., 80
passion, 40, 60, 68, 72
PBS. *See* Public Broadcasting Service
PBS-ALS. *See* Public Broadcasting
    Service Adult Learning Service
Pearson eCollege, 150
Pearson Publishing, 150
pedagogical strategies, 91
pedagogy, 119
Pennsylvania State University, 7, 204
    Independent Learning System at,
        52–53
    Institute for Online Learning at, 205
    leadership development program at,
        24
    Online Coordinating Council at, 61
    Online Initiative at, 61
    Online Steering Committee at, 61

Outreach unit at, 25, 52–53
Pennsylvania State University World
    Campus, 2, 204
    Academic Council for Undergraduate
        Education at, 34
    Advising and Learner Success unit
        at, 69
    business model for, 28
    Corner of College and Allen blog
        at, 69
    enrollment at, 54, 56, 72
    Faculty Senate and Graduate Council
        at, 31, 34
    institutional culture at, 33–35
    as model, 25–26, 36
    program development at, 31, 52–54,
        165
    services at, 31
    Smutz on, 54–57, 64, 65, 68–73
    Strategic Management Group at, 55
    vision of, 56–57
performance, 50, 94
personalization, 19
Peterson, R., 157
Pew Charitable Trusts, 152
Phoenix, Arizona, 27
pillars, 9. *See also* Five Pillars of Quality
    Online Education
Pitinsky, Matt, 150
planning, 46
PLATO (Programmed Logic for
    Automatic Teaching Operations),
    8, 149
Polis, Jared, 196
President's Forum, 195
Princeton University, 8
*Principles of Good Practices for
    Electronically Offered Academic
    Degree and Certificate Programs*
    (Shea & Armitage), 134
professional associations, 184, 195,
    200–201, 202–3
    adult education, 207
    distance education, 206–7

faculty research, 208
international, 207–8
online learning, 206
open education, 208–9
product user, 208
sector-based, 205–6
proficiencies, 93
Programmed Logic for Automated
Teaching Operations. *See* PLATO
Project for Assessing Long-Distance
Learning via Telecommunications
(Project ALLTEL), 194–95
provost, 28
prudence, 42
psychology, 69
Public Broadcasting Service (PBS), 7
Public Broadcasting Service Adult
Learning Service (PBS-ALS), 7
public information, 9
public policy
Chaloux on issues of, 218
on education, 19–21
Schroeder on issues of, 217–18
Swan on issues of, 218
public television, 6–7
Pullan, M., 138

QM. *See* Quality Matters Rubric
Standards
Quakerism, 62
Quality Matters Rubric Standards
(QM), 87–88, 103–5, 117

radicalism, 59
Ragan, Lawrence C., 75
on accreditation, 220
on disruptive innovations, 216
on distance education, 211
on faculty, 227
on focus of online learning, 229
on for-profit providers, 219
on higher education, 232
on mainstream, 225
on online learning, 214

on online learning structure, 223–24
on open educational resources
movement, 231
on skills, 227–28
on technology, 230
railroads, 4
Raphael, A., 138
realism, 41–44, 45–46
Redecker, C., 19
registration, 18
Renaissance, 5
research, 15, 59–60
respect, 44, 48
responsibility, 44
retention
associated with student services,
10, 139, 140, 192
learner, 92
revenues
distribution of, 67
sharing of, 67, 190
tuition, 18, 28
Rio Salado College, 132n1, 135,
141–42
business model for, 28
institutional culture at, 33–36
as model, 27, 36
program development at, 31
services at, 31, 144
risk taking, 58–59
Romeo and Juliet, 69
Rubric for Online Instruction, Chico,
87, 89
Rural Free Delivery, 5, 11
Ryan, Jim, 53–54

Sadera, W. A., 140
Sakai, Hiroyuki, 150
Sakai project, 150
Sangamon State University.
See University of Illinois
Springfield
SARA. *See* State Authorization
Reciprocity Agreement

satisfaction
    faculty, 10, 39
    learner, 92
    levels, 10
    student, 10, 39, 83, 192
Schiffman, S., 23
scholarship, nature of, 59–61
school districts, 6
Schroeder, Raymond, 33, 34, 75,
        76, 127
    on accreditation, 221–22
    on disruptive innovations, 215
    on distance education, 211
    on faculty, 226
    on focus of online learning, 229
    on for-profit providers, 220
    on higher education, 233
    on mainstream, 224–25
    on online learning, 213
    on online learning structure, 223
    on open educational resources
        movement, 231
    on public policy issues, 217–18
    on skills, 228
    on technology, 230
Schwartz, Peter, 43, 46
Seaman, J., 12, 21, 29–30
Second Morrill Act of 1890, 5, 179
"Seeking Evidence of Impact:
        Opportunities and Needs," 84
self-accountability, 44
self-awareness, 44, 73
self-confidence, 48
"Serenity Prayer," 43
Serviceman's Readjustment Act of
        1944, 179–80
Shea, P. J., 89, 134
Showkeir, Jamie, 63, 66–67, 72
Showkeir, Maren, 66–67, 72
skills
    Chaloux on, 228
    innovations and, 11
    leadership, 201
    Miller on, 227

Ragan on, 227–28
Schroeder on, 228
society, 12
teaching, 108–9, 122
Sloan Consortium (Sloan-C), 145, 178,
        184, 195–96, 202, 205–6
    funding by, 126–27, 128, 135
    Outstanding Program Awards of, 55
    scorecard of, 133–34
    study, 29–30
Smutz, Wayne, 2, 33, 34
    on accreditation, 221
    on disruptive innovations, 216, 217
    on for-profit providers, 219–20
    on leadership, 48–50, 51, 54, 55, 58,
        60, 62, 68–73
    on mainstream, 225–26
    on online learning, 213–14
    on online learning structure, 223
    on Pennsylvania State University
        World Campus, 54–57, 64, 65,
        68–73
social needs, 3–4, 11
social networks, 90
social objectives, 39
social organizations
    elements of, 40–41
    higher education as, 2, 39, 40–41
    purpose of, 39
social presence, 82–83, 106–7
social transformations, 5
Society for the Study of Emerging
        Adulthood (SSEA), 208
Southern Regional Education Board
        (SREB), 186–87, 195–96
Soviet Union, 180
Spain, 204
Spanier, Graham, 52, 59, 61
Speak Easy and Student Café, 139
sports, 55
Sputnik, 180
SREB. See Southern Regional
        Education Board
SRI International, 78–79

SSEA. *See* Society for the Study of
    Emerging Adulthood
stakeholders, 159
Stanford University, 8, 126, 150
state
    financial aid, 20, 50, 191–92
    funding campus and, 189–91
    role in e-learning,
      181–82, 201–2
State Authorization Reciprocity
    Agreement (SARA), 195, 197
State University of New York (SUNY),
    135, 142, 201–2, 204. *See also*
    Empire State College
    faculty development programs
      at, 110
    Learning Network, 13–14, 89
student
    -centered environments, 76,
      80–81, 134
    centric, 191–92
    e-learning, 185
    empowerment of, 155
    engagement of, 140
    higher education of, 12, 14, 20
    markets for, 4, 12, 21, 178
    needs of, 137–38
    nontraditional, 13
    population of, 14
    resources for, 16
    role of, 51
    satisfaction, 10, 39, 83, 192
    swirling, 188
    traditional, 12, 13
student performance, 50, 94
student services, 17, 18, 32, 86, 145,
    192–93
    case studies of, 142–44
    challenges in, 135–36
    drop-in hours as, 143
    leadership, 133
    national quality standards for,
      133–35
    needs for, 137–38

perspectives and role of, 133
resource issues with, 136–37
retention associated with, 10, 139,
    140, 192
staff, 136–37
sustainability models for, 136–37
trends in, 141
student success
    leadership and, 68–69
    predictor of, 86
student support, 166–67, 192–93
    access to, 9, 134
    areas of, 9, 86–87
    effectiveness of, 132, 139
    empowerment of, 155
    functions, 24
    help desk as, 9
    online, 32
    provision of, 132–33
Stukel, James J., 126, 205
success, 44, 57
    faculty, 108, 112
    leadership and organizational, 66,
      69–72
    teacher, 108, 112
Sunrise Semester, 6
SUNY. *See* State University of
    New York
supply chain, 11–12
surveys
    APLU, 78
    CoI, 106–7
    faculty, 15–19, 30
    online programming, 29–30
Swan, Karen, 75, 88, 132n1, 152, 205
    on accreditation, 220
    on disruptive innovations,
      214–15
    on faculty, 226
    on focus of online learning, 229
    on for-profit providers, 219
    on higher education, 232
    on mainstream, 224
    on online learning, 214

on online learning structure, 223
on public policy issues, 218

Tannen, Deborah, 60–61
teacher, 91
-centered environments, 80–81
role of, 108–9
success, 108, 112
teacher presence, 82–83
establishment and maintenance of, 114
statements regarding, 106
teaching, 19, 59–60, 125
accountability and, 77
models, 151
quality of, 23
skills, 108–9, 122
technology interface and, 116–17, 119, 120, 127–28
technical quality, 9
technical support, 134
technology, 65, 136
affordability of, 155–56
buffet model of, 152
Chaloux on, 230–31
content sharing of, 154, 157–58
costs, 10, 190–91
course, 80, 105
current, 149–51
curricular requirements for, 156
delivery, 9
digital, 51–52
emporium approach to, 152
as empowerment tool, 154–55
environments and supports, 86
infrastructure, 110, 155–59, 166
interactive, 79–80
interface and teaching, 116–17, 119, 120, 127–28
mainstream, 156–57, 159–60
Miller on, 230
online, 75
personalization of, 158–59
policy implications for, 156–57
Ragan on, 230

replacement model of, 152
role of, 50, 51
satellite, 6–7, 19
scalability of, 156
Schroeder on, 230
supplemental model of, 152
support, 156
telephone, 7
training requirements for, 156
types of, 78–80, 91
Telecourse People, 6
telecourses, 6–7
telephones, 7
tenure, 15, 18, 38, 53, 121, 125
thinking, 44–45, 56
time management, 115–16
Tinto, V., 140, 141
Title IV financial aid, 184, 194
transfer credit policies, 188–89
transportation, 4
trust, 48, 63
tuition
costs, 134
electronic, 187
increases in, 50
policies, 186–87
residency and, 187
revenues, 18, 28
tutoring, 9, 142–43
Twigg, Carol, 152–53

UIS. See University of Illinois Springfield
United Kingdom, 6
United States (U.S.), 5, 90, 152, 179–81
United States Distance Learning Association (USDLA), 207
United States Distance Learning Consortium, 184
Universitat Oberta de Catalunya, 208
universities
Black, 5
ethical realism and, 41–44, 45–46
land grant, 4–5, 12, 26, 179

microcontext of, 59–61, 112
open, 6
outreach programs of, 5
public, 6, 21, 153–54
public research, 15
University Continuing and Professional
    Education Association, 201
University of British Columbia, 149
University of California, Berkeley,
    58, 60
University of Catalonia, 204
University of Central Florida, 110,
    135, 203
University of Chicago, 5–6
University of Illinois, 167
    Learning Outside the Classroom at,
        126
    Online program at, 126–27
    programs at, 126–28
    web browser launch by, 7–8
University of Illinois at Chicago,
    26, 127
University of Illinois at Urbana-
    Champaign, 26, 127
University of Illinois Springfield (UIS),
    135, 204
    business model for, 28
    case study, 109
    Center for Online Learning,
        Research and Service at, 26, 33,
        127–28, 205
    Community of Practice in e-Learning
        at, 33
    institutional culture at, 33–35
    as model, 26, 36
    Office of Technology-Enhanced
        Learning at, 127–28, 165
    program development at, 31
    services at, 31
    Teacher Leadership program at, 91
University of Maryland, 135, 204
University of Maryland University
    College, 6, 7–8, 203
University of Massachusetts Lowell, 135
University of Michigan, 126, 150

University of Wisconsin, 5–6, 204
University Professional and Continuing
    Education Association (UPCEA),
    195, 205
urbanization, 5
U.S. *See* United States
USDLA. *See* United States Distance
    Learning Association

values, 48–49
    attitudes and, 64, 86
    leadership's principles and, 42–44,
        67–68
    of operational leadership, 169–70
    organizational culture and, 65
    of realism, 42
    of strategic leadership, 169–70
vendors, educational, 185
Vietnam War, 60
virtual offices, 32
vision, 8
    leadership and, 29, 50, 54–57, 109
    long-term, 46
    mission and, 45
    for online distance education, 24,
        29–30, 32
    of operational leadership, 171–72
    of Pennsylvania State University
        World Campus, 56–57
    statement, 45
    strategic, 43, 50
    of strategic leadership, 171–72

Washington State University's Extended
    Degree Program, 139
Waters, T., 94
WCET. *See* Western Cooperative for
    Educational Technology
Web-based Course Tools (WebCT),
    149–50
Wellins, Richard, 163, 169
Wenger, Étienne, 124
Western Cooperative for Educational
    Technology (WCET), 134, 146,
    184, 202, 206

Western Governors University, 8, 137, 141–42
Western Interstate Cooperative for Higher Education (WICHE), 8, 206
Wiggins, G., 92–93
WikiEducator, 208

Wisconsin, 45
workforce, 11–12
The World Is Flat (Friedman), 11
World War II, 179
World Wide Web, 7, 8, 149, 164

Yale University, 8

OLC MEMBERSHIP

Membership in the Online Learning Consortium provides knowledge, practice, community, and direction for educators.

ONLINE WORKSHOPS

Nearly 100 workshops annually designed to meet your entire faculty and staff's online teaching and learning needs.

OLC ONLINE TEACHING CERTIFICATE

Consisting of a 9-week foundation course and three electives, this program prepares educators to teach and improve online courses.

ANNUAL CONFERENCES

- Emerging Technologies for Online Learning
- Blended Learning Conference & Workshop
- Annual Online Learning Consortium International Conference

MASTERY SERIES PROGRAMS

The OLC Mastery Series emphasizes theory and application of research on key topics and culminates in a Recognition of Mastery in a topic.

ONLINE LEARNING™
CONSORTIUM
FORMERLY THE SLOAN CONSORTIUM

Join The
Online Learning Revolution

The Online Learning Consortium (OLC) is the leading professional organization devoted to advancing the quality of online learning worldwide. The member-sustained organization offers an extensive set of resources for professional development and institutional advancement of online learning, including, original research, leading-edge instruction, best-practice publications, community-driven conferences and expert guidance. OLC members include educators, administrators, trainers and other online learning professionals, as well as educational institutions, professional societies and corporate enterprises.

ONLINE LEARNING™
CONSORTIUM
FORMERLY THE SLOAN CONSORTIUM